Roundtable Justice: Case Studies in Conflict Resolution

Other Titles in This Series

The War System: An Interdisciplinary Approach, edited by Richard A. Falk and Samuel S. Kim

Bibliography on World Conflict and Peace: Second Edition, compiled by Elise Boulding, J. Robert Passmore, and Robert Scott Gassler

Conflict Regulation, Paul Wehr

The Myth of Victory: What Is Victory in War? Richard Hobbs

Also of Interest

Environmental Mediation: The Search for Consensus, edited by Laura M. Lake

The ELF Odyssey: National Security Versus Environmental Protection, Lowell L. Klessig and Victor L. Strite

Westview Special Studies in Peace, Conflict, and Conflict Resolution

Roundtable Justice:
Case Studies in Conflict Resolution
REPORTS TO THE FORD FOUNDATION
edited by Robert B. Goldmann

This book describes seven cases in which third-party intervention was employed to settle complex social and economic disputes ranging from conflict among developers, farmers, environmentalists, and others over the construction of a dam in Washington State; to school integration conflicts in Atlanta, Georgia, and Dayton, Ohio; to the claims of the Mohawk Indians in the state of New York. All the disputes had been headed for litigation; however, responding to leadership from the government and other concerned sources, those involved agreed to mediation and negotiation as an alternative.

The authors provide detailed accounts of how mediation came about in each case, how it was conducted, the settlements that resulted, and the follow-up that was required. Demonstrating the potential of third-party intervention for resolving the growing number of disputes in society today, they also show how, in practical terms, conflicts can be resolved.

Robert B. Goldmann is a program officer, Division of National Affairs, with the Ford Foundation. He has also served as deputy director of the Governor's Commission on Civil Disorders in New Jersey and as director of public affairs for the New York City Human Resources Administration.

Roundtable Justice: Case Studies in Conflict Resolution

Reports to the Ford Foundation

edited by Robert B. Goldmann

Westview Press / Boulder, Colorado

Westview Special Studies in Peace, Conflict, and Conflict Resolution

Published in 1980 in the United States of America by
Westview Press, Inc.
5500 Central Avenue
Boulder, Colorado 80301
Frederick A. Praeger, Publisher

Library of Congress Cataloging in Publication Data
Main entry under title:
Roundtable justice, case studies in conflict resolution.
(Westview special studies in peace, conflict, and conflict resolution)
Includes index.
1. Justice, Administration of—United States—Addresses, essays, lectures. 2. Courts—United States—Addresses, essays, lectures. 3. Compromise (Law)—United States—Addresses, essays, lectures. 4. Arbitration and award—United States—Addresses, essays, lectures. 5. Third parties (Law)—United States—Addresses, essays, lectures. I. Goldmann, Robert, 1921– II. Series.
KF384.A2R68 347.73'1 80-13357
ISBN 0-89158-962-7
ISBN 0-86531-139-0 pbk.

Printed and bound in the United States of America

Contents

Preface

For close to a decade, the Ford Foundation has supported a variety of efforts to advance both knowledge about and the use of alternatives to the adversary process for the settlement of disputes. The Center for Dispute Settlement of the American Arbitration Association; the Institute for Mediation and Conflict Resolution in New York City; the Center for Community Justice in Washington, D.C.; the Institute for Environmental Studies at the University of Washington in Seattle, Washington; and the Office of Environmental Mediation at the University of Wisconsin have played a major role in advancing the state of the art in the disposition of major disputes as well as in introducing mechanisms for grievance management and conflict resolution.

The foundation remains committed to this work because it foresees the need for more rather than fewer efforts to find ways to resolve disputes fairly and efficiently. Beyond third-party intervention, which will always be central in such efforts, the foundation is now exploring ways to help groups concerned with improving procedures of existing institutions, including the courts and administrative and regulatory agencies.

The documentation of the cases in this volume is not limited to work done by grantees of the foundation. The selection of cases was based on substantive criteria, in the hope of making through this volume one more contribution to knowledge about conflict resolution in our society.

The book represents a truly cooperative endeavor. The authors of the chapters participated in the development of the guidelines of the research. Each author reported and wrote on his case or cases. The editor's task was to coordinate the work of the authors. It was a stimulating job, because each author brought special experience and insights to the work. I am grateful to Richard Kwartler, Stephen Gillers, Lee Dembart, Joel Fleishman, and Graham Finney, who have documented and illustrated a growing trend toward making this a fairer and more resilient society.

Robert B. Goldmann

The Contributors

Robert B. Goldmann (editor) has been a program officer in the National Affairs Division of the Ford Foundation for the past twelve years. He was previously an editor of *Vision,* the Latin American news magazine, and public affairs director of the New York City Human Resources Administration. Earlier in his career, Mr. Goldmann served in the federal government as director of news of the Voice of America (1958–1962) and as director of public affairs of the Alliance for Progress, the U.S. aid program for Latin America (1962–1965).

Richard Kwartler is executive vice-president of the Criminal Justice Institute, a nonprofit agency in New York City that operates the National Center for Correctional Mediation. He is the editor of *Behind Bars: Prisons in America.* In 1974 he founded *Corrections Magazine* and served as editor and publisher for three years. Previously, Mr. Kwartler helped establish the first national program to train members of minority groups for careers in broadcast and print journalism.

Stephen Gillers is associate professor of law at New York University. He is the author or editor of half a dozen books on law and law-related subjects and has contributed to numerous periodicals. Before teaching, he practiced law for ten years.

Lee Dembart is a science writer for the *Los Angeles Times.* He was formerly city hall bureau chief of the *New York Times.*

Joel L. Fleishman is professor of law and public policy, director of the Institute of Policy Sciences and Public Affairs, and vice chancellor of Duke University. Before moving to Duke in 1971, he was associate provost for Urban Studies and Programs, as well as associate chairman of the Center for the Study of the City, at Yale University. He has written extensively on political finance reform, ethics of public office holding, and a variety of topics in public policy. He is the president of the Association for Public Policy Analysis and Management for 1979–1980.

Graham S. Finney has had wide experience in planning and managing urban activities, including city planning, school administration, and drug abuse and other human service programs. His current work centers on the changing roles of the public and private sectors in urban America and problems of energy conservation. Based in Philadelphia, Mr. Finney lectures at the Wharton School, University of Pennsylvania.

Roundtable Justice: Case Studies in Conflict Resolution

Introduction

Robert B. Goldmann

The American society of the sixties and seventies has been called the litigious society. During that period more groups asserted rights through the courts than ever before or than judges, policymakers, or scholars had ever envisaged would do so.

After the civil rights movement, other minority groups became aware that they had been and were underrepresented in the places and processes where decisions were made about the allocation of resources and opportunities. Spanish-speaking people and Native Americans followed the lead of Blacks. The women's rights movement gained momentum. Concern for the nation's and the world's natural environment and worry about the seemingly heedless use and abuse of natural resources gave rise to a dynamic environmental movement that soon found itself at odds with business, organized labor, and minority groups who were pressing for more growth and more jobs. Consumers organized to press their claims for quality products at reasonable prices. New constituencies continued to develop at an astounding rate, and many institutions—corporations, labor unions, schools, colleges, and government agencies at all levels—were and continue to be involved in conflicts of one sort or another.

The courts are not only overburdened by an unprecedented workload, making for lengthy delays and a diminution of justice; they are also saddled with cases that do not necessarily fit the traditional adversary model. The rules of evidence and other limits on judicial fact-finding may make fair resolution of some disputes difficult, if not impossible, since the courts must depend only on litigants for the facts. There is also the question of timing. Courts generally cannot enter a dispute, even one that is justiciable, until it polarizes or becomes "ripe" for judicial action. In many cases it may not be best for society to wait that long.

It is in this context that new and different methods for settling disputes are being sought and developed. Some of the new techniques are based on the model of mediation and arbitration that has been used by business and labor organizations for many years. Neutral third parties have entered social disputes in various stages of crisis and have sought to work out compromises that accommodate the interests of all parties. Unlike a court, an intervenor often can begin operating before the parties are polarized and positions are frozen. Thus, a settlement that satisfies all parties may be reached more quickly and more easily than if the dispute had reached the courts.

This book examines a representative group of mediated disputes and suggests some conclusions based on the successes and failures of these efforts. It is *not* designed to present a definitive theory of the mediation of social disputes. At this stage, gathering evidence may be as useful as expounding on it.

Many recently mediated social disputes involved complex networks of relationships, needs, and issues that third-party intervenors must learn to deal with. A study of significant or representative cases, such as this one, can serve the following purposes.

- It can help government and private bodies assess the merits of alternate methods of dispute resolution so they can determine which path to follow in a specific dispute or in disputes in general. Some administrators may be unaware of the possibility of third-party intervention. Others may want to know more about the mix of variables involved in social disputes and what they augur for successful mediation.
- It can provide some insight into the qualities needed by persons who attempt (through mediation, arbitration, or any other method) to intervene in an incipient or full-blown dispute.
- The growing corps of mediators may learn more about the pitfalls and failures of mediation as well as about methods and approaches that have been successful.
- The study can inform the general public about alternative institutions and approaches for dispute resolution and about what can be accomplished through these mechanisms.

Four aspects of disputes were identified as a result of reviewing and discussing a variety of disputes with individuals and members of several institutions engaged in third-party intervention. Utilizing those characteristics, we selected cases that would be most useful to policymakers, administrators, and others eager to find alternatives to mechanisms now available or known to them.

1. *The Nature of the Dispute*

Intensity. Has the dispute been polarized or inflamed? How defined is it? To what extent do neutral persons or institutions still exist within the dispute community? To what extent do the participants and potential participants see themselves as being involved in a dispute? How strongly do they feel about the issues?

Time pressure. Must something be done quickly to avoid other dangers? Has the dispute gained visibility as the result of some clash or conflict? Or is it a dispute that the intervenor may have "discovered" on his or her own?

Size. How many participants are involved in the dispute?

History. What came before the dispute? What are the relationships among the participants?

The need for resolution. How threatening is the possibility of nonresolution? Do some participants have a vested interest in the dispute not being solved? How great is the motivation to settle?

Legitimacy. Is the dispute sufficiently justified to require the cost of social intervention? Is it a "strike" suit? Is it frivolous? What is meant by a "frivolous" dispute?

2. *The Community Within Which the Dispute Exists*

The dispute community. Are there overlapping communities? Can the dispute be resolved without also resolving other problems radiating from the dispute? What kind of community does the dispute exist in: a neighborhood? an institution? How defined is the community?

The community interests involved. What are the particular interests of the parties to the dispute? Are they economic, political, ideological (e.g., having to do with the environment or civil rights), "negative" (fear of crime, fear of racial minority, fear of change)? How many adherents does each interest have? How passionate are the adherents about their point of view? How articulate and vocal? What is the source of the authority, or the legitimacy, of those who speak for different sectors of the community?

Local and national disputes. Is the dispute a national one, or if local, one that will have national consequences (perhaps it is the first of its kind)? If local, has national attention been drawn to it? How has news media attention affected the community within which the dispute exists?

3. *The Purpose of the Intervenor*

Retrospective or prospective function. Is the intervenor attempting to resolve something that has already happened or to set up a structure for the resolution of future problems? Does the intevenor find the facts or suggest solutions? Are the suggestions binding? What methods are used to fulfill the tasks?

Implementation or monitoring of the resolution. Will the resolution be self-enforcing? Should or does the intervenor provide a means of implementation or monitoring? If not, how will a settlement be enforced and related community needs met?

4. *Nature and Qualities of the Intervenor*

Relation to the community. Does the intervenor come from inside or outside the community within which the dispute exists? Does the intervenor expect something from the community (as a politician might expect votes)? Must he or she continue to live in the community after the resolution?

Source of intervenor's authority. Where does the intervenor's authority come from? Is he or she appointed by a public body with power to take unilateral action if intervention is not successful?

Personal characteristics of intervenor. What personal qualities does the intervenor have? What qualities are called for in the particular dispute?

The Forest Hills dispute (Chapter 4) was very intense, with a potential for violence and a significance far beyond its immediate boundaries. A policy of city government was challenged; the Mayor intervened; and a mediator of high visibility (Mario Cuomo), backed by considerable power, was brought into the dispute.

In sharp contrast to Forest Hills, the Snoqualmie Dam controversy (Chapter 3) was persistent but of low intensity. The interests and the issues did not require urgent action. No immediate crisis and certainly no violence were in the offing. Yet there was a conflict of interests that sooner or later needed to be resolved for the sake of balanced growth, environmental health, and economic equity of a large area and a sizable population. Here mediation could proceed at a less rapid pace, over a longer time span, and the mediator did not need or want the high visibility and political power that were required in Forest Hills. The mediation was successful, but problems arose in implementation, and this experience, too, holds lessons for the future.

Chapter 7 on the Dayton school problem covers merely one segment of a long and continuing dispute. The work of a federal service in creating the atmosphere for implementing a court decision is documented in this chapter. In all cases, the decision or the settlement is merely the beginning of resolution. The hard work of carrying out the terms and of getting people adjusted to what the courts have decided or what their representatives have agreed to in mediation is the less publicized but vital ingredient that gives meaning to signatures on documents.

The Atlanta case (Chapter 6) tells us much about that city—a community that was determined to resolve a seemingly intractable issue with its own leadership resources. The dispute in St. Louis (Chapter 5) was another of high intensity and urgency, and there seemed to be only one person who was acceptable to all parties to resolve it—and he did the job. In the case involving the Mohawk Indians and New York State (Chapter 1), Mario Cuomo again played a role (but a very different one from his role in the Forest Hills dispute). Chapter 2 describes dispute resolution within a California prison system. Similar approaches could be used by school systems, by colleges and universities, and by individuals dealing with governmental systems, such as social security or services for the aged and handicapped, where challenges to decisions or awards either go unanswered or wend their way through complicated, time-consuming and costly processes.

1
"This Is Our Land": *The Mohawk Indians v. the State of New York*

Richard Kwartler

Introduction

If we have come to fight,
  we are too few.
If we have come to die,
  we are too many.
–Statement attributed to anonymous
Indian chief on the eve of battle
more than 175 years ago.

In some respects, little has changed. There are still some Indians ready to fight if they must and prepared to die if it is absolutely necessary. For them, the reason is compelling–part of it concerns their commitment to settling a question for which there may never be a mutually acceptable answer: Who really owns the land on which much of America stands?

They don't want to fight or die, but they are motivated to take great risks by what for them are real fears of cultural extinction. They see only bleakness ahead if they do not obtain land–land on which they can return to the agriculturally self-sufficient life of their forefathers, and land on which they can freely bring up their children with Indian cultural and religious values and without the alcoholism, mental illness, and other pathology of the existing reservations. As for living elsewhere in America, these deeply committed "traditional" Indians want no part of it that isn't totally their own.

The problem, of course, is that all of the land Indians want is spoken for. Some of the land is government-owned and set aside as parks or "forever wild" areas upon which nothing is supposed to be built, while the rest has on it the homes, farms, schools, businesses, and government buildings constructed by people and agencies convinced that they own that terra firma. They contracted for it and paid for it, and they have the deeds and mortgages to prove it. They also have the support of government officials who cite the long line of treaties that changed the ownership of tens of millions of acres that unwind across the scenic majesty that is the United States of America. The treaties, say the officials, are valid. Other Indian land was given away, abandoned, or captured.

For at least a thousand years before the Pilgrims landed at Plymouth Rock in 1620, the varied Indian nations on this continent controlled those acres. The Iroquois Confederacy (Mohawk, Oneida, Onondaga, Cayuga, and Seneca), the Passamaquoddy and Penobscot, the Sioux, the Pueblo, the Navaho, and many others were among the peoples who once owned vast acreage. Today, members of these and other Indian nations are seeking to regain control of some of that land. They maintain that many of the treaties are illegal, and that fraud was present in a great many cases in which land changed hands. The nature of the claims and of the goals varies from group to group. The issues are complex, and there is a diversity of opinion. Millions of dollars have already been paid in Indian claims.

Some Indians want land and money. In Maine, the Passamaquoddy and Penobscot tribes asked the federal government in 1978 to intervene on their behalf and seek 350,000 acres and $300 million in damages from the state of Maine, but not to sue private landowners. The Indians contend that 12 million acres were taken from them illegally. Some Indians seek land only; they are committed traditionalists who value the old ways and see the land as something sacred that cannot be bought or sold as in the non-Indian world. Traditional Indians are also concerned about maintaining numerical Indian identity by discouraging intermarriage with whites. Today, there are an estimated 750,000 to 1,000,000 Indians in the United States, but no one knows for sure, just as no one is sure how many Indians were here prior to Columbus. Some estimates place the total at that time at around 25 million—but that includes all of North America. Other estimates go much lower.

Indian land claims, however, are diverse and are not easily cataloged—some traditionals seek money as well as land; so do some "elective" Indians. An estimated three-quarters of the Indians in the United States are known as elective because they have opted for the non-Indian way of life and believe in assimilation.

What has eluded the courts, the state and federal agencies, and the individual participants involved in disputes from Maine to Washington State is a formula for settlement. The conflicts drag through the courts for years. A number of Indian leaders have called for a meeting with President Carter or a White House conference to consider the overall question of Indian claims.

There are in New York State a number of people who believe that the formula for resolving a number of the existing Indian disputes may have already been found—and used—to produce an interim solution to the May 13, 1974, seizure by armed Mohawks of 612 acres of New York State land. The land, said the Mohawks, was seized as a symbol because it is part of 8 million acres in New York and 1 million acres in Vermont that together make up the original Mohawk homeland. The Indians claimed that all 9 million acres still belonged to them because the treaties the states relied upon for ownership were invalid. The 612 acres are located at Moss Lake, about fifty miles from Utica, in the Adirondack State Forest Preserve. The land had once been used for an exclusive girls' camp for children from families like the Rockefellers and Roosevelts.

It could have become, in the opinion of many, including the State Police, a bloody battleground that would have made "Attica look like a Sunday school picnic." That was the opinion of former State Police Major Robert S. Charland, who was in command of the troop that covered the Moss Lake area when the Mohawks took control. Charland asked his superiors for permission to remove the Indians, whose strength he estimated at about one hundred men, women, and children. Permission was denied, and the Indians stayed; three years were to go by before an interim agreement was reached that arranged for the Indians to move to a new site in New York's Clinton County near Plattsburg and the Canadian border.

Charland still thinks it would have been right to remove the Indians on that first day "since they took a piece of property in a fashion that led to violence." There were a number of shooting incidents involving Indians and local residents who opposed the takeover, but no one was killed "due mainly to the efforts of the State Police." Charland, 46, a native of Brooklyn, New York, is a man who follows the law no matter who is involved–Indian or white–and it is a mark of the extraordinary circumstances surrounding the Moss Lake settlement that one of Charland's strongest supporters is Kakwirakeron (pronounced Gah-Gwee-La-Geh-Lu), a key Mohawk leader. Kakwirakeron is 35; his English name is Arthur Montour. All the non-Indian participants in the Moss Lake controversy agree that if the date were 1600, Kakwirakeron would be a famous chief. His commitment to the Mohawk cause is total, and he said at one point during the occupation of Moss Lake: "We realize we're in a very dangerous position and we know we are in a life-and-death situation–literally, figuratively and culturally. There's always the possibility of death."

Charland retired from the State Police in August 1976 and went to work for the same Rochester utility that employs the man who is considered by most of the other participants to have played the major role in effecting the interim settlement–Howard Rowley. Rowley is a part-time mediator for the American Arbitration Association's (AAA) Community Dispute Services (CDS), and he believes that it was the use of a carefully formulated mediation process that enabled both sides to agree finally on the imaginative use of a trust to hold the Clinton County land for the Mohawks. Rowley, 50, started out as a laborer and now is director of urban affairs for the Rochester Gas and Electric Company. He recently won a $10,000 Rockefeller Public Service Award for his work as a mediator.

The mediation effort lasted thirty months, and during the final ten months New York Secretary of State Mario Cuomo represented Governor Hugh Carey at the sessions. Cuomo is credited with securing acceptance of the interim settlement from Albany, and he played a role in hammering out the agreement.

Cuomo was the fact finder in the Forest Hills housing dispute (see Chap. 4). In discussing that conflict, he said: "In the end we prevailed because we were right, and when is the last time that that happened?" Later on he said:

> I think that it happened again with the Mohawks. We got the State to do something there that everyone said was not doable and everyone said that [State Attorney General] Louis Lefkowitz would never agree to the legality of this arrangement, and he did. . . . I think the best thing

> about the Mohawk situation was not what it does for these Indians and their traditional way of life because it does very little. . . . But it is symbolic—it was that you can arrive at an arrangement. You can make this kind of implicit confession of past failure on our part as the white society. I think it was the right thing. The way we handle the Indians is a real test of ourselves as Americans, and what we like to boast makes us different from the rest of the world—freedom, compassion, equity. There is a moral claim. We took it [the land] from them; everybody knows that.

The theme of "past failure"—in effect, white guilt—was present during the entire Moss Lake conflict. It was felt by many participants that perhaps no other group except Indians could have seized state land and stayed there for three years without being put out forcibly. Cuomo also touched on another element on which there was widespread agreement: the courts were not the place to solve disputes of this kind.

> The Mohawk settlement has moved us toward a realization that the way to resolve these things is not by letting them go to court because if the Indian goes to court and wins then the court will say that the land belongs to the Indians. If the land belongs to the Indians, the court will not actually deliver the land to the Indians because the legislative process will then intervene to say that's an absurd result—for example, to give the whole City of Saratoga to the Indians. We must find a different process—conflict resolution without litigation, a process of negotiation.

Now, both Rowley and Cuomo have kind words for each other. But during the negotiating and mediation process they had some volcanic disagreements on strategy. The problem may have been analyzed best by Cuomo when he mentioned in passing, "I mean, you can't have two mediators."

Moss Lake

Kakwirakeron said that the Indians who seized Moss Lake came from Canada and the United States. They had rifles and a commitment to stay and defend themselves against any attempt to drive them off the property by force. They renamed the lake Ganienkeh, which in the Mohawk language means "Land of the Flint" or "Mohawk Nation." Karoniaktajeh (pronounced Geh-lon-yeh-dah-jeh), another Mohawk leader, said of Moss Lake during the occupation: "This is not a gentle place. We'll fight for it with guns."

What the Indians wanted first was recognition by the state and federal governments that the 9 million acres actually still belonged to the Mohawk Nation. That never came, and the Iroquois Confederacy is still reviewing the matter. Since the Mohawk Indians are part of the confederacy, they secured approval of its Grand Council in making their claim for the 9 million acres and in seizing Moss Lake. Mohawk attorney Robert T. Coulter of the Indian Law Resources Center in Washington, D.C., said the overall land claim was "under study." When Moss Lake was seized, the Indians did not ask that the 9 million acres be turned over at once in total. Nor did they ask for money. And, according to Kakwirakeron, they never will.

> We are different than other minority groups in our cultural values—especially as they relate to land. We place more emphasis on land as belonging to all the people—past, present and future. We hang onto our values and look out for coming generations. Other societies take money for land—for us that's out of the question. We consider the land to be "our mother, the earth," and there's no way one can sell his mother. It takes a while for non-Indians to understand our values and goals.

In an interview during the Moss Lake occupation, Kakwirakeron said:

> All Indians have asked of the whites is that they respect the Indian way of life. We have our own form of government, our own form of religion, our own way of life. We have practiced these ways for thousands and thousands of years.
>
> The white people have their own ways. If they want us to respect theirs, they should respect ours.
>
> We've never forced our language, religion or laws upon you. Ours is a mutual respect. People don't have to agree with our ways. They must just let us be. We are concerned not so much with the present, but with the future, with our children and grandchildren.
>
> As long as this is recognized we can live side by side with the white man.
>
> There are worse ways to die than by a bullet. If we go back to the cities and reservations our children will die from alcohol, drugs, depression and suicide.

Kakwirakeron has eleven children, four from a former marriage and seven with his present wife. He was a steel structure worker earning about $25,000 a year when he was injured in an accident. "When I was down and out," Kakwirakeron said, "I realized how most Indians live. So I got involved in pro-Indian activities." To understand the determination of the Moss Lake Indians, it is first necessary to try to grasp the commitment of men like Kakwirakeron, who talk about how the despair and hopelessness of Indians on and off the reservations leads to unemployment, alcoholism, and mental illness rates that run in multiples of the rates for the white population. The reasons they cite for these high rates are the loss of Indian identity and cultural values and unfair pressure to assimilate. Said Cuomo of Kakwirakeron:

> He has what most of us lack, an undeviating belief in something. That's the secret to his strength and to most geniuses and great achievers. They believe something deeply. There are plenty of people floating around with enormous talent who don't know what to believe, and the result is dissipation, frustration, non-achievement, but Kakwirakeron believes something deeply. [The absence of belief is] one of the great gaps in our society, I think.

Following their request for recognition of the 9-million-acre claim, the Indians at Moss Lake sought, as Kakwirakeron put it, enough land so that "our people could live and carry out our way of life on the unoccupied portions of the land." How much land is that?

"We are probably talking about a minimum of 500,000 acres," said Kakwirakeron. But when the Mohawks left Moss Lake after the settlement to take up residence in Clinton County, they went to two sites that totaled only about 6,300 acres provided by the state of New York. Additional land is being purchased with private funds.

Mediation Begins

The mere existence of the Moss Lake occupation cast a cloud on land titles in the surrounding area and did not endear the Mohawks to their involuntary neighbors, some of whom had read the Ganienkeh Manifesto issued by the Mohawks soon after they arrived: "The Mohawk Land was lost in an earlier century by fraud and its possession by New York State and the State of Vermont constitute illegal usurpation."

During the summer of 1974, according to the Indians, there were a series of incidents involving shots being fired into the Indian camp from passing cars. Kakwirakeron said the Indians did not return the fire for a long time. No one was injured in the camp. In October, two whites were shot in separate incidents in which the Indians maintained that they had responded to shots being directed toward the camp from cars in which the two had been passengers. In the second incident, a nine-year-old girl was hit in the back and severely injured, apparently by a ricochet from the trunk of the car. Major Charland said his men investigated and could find no evidence of any provocation that might have led the Indians to fire at the car. He still regrets not finding the people responsible for the girl's injuries.

Charland had always talked about seeing "the right thing done" and avoiding violence at all costs. Perhaps this explains the Indians' respect for him. Said Kakwirakeron: "He played an important role in preventing conditions that might have led to an incident that could have been the most violent and bloody ever seen in this country. He's an exceptional type of person. He used a clear mind and tried to put the human element into the proper perspective."

Charland said that many residents of the area (rugged individualists and backwoods types) were armed after the October incidents and wanted to use their weapons to "defend women and children." He added that state and local officials, as well as local residents, advised him on the kinds of action they would have liked taken against the Indians: "Bomb them, use flame throwers, napalm, tanks. You wouldn't believe what they wanted."

In December, Rowley made his first appearance to determine whether mediation would be possible. He had been asked to take a look at the Moss Lake situation by the YMCA in Rochester, which owned a summer camp adjacent to the camp the Mohawks were occupying. The "Y" was concerned about its camp if the trouble continued at Moss Lake. Rowley was a natural choice since he had started his community affairs work in Rochester as a part-time street-gang worker and counselor for the "Y" in 1959. He had worked part-time with the AAA since 1972, and the "Y" knew that, too. So they asked Rowley to take a look. Charland later described Rowley's arrival at Moss Lake in the middle of a raging blizzard:

> My first sergeant comes in and announces that Howard Rowley is here with some guests. In marches Rowley, who looks like a typical

> WASP, conservative, white hair and all; next comes Josh Stulberg, a very Jewish lawyer from the AAA, pensive, thoughtful and smart; then a black militant named Earl Brown from Cleveland, and finally, as the frosting on the cake, an Indian from Minnesota named War Cloud, with peace patches and [cutouts] of clenched fists [sewn on his jacket]; he makes Brown look like a lollypop. "My cup runneth over, I thought."

Rowley began what he calls his "standing on the corner" technique to determine whether AAA should become involved in trying to mediate the dispute. "My style is to get to know people," he explained. "I think you are a lot more successful, particularly in crisis intervention, if you know the people you are working with and dealing with and they know you so that you don't have to go through an identity process in the critical stages of a dispute. I mediate very openly." Rowley, who has since worked on other disputes involving Indians, decided to recommend that AAA's CDS take on the mediation job. The recommendation was accepted and Rowley became the mediator. "I didn't have a full weekend off for the next three years," he said. "And during most evenings at home, I spent two to three hours on the phone working on the mediation effort," he added.

Rochester Gas and Electric, which is a public-spirited company, allowed Rowley to take time off to do his mediating. The company did the same for Charland, who is also on the part-time staff of CDS, which has an office in Rochester. AAA, the parent agency of CDS, is a private nonprofit organization. Charland has assisted Rowley in mediating other current Indian disputes. At the utility, Charland is manager of security.

During the thirty-six months that followed his appointment as mediator, Rowley attended at least a couple of hundred meetings that were part of the mediation process. That process extended to minor problems the Indians had when about thirty Mohawk families moved in stages from Moss Lake to Clinton County after the interim settlement was reached in May 1977. To this day, Rowley still keeps an eye on things in Clinton; so does his son, Richard, who is a full-time mediator for CDS.

Kakwirakeron, who attended many of the mediating sessions along with other Indians and various state officials, described the Indians' impression of Rowley as follows:

> When we first met Rowley I remember the white hair which he has,

> and the type of face he has is to me an honest face. And he always had the ready smile, which is a genuine smile, not just for the show of it. He had a manner, a very easy manner which is easy for us to identify. He . . . really doesn't have a mask on. He is not trying to put on a show or an air of importance. He is just honest and straight-forward and our first impression of him held up all the way through.

Kakwirakeron believes the CDS role as mediating agency was an extremely important development.

> It marks the first time that a neutral force has been available to the Indian people for assistance in settling a major dispute. Previously, a federal agency or some organization connected to the government functioned in that role and placed the Indians in a great disadvantage. In our experiences in the past, if there were a person who described himself as a mediator they were always part of or belonged to some agency or branch of that particular government, whether it be state or federal, and therefore, their income or their pay was always tied to, in effect, their loyalty to their government, to their cause, so that the experience has been that whoever the mediator was, in those circumstances, they would generally, if not always, be a little more openly biased towards the government.

The Indians, Kakwirakeron continued, realized that Rowley was not subject to any job pressure and could be totally impartial. "We were comfortable and satisfied in the manner in which AAA acted."

Rowley used the word "process" to describe the CDS technique.

> First of all, what the process is, is a mechanism for non-violent conflict resolution. It is the process of bringing disputing parties together to resolve their problems collectively and to reach a solution acceptable to everyone. . . . Reach a decision that is acceptable to everyone and which allows, in my opinion—and you won't find this phrased this way in textbooks, perhaps—for no big winners and no big losers. So it is a process in which you can settle a dispute without embarrassment and with dignity to all the parties involved.
>
> Hopefully, the solution, and it has to work this way, the solution allows for the creation of further mechanisms to prevent this same thing from occurring constantly. You know, hopefully, a big part of the process is teaching people how to communicate and how to solve their own problems in an atmosphere other than a hostile atmosphere. Also, we

> won't have done our job if we don't initiate some mechanism that will take care of those small irritants that constantly come up and suddenly blossom into one great explosion.
>
> Another key part of the process is that we don't sign contracts. For example, any one of the parties to a dispute can say, "Hey, Rowley, we don't like what you're doing. You're too much this or too much that," and that's the end of it. We can go out as quickly as we came in. Mediation is a very fragile process. One of the things I usually talk about with people when we are sitting down together is the fragility of the process. I believe that's what makes the process work because everybody has to want it to work. And anybody, any one of the parties at any time, can blow it apart if they so desire. The fact that we are an independent, private group means that the Mohawks can deal with us and they do not have to deal directly with the State of New York, which would violate the principle of sovereignty.

Sovereignty is a key word to the Mohawks. They insist without waivering that the Mohawk Nation is an independent sovereign government that cannot deal with a state or municipality, but must, like any other nation, conduct negotiations directly with the federal government. But the United States did not want to be drawn into the Moss Lake dispute, and so there were no federal officials at the mediation session. In their eyes, the Mohawks did not deal directly with state officials at the meetings, but worked with Rowley and other CDS personnel, maintaining their sovereignty.

Interim Agreement

The state of New York had moved unsuccessfully in federal district court to force the Mohawks out of Moss Lake—the suit had been directed against the individual Indians on the site, but in dismissing it the court said it should have been directed against the Iroquois Confederacy and the Mohawk Nation. Yet since each had sovereign immunity neither could be sued without its permission.

The Mohawks finally decided themselves, as the mediation effort wore on, to give up Moss Lake as part of an interim settlement that would give them an alternate site where local opposition would not be nearly as great and where they could set up a viable agricultural community while deciding how best to pursue their 9-million-acre claim. They had learned also that private funds could be secured to buy private land adjacent to any new-site acreage.

The state, of course, was eager to see the Indians depart Moss Lake and had decided to provide another site. But for a while a plan could not be worked out that would enable the Indians to accept state land without entering into direct negotiations with the state, thereby impairing their sovereignty. The solution was not unique but it was inspired. It cannot be determined if there was a sole author, but it appears that Rowley, Cuomo, Coulter, and perhaps others were thinking along the same lines—the establishment of a trust agency that would accept the new site from the state and then would turn it over to the Mohawks, who would deal only with the private, nonprofit trust agency. That worked.

That agreement gave birth to the Turtle Island Trust, which was created for "charitable, religious and educational purposes." Among its main purposes are: "the preservation of the traditional culture, heritage, history, religion, language and arts of the Indian Nations of North America" and the "promotion of racial and cultural harmony and understanding between members of the North American Indian Nations and citizens of the United States." The trustees of Turtle Island are Ann Louise Maytag, who arranged for the private funds to purchase additional land; the Reverend John L. Reiger, executive director of the New York State Council of Churches and an interested on-site observer at Moss Lake; and Robert S. Charland.

The trust accepted and later turned over to the Mohawks two sites in Clinton County about twenty miles from Plattsburg and sixty miles from Montreal in the northeastern corner of the state. One site, of 720 acres, is in the town of Altona and is called Minor Lake Park; it has been leased to the trust with five-year options to renew. The other site, of 5,500 acres, on the Macomb Reservation is in the town of Schuyler Falls. It was provided under a revocable permit arrangement that continues indefinitely unless cause is given for revocation. The Mohawks can build homes and farms and can keep their livestock on the 720-acre tract, and they are using the private funds to buy adjacent land. By mid-June, an estimated two hundred Mohawks lived on this acreage. Under terms of the trust's lease with the state, the Mohawks will set up an educational museum to demonstrate their traditional way of life to white visitors. Otherwise, non-Indians are not permitted on either parcel. On the Macomb land, the Indians are restricted to hunting, fishing, and trapping, but cannot build structures.

No one can foretell what will happen to the 9-million-acre claim. But it is land that the Mohawks now deem as the greatest prize. "No amount of money would be acceptable in place of land," said Kakwirakeron. "The only way our children in coming generations can have any future is with the land. Any money, no matter how many millions of dollars we get today, is nothing against the value of the land itself. The land is priceless."

2
Dispute Resolution in Prison: The California Experience

Stephen Gillers

Introduction

Jim, a seventeen-year-old boy in a California Youth Authority (CYA) institution, summed up CYA's grievance procedure: "Without grievance, we wouldn't have rights. Rights would be meaningless. They would be favors." The difference between a favor and a right is power. In a prison, the people with power are "the authorities"—the guards, the administration, the warden. The only check on the arbitrary exercise of that power lies with the courts; but the courts, traditionally and even today, are reluctant to intervene between people in prison and prison authorities. The result is a real potential for arbitrariness, especially about "small" things, where judicial help is even less likely.

But what is "small" to outsiders may be magnified many times to a person with no control over his world, no power to retreat and hide, no freedom of choice. The ability to enforce the decision to keep a favorite wall poster in one's room or to have the full twenty-five minutes allotted for dinner is important because, cumulatively, such decisions allow people whose freedom has been denied the power to still mediate their environment, to organize, however modestly, the world about them. Multiply dozens or scores of irritations, and place them in the atmosphere of a prison, and you have the mix that can make for an explosion if the spark is set off at a time when pressure is high.

Against this background, the availability of a grievance procedure becomes important. And although the cases dealt with may appear trivial to the outsider, they are not to the prisoners. California's experiment with a ward (or inmate) grievance procedure in Youth Authority institutions is a middle way to protect inmate rights on issues the courts cannot easily handle. It is a way to promote human autonomy within walls. It recognizes that the inability to assert minor, even petty, claims when the sense of fairness is challenged, takes on tremendous importance to people who are locked up. Consider, for example, the cases of Charles and Theresa.

Charles and Theresa

Charles, a young man in his late teens, was incarcerated at an institution run by the CYA. He was permitted to keep his own money in an account at the institution and to use it to make purchases from the canteen. One day, he was transferred to a different CYA institution. But his money took six weeks to follow him, and for six weeks he was unable to make canteen purchases.

Charles complained. He filed a grievance asking that CYA policy be changed so that a ward (as inmates are called) who was transferred would promptly be credited with his or her funds by the new institution. Three days after Charles filed his grievance, a committee of two wards and two staff members listened to his complaint and unanimously agreed with him. They recommended that action be taken. Three days later, a higher-ranking staff person at the new institution considered the recommendation. He concurred and referred the proposed change to the superintendent.

On that same day, the superintendent reviewed the grievance and the recommendation and concluded that the argument had merit. But since a change required departmental action—because the issue affected the entire CYA—the superintendent wrote to the director. He informed her of his "full agreement" with the original finding and of his conclusion that documents and materials from his institution "relating to trust accounts could be forwarded directly with the ward to the receiving institution."

Three days later, or nine days after Charles had filed his original grievance, the director of the CYA, Pearl West, wrote him that she understood "the reasons from your grievance and I believe you have raised an important and valid issue." She told Charles of the practices at some of the other CYA institutions. She approved of the superintendent's request to implement a direct forwarding procedure immediately. Finally, she revised the applicable section of the CYA manual so that "all wards will be assured of a timely transfer of trust funds and thus be able to predict within the institution canteen rotation when they can purchase items." In conclusion, the CYA director informed Charles that if, for any reason, he was dissatisfied with her response, he had the right to have his grievance referred to a "neutral person outside the Youth Authority" for arbitration.

At about the same time that Charles filed his grievance, Theresa, a ward at a different CYA institution, also had a complaint. She thought the heating equipment at her institution was malfunctioning because it seemed that only cold air circulated through the vent. If the equipment was not malfunctioning, then Theresa believed the thermostat should be reset ten degrees higher.

On the same day that Theresa filed her grievance, it was heard by a grievance committee of two staff persons and two wards. They concluded that the thermostat should be reset ten degrees higher. This recommendation was forwarded to the superintendent of Theresa's institution, who disagreed with the grievance committee. The superintendent explained that thermostats were set at sixty-five degrees in accordance with a memorandum from state officials and did not feel she had the authority to modify this policy. The grievance was eventually sent to the office of the CYA director for review.

The director denied the grievance. In a letter, she explained to Theresa that California and the nation were facing a serious energy crisis that required an effort to conserve fuel. The director said she was going to ask the superintendent to check Theresa's room to make sure there was adequate ventilation. She also suggested various alternate ways of keeping warm. Finally, the director emphasized that the heating level of state institutions was outside the control of the CYA. For that reason, the issue was not grievable. A grievance, the director explained, is "a complaint about the substance or application of any written or unwritten policy of the Department of the Youth Authority or of any of its program units, or a complaint about any behavior or action directed toward a ward by staff or other ward."

The director concluded her three-page letter by informing Theresa that if she disagreed with the director's judgment that her complaint was not grievable, Theresa could appeal "this issue of jurisdiction to independent review." The time between the filing of the grievance and the director's response was twenty-nine days.

The California Experience

Charles and Theresa were using what the CYA calls its Ward Grievance Procedure (WGP). The WGP was started in the fall of 1973 by then-CYA director, Allen F. Breed. It began as an experiment at one of the CYA institutions, the Karl Holton School for Boys in Stockton, California, and then spread to other Youth Authority facilities. Today, it is required by law. In 1976, the state legislature passed, and Governor Edmund G. Brown, Jr., signed, a bill directing the head of the CYA to "establish and maintain a fair, simple and expeditious system for resolution of grievances" of all CYA wards. Grievances to be covered were those arising out of written or unwritten policies or rules of the Youth Authority or out of any decision or action taken by a Youth Authority employee or another ward. The procedure even applies to the policies and actions of persons who are only contractors or agents of the Youth Authority. The CYA grievance procedure was the first of its kind for any youth institution in the United States.

The CYA definition of "grievance" makes nearly all ward (and even many staff) complaints grievable. However, it does exclude complaints dealing with ward discipline, which are handled by a separate procedure called Disciplinary Decision Making System (DDMS). Notably, though, DDMS does not have provision for ward participation or outside review. There are also separate procedures for review of CYA decisions regarding conditions and time of release.

The law does not explicitly define the exact procedures to be implemented for grievance resolution, but it does establish certain minimal requirements.

- Staff and wards must participate "on as equal a basis and at the most decentralized level reasonably possible."
- The system must provide ("to the extent reasonably possible") for the selection by their peers of the wards who will participate "in the design, implementation and operation of the system."
- The system must provide for "written responses with written reasons in support thereof to all grievances at all decision levels."
- There must be a provision allowing priority processing of emergency grievances, such as grievances that if subject to the

"passage of time required for normal processing [would] be made moot, and matters in which delay would subject the grievant to substantial risk of personal injury or other damage."

- A grievant must have the right to be represented by a ward, a staff person, or anyone else, including a CYA volunteer.
- There must be provisions to assure the wards who grieve or participate in the resolution of grievances do not suffer reprisal.
- There must be provision for a "full hearing of the grievance at which all parties to the controversy and their representatives shall have the opportunity to be present and to present evidence and contentions regarding the grievance."
- Finally, there must be an appeal process, including a final right of appeal to "advisory arbitration of the grievance by a neutral person not employed by" the CYA. Although the arbitration is advisory only, the CYA must adopt the arbitrator's decision unless it is illegal, would result in physical danger to any person, would require expenditure of funds not available, or (and this is the only real "loophole") "in the personal judgment of the Director, would be detrimental to the public or to the proper and effective accomplishments of the duties of the department." In the more than four years that the grievance procedure has been in operation, the director has apparently only once concluded that an arbitrator's decision (that a ward should have the right to hang pro-Nazi material on the wall of his room) should not be implemented for policy reasons.

Introduction of a grievance mechanism to the California Youth Authority was the result of the work of many people and organizations. Linda Singer, a Washington, D.C., lawyer and head of the Center for Community Justice, was an important force in its creation. Singer, her deputy (Michael Keating), and the staff of the center designed the grievance mechanism and did early monitoring of its operation. The Youth Authority and the center also enlisted the help of the Manhattan-based Institute for Mediation and Conflict Resolution (IMCR) to train CYA administrators and wards and staff at the Holton School—the site of the first grievance procedure—in the techniques of conflict resolution.

The operation of the CYA's grievance mechanism cannot be fully appreciated without a sketch of the ward population. George Nicolau of

IMCR, who was instrumental in its CYA training efforts, described the CYA population.

> The term Youth Authority [YA] is misleading to those on the outside. The image is that of kids, truants or runaways, but the reality is that the YA inmates, who in theory range from 13 to 25, are not that different from their adult counterparts. Recently, over 50 percent of all YA commitments have been from the adult criminal courts (young men over 18). More than half of those in YA institutions are from minority groups; the same percentage has committed crimes of violence and been involved with drugs. Assault, robbery and homicide are almost as common among the YA prisoners, euphemistically called wards, as among adult inmates.

What are the alternatives to an institutionalized grievance mechanism? In a prison population, they are surely not attractive. The primary purpose of grievance is to permit change. Even where the grievant is complaining about a past event, the grievance proceeding is concerned not only with the grievant's feeling of having been unjustly dealt with, but also with educating and explaining so that the same or a similar incident will not recur with the same or with another grievant. If a mechanism in which inmates could participate to change policy and to review charges of injustices were not available, would-be grievants could be left with less constructive remedies (which could range from pleading with appropriate staff persons for relief to resorting to violence). Often, complaints expressed by prisoners during or after a riot seem reasonable and one wonders why the prison administration was not able to respond to them before the outbreak of violence. It is the purpose of the grievance mechanism to make complaints known so that they can be fairly dealt with as they arise. The fact that the grievance procedure is institutionalized—that is, the grievant has *rights* within the procedure—encourages expression and resolution of conflict rather than repression and outburst.

Each of the CYA institutions has fashioned and implemented its own grievance structure, although all must follow the minimum requirement of the state law. Generally, one or more grievance clerks service each of an institution's housing units. The clerk informally reviews new grievances and assists the grievant in filling out the appropriate complaint forms. Sometimes a grievance clerk can and does resolve a dispute through informal discussion before it ever gets to the grievance stage.

Once a dispute is grieved (formally submitted to the process), it is generally heard by a committee of two wards and two staff people. A fifth member (a ward or a staff member), who does not vote, acts as moderator. The grievant is entitled to be represented by another ward, a staff member, or anyone else. There is a second level of review, generally by the institution's superintendent or his or her representative, followed in some cases (for example, when CYA departmental policy is involved) by further review by the CYA director.

Finally, a grievant unsatisfied with the superintendent's or director's decision can seek advisory arbitration. There are three arbitrators. One is selected by the grievant and can be another ward, a staff person, or an outside volunteer. One is selected by the CYA director or facility superintendent. The third is chosen by the other two from a pool of volunteer professional arbitrators secured through the offices of the American Arbitration Association.

The provision for outside arbitration is perhaps the most innovative part of the grievance procedure. Although the arbitration is "advisory" in the sense that the director of the CYA can overrule the arbitrators' award under certain circumstances, the award itself carries a certain force of its own which, together with the commitment to the idea of outside review in the first instance, makes it difficult to reject the arbitrators' decision. Issues that have been arbitrated have led to decisions granting wards the right to grow beards and requiring that discipline for minor infractions be subject to review prior to the imposition of the discipline. Charges of staff threats against wards have also been dealt with in arbitration. In the beard case, the director had rejected a change of the rules permitting wards to grow beards; but the arbitrators, in a two-to-one decision, ruled that wards who have been referred to parole should be allowed to grow beards. The director let the arbitrators' decision stand.

A study by the Law Enforcement Assistance Administration (LEAA) for the twenty-month period ending April 1975 showed that of about 1,400 grievances, 17 percent were resolved informally prior to a hearing, 42 percent were resolved at the ward-staff committee level, and 25 percent were resolved by the institution's superintendent. The balance were reviewed by the CYA director or referred to arbitration. In 1978, there was a shift from committee to informal review. The breakdown by mode of resolution was: informal, 36 percent; committee, 22 percent; superintendent, 29 percent; CYA director 0.3 percent; arbitration, 0.5 percent. The remaining 10 percent of the cases are still going though various stages of the process. Thus, almost 60 percent of the grievances were settled infomally or by the ward-staff committee. Those that went higher did so because the issues involved institutional or departmental policy that could only be resolved by the superintendent or the CYA director.

The LEAA study also broke down the grievances by type. The largest category, accounting for some 40 percent of all grievances, involved individual problems—such as a complaint about how an institutional rule was being applied to a particular ward—rather than a challenge to the rule itself. A third of the grievances involved challenges to a rule or policy. Fewer than one-fifth of all grievances were charges by a ward that a member of the staff had acted arbitrarily toward him or her. The balance of the grievances, about one-tenth, include complaints by one ward against another and complaints about faulty equipment or inadequate physical facilities as well as other issues. In 1978, 52 percent of grievances involved the application of rules; 18 percent were challenges to the rules themselves; 21 percent involved staff action; 3 percent were complaints against peers; 5 percent were complaints about equipment or environment; and the balance concerned miscellaneous topics.

One possible indicator of the success of the grievance procedure is the extent to which it is used. In the first forty months of operation, between September 1973 and December 1976, approximately 15,000 grievances were filed (about 375 per month). In 1978, there were between 500 and 600 greivances filed each month. Some have argued that a small number of grievances at a particular institution may simply reflect good staff work, but others feel that conflict is inevitable within an inmate population and that a low grievance rate may actually reflect fear of retaliation or ignorance of the existence of the grievance operation.

The possibility of retribution by a staff member against a ward who files a grievance is a primary concern of both Linda Singer and CYA personnel. Singer acknowledged that there is no absolute way to anticipate reprisals. Furthermore, the danger of reprisal is especially great in states like California, where, until recently, sentences were indeterminate or open-ended. One precaution Singer suggested was to prohibit indication on a ward's record of the filing of a grievance. But this would not exclude other means of retribution. For example, as David Dillingham, a research analyst at the Youth Authority, explains, the major danger of reprisal is that a staff member will begin to "write the ward up" for failure to observe institution rules. Since every institution has hundreds of rules, a staff person can easily find violations.

The grievance procedure has some incidental advantages in addition to its value as a means of dispute resolution. Dillingham believes that the grievance process is therapeutic as an end in itself. It shows the ward that his or her point of view will be heard and this itself has a rehabilitative effect. The grievance system also has a collateral educational value. Some wards became eloquent representatives of their "clients" during grievance hearings. At the advisory arbitration stage, wards have written sophisticated legal briefs, complete with case citations.

To assure continuity and consistency of the grievance procedure, all grievances and their resolutions are summarized and digested periodically. These digests are placed in the law libraries (located in each institution) to which all wards have access.

One problem for professionals in the corrections community is how to weave the grievance theory into the various approaches to incarceration, especially incarceration of young people. Richard Kolze, who was the superintendent of the Holton School when the grievance procedure was first instituted, and who is a strong advocate of it, suggested that grievances could be seen from four perspectives: the legal rights perspective, the treatment perspective, the humanitarian perspective, and the "militancy" perspective. The last perspective advances the notion that grievances are necessary because institutions are inherently inimical to wards.

Kolze said that it was important for him to convince his staff, when grievance mechanisms were instituted at Holton, that he did not have a "militancy" perspective. Rather, Kolze said, he explained that he favored grievance procedures for humanitarian reasons. Everyone should have "the means to mediate their environment," Kolze maintained. Social workers and teachers, operating from a treatment model, have the greatest problem with a grievance mechanism, Kolze said. Some social workers, he added, believe that if a ward has a complaint, it is the ward's problem since everything that is being done is for the ward's benefit. Teachers were able to accept the grievance procedure only outside the classroom, since they considered themselves professionals who should not be subject to a grievance mechanism.

Whether an argument for exemption from grievance mechanisms is based on professionalism or on inconsistency with one or another rehabilitation theory, power issues are always present as an undercurrent. Linda Singer recognizes that in instituting grievance procedures, an institution is really redistributing power. Although grievance procedures result in a transfer of power from staff to inmate, prison administrators lose relatively little. And while, in theory, grievances can be filed against wards by other wards, in fact, this rarely happens. Ward-against-ward grievances are not tolerated in the delinquent subculture. If they occur at all, Kolze said, they usually involve petty complaints (such as the failure to take a shower), but nothing as substantial as an allegation of stealing or a charge relating to sexual issues.

The notion that the grievance mechanism has the primary effect of making the staff accountable—without threatening the administration or the ward population—was repeated several times in interviews with CYA personnel. Robert Mabbutt, deputy director of CYA, confirmed that the staff sees the Ward Grievance Procedure as a threat. Some staff members, therefore, opposed outside arbitration of grievances against employees, Mabbutt said; and, as a compromise, two "protections" sought by staff members were built into the system. First, although the existence of a staff violation is still grievable, any penalty must be administratively determined within the CYA and is not subject to the grievance mechanism. Second, if a staff member is grieved against for conduct that could result in punitive action, the advisory arbitration is before a single arbitrator rather than a panel of arbitrators that would include a ward representative.

Both Mabbutt and Kolze believe that to win staff acceptance of a grievance procedure, it is necessary to involve all levels of the staff in both developing and implementing it. Mabbutt suggested that any state considering a grievance mechanism should first look to California, fully explore its system, and then, if it decides to go ahead, make an effort to convince its own correctional staff that the grievance procedure will benefit them.

The Procedure at Work

The Northern Reception Center Clinic

The Northern Reception Center Clinic (NRCC) houses forty wards (mostly young men) with psychological or medical problems. The unit is run by John Holland. Four grievances that were heard at NRCC demonstrated that many complaints can be comparatively minor. Some personnel said that in the early years of the grievance procedure many antiquated policies at CYA institutions and in the central CYA administration itself were successfully challenged. After these policies were weeded out, the percentage of grievances involving less serious, or personal complaints, increased.

The grievance procedure at NRCC resolved the following issues:

1. One ward complained that he did not have a desk in his room. Another ward had offered him a desk, but the grievant felt that it was too small. Although new desks had been ordered, they were not expected to arrive for several months. The grievant claimed that he could not spread out his books and maps and do his homework without a desk. After discussion, one of the two wards on the ward-staff committee offered to give the grievant his own desk in a few weeks when he was scheduled to be released. This was acceptable to the grievant and the matter was closed.

2. There were two showers in the unit. When only one shower was operating, the hot water was too hot. To prevent this, one ward had the responsibility of assuring that both showers were going at the same time. Because he failed to do this on one occasion, the grievant had taken an unexpectedly and unnecessarily hot shower. The matter was resolved with an understanding that closer attention would be paid to this problem.

3. Wards were allowed twenty minutes to eat meals. Some staff members were measuring the twenty minutes from the time that the first ward went through the meal line, with the result that the last ward had only about ten minutes to eat. It was agreed that staff would be reminded that wards were to have a minimum of twenty minutes measured from the time the last ward went through the meal line.

4. Wards were required to shut their room lights by 10:00 or 11:00 P.M. on weekday and weekend nights, respectively. The grievant felt this was too early. He said that since wards did not leave their rooms

the following morning until 7:00 or 8:00 A.M., respectively, it meant that they were in their rooms with lights out for nine hours, although they only needed eight hours of sleep. One panel member pointed out that the sun rose well before 7:00 or 8:00 A.M., so that the wards were not in complete darkness. The Youth Authority had a departmental law requiring lights out by a certain time, even earlier than the particular institution allowed. The ward-staff committee declined to create any additional exceptions to the departmental rule. The grievant chose to appeal to the superintendent.

Holland feels that it is important for a grievance to reach the hearing stage. Research in dispute resolution has shown that when a resolution is reached through a formal hearing, rather than through informal methods, the grievant has a greater sense of fairness. This is true, Holland believes, even though the same resolution may be reached in either case. In his unit, therefore, he does not emphasize informal settlement of grievances before hearings.

Holland also believes that the grievance mechanism could work as well with the youngest wards as it does with adult prisoners. It will work better, he said, if the superintendent is behind it and if the fear of reprisal can be dealt with. Holland feels that the staff members' fears of reprisal from the administration as a result of being grieved against will be communicated to the wards, who, in turn, will fear reprisal from the staff. Recently, when a staff member was accused of hitting a child, and the grievance procedure resulted in a letter being placed in the employee's personnel file, Holland went out of his way to make sure that everyone understood that making grievances or being grieved against would not automatically result in reprisals by the administration.

DeWitt Nelson Training Center

At the DeWitt Nelson Training Center in Stockton, Dan Fishman, a transplanted New Yorker, is the school's social worker and chief of its grievance committee. Fishman acts as the fifth man, or the neutral, at first-level hearings. DeWitt Nelson has a population of 250 (it was built for 400), about 100 of whom go outside the gates each day to work or be trained. The wards live in dorms of 50 each.

When the DeWitt Nelson center was instructed to set up a grievance mechanism, it adopted a three-tier system. The first tier is a ward-staff committee on an institutional level. While other schools created similar committees at the unit level, DeWitt Nelson decided on one that was facility-wide. The second tier is an appeal to the superintendent of the facility or to the CYA director, depending upon who has jurisdiction over the particular issue grieved. The final tier is advisory arbitration.

Fishman acknowledged that there was initial staff resentment to the grievance procedure and, in fact, said resentment still exists. He shares the view held by others that the grievance mechanism dissipates the power of the staff over the wards. As he put it, the grievance mechanism "moderates or mediates" staff power. In order to work, Fishman said, staff and wards must trust the administration and the administration must be knowledgeable about the ways in which grievances can be abused. Fishman believes, for example, that wards sometimes organize to "get" a particular staff member by filing many grievances against that employee. When the procedure was instituted, the administration was not completely aware of how the grievance mechanism could be abused, Fishman maintained, but he believes this is no longer so.

Fishman sees the grievance mechanism as one additional avenue for dispute resolution. "Whether it's written down or not, you've got to settle problems," he said. The grievance procedure is "one additional way to do it but it should not be seen as the only way and it should not be the only way." Staff members must also be able to use their skills to settle problems outside a grievance mechanism.

DeWitt Nelson averages about twenty grievances per month, comparatively low for the Youth Authority. Fishman believes that the low figure is due, in part, to the fact that first-level grievances go to a facility-wide committee rather than to a unit committee. This tends to increase the stakes in the eyes of a grievant.

What kind of complaints have been made at DeWitt Nelson? Fishman cited one by a ward to the effect that a staff person, in searching the ward's bed and locker, had left the lock and bedding on the floor. At the grievance hearing, the staff person said that he did not believe he had violated the rules and had in fact not done what the ward said. Although the issue of veracity was not resolved, it was agreed that the staff person would be more careful in the future. The ward accepted this resolution. Fishman, recognizing that the grievance mechanism did not really determine the facts of this case, explained that the committee has no extensive "investigatory power."

When a grievance comes in, Fishman does preinvestigative work to define the issues for a hearing. More than the others, Fishman sees the hearing as a mechanism for discussing and resolving the dispute by agreement. He is opposed to using it to assert adversary positions. Ward and staff members are selected for the grievance committee by a trainee advisory committee consisting of ward grievance clerks and by a staff advisory committee. The trainee advisory committee nominates six potential ward hearing officers and the staff committee does the same from among its members. The wards then select three of the six nominated staff members to serve on the hearing committee and the staff selects three of the six nominated wards. In this way, wards and staff members each have a say in the other's representation. Each committee member serves for six months.

Initially, the DeWitt Nelson staff was hostile to the grievance procedure but the hostility lessened as the staff realized that the procedure was not instituted to "get" them. Many felt that the success or failure of the grievance mechanism depended on staff attitude and that staff attitude depended on two things: the amount of training the staff received prior to the institution of grievance procedures and the staff's perception of the administration's fairness and commitment to the process.

Ventura School

At the Ventura School in Camarillo, just north of Los Angeles, most of the wards are high school or college students. Ventura also houses most of the females committed to CYA custody. Susan Hooper is the superintendent; Patricia Wolfgram is the grievance coordinator.

Ventura is set up on a cottage system. There are six cottages with up to forty-nine wards in each. High school wards are separated from college wards and men are separated from women. Unlike the facility-wide committee at DeWitt Nelson, each cottage has a separate grievance committee composed of two wards and two staff members. Like Fishman at DeWitt Nelson, Wolfgram is the constant "neutral" on each grievance committee. Each cottage also has a grievance clerk and an assistant grievance clerk whose jobs are to receive grievances and assist wards in preparing them. Grievance clerks meet on a weekly basis to review the "state of the law"—to discuss the written account of departmental grievances received at each institution and placed in its law library.

Echoing a concern voiced by John Holland of NRCC, Hooper and Wolfgram said that they had "mandated out" the informal resolution of grievances because of the "potential for abuse": serious grievances could be deflected or compromised. Only grievances involving ward-staff relations are excepted from this ruling. Hooper and Wolfgram believe that wards and staff members should be able to resolve their problems informally.

Hooper and Wolfgram expressed concern that most grievances were filed as emergencies, even though they were not emergencies. Only about 5 percent of the claimed emergencies really deserved that label, they maintained. If a grievance is filed as an emergency but is then judged not to be one, thereby requiring no priority treatment, it can be dismissed. The ward is then free to refile the grievance on a nonemergency basis. But Hooper and Wolfgram said that refiling rarely occurred.

As many as 70 to 80 percent of filed grievances were designated emergencies by those filing, who, Hooper and Wolfgram believe, did so in anger. Although the grievance clerk is supposed to screen grievances, the ward has a right to file a grievance as an emergency even if the grievance clerk disagrees.

Hooper and Wolfgram believe also that there should be some limit on outside arbitration, as in the case of a ward's complaint that the school refused to subscribe to *Easy Rider* magazine at school expense. The school subscribes to various magazines, but decided against ordering *Easy Rider*. The ward was free to use his own money to subscribe to the magazine, but he did not want to. The ward grieved the issue.

Hooper mentioned an additional example of a dispute that should not go to arbitration. In her view, the arbitrator did not understand the school's setting and therefore could not rule wisely. A student had been disciplined at Level A, a designation defining minor infractions. The severest sanction that can be imposed for a Level A infraction is a twenty-four-hour lockup. The school has a two-stage review and an appeal procedure for a Level A infraction. But Ventura routinely imposed the Level A sanction before a review was held. One student grieved, claiming that if the sanction were removed after review or appeal, the student would already have suffered the twenty-four-hour lockup. The school responded that the record of the sanction would be taken out of the student's file if the sanction were removed after review or appeal. The student thought this was not sufficient. The arbitrators ruled that the sanction could not be applied until the review process was concluded, but that it could be applied prior to appeal. The issue went to the director of CYA.

Hooper and Wolfgram reported that the number of arbitrations at Ventura decreased because the administration has succeeded in talking students out of going to arbitration. In 1977, about twenty wards were dissuaded from arbitrating a grievance, in some cases, apparently, after a settlement in which the school agreed to a compromise. While it was obvious that Hooper and Wolfgram do not like arbitration and see it as an infringement of their own authority over the institution, Hooper said that talking a ward out of arbitration often took so long that it was just as easy to arbitrate.

Three grievance clerks interviewed at Ventura agreed that the emergency procedure was abused and said that they often had tried unsuccessfully to talk wards out of filing such grievances. The grievance clerks explained that, according to the rules, a ward filing an emergency grievance was entitled to a verbal response within twenty-four hours and a written response within three days. Emergency grievances were filed, said the clerks, because grievants did not want to wait for a longer period. One of the clerks thought that resorting to the emergency designation reflected a lack of maturity on the part of grievants. The three also suggested that the best way to deal with the problem would be to have a two-week course on the grievance procedure for all incoming students, including a lecture on proper use of the emergency grievance.

One clerk cited a recent case in which a ward had complained about the time of church services. Catholic services were routinely held at 8:30 A.M., while Protestant services were held at 10:00 A.M. The grievant, who was Catholic, said that this discriminated against Catholics because they had to get up earlier. The committee recommended a change in policy so that Catholic services would be held at 8:30 A.M. for six months and then at 10:00 A.M. for the following six months. This modification was adopted by the superintendent.

Another clerk said that without the grievance procedure he would not even be at Ventura. Apparently, when he was a ward at the NRCC, he had been transferred to Ventura by the CYA board. When NRCC decided not to send him to Ventura, he complained that the NRCC staff could not overrule the board and he filed a grievance. The NRCC staff told him that if he were willing to withdraw his grievance, he would be sent to Ventura the next day. He agreed.

All three wards emphasized that they would be "lost" without the grievance procedure. They could not have obtained television sets or radios. They could not have grieved policy issues (such as hair length, facial hair, and pants for women) or won the right to see the staff psychiatrist. One ward summed up the grievance procedure by saying that without it, "the rights of wards would be meaningless."

Ward-Staff Consensus

A noteworthy aspect of the operation of the grievance mechanism in CYA facilities is that, with few exceptions, wards and staff generally agree on the resolution of particular grievances. Some believed, before the procedure was instituted, that grievance panels composed of two staff members and two wards would, with regularity, split down the middle. But this did not happen. According to Singer, the resolution is usually unanimous.

Unanimity can be explained in many ways, including a hesitancy to disagree. But supporters of the grievance procedure would argue that unanimity means that the procedure is working well, that all of the arguments and facts for and against a particular resolution are revealed, and that four people who share a community—although playing different roles in it—understand what is necessary and fair in their special world.

3
The Snoqualmie River Conflict: Bringing Mediation into Environmental Disputes

Lee Dembart
Richard Kwartler

Introduction

All British diplomats, it is said, are given three rules to follow: never lie, never tell the whole truth, and never miss a chance to go to the bathroom. That advice might also be given to those involved in an endeavor requiring the same interpersonal skills and sensitivities as diplomacy—mediation. And in none of the new fields to which mediation has come in recent years is the need for such talent greater than in environmental affairs. Like the diplomat, the environmental mediator often works with disputes that have divided communities or regions for a decade or longer. A leading environmental mediator, in a frank discussion of his field, said recently: "Mediation takes power and the only basis for mediating disputes is fear—fear that something worse will happen" if there is no mediation. Change the word mediation to diplomacy and you might have had a diplomat speaking.

The environmental mediator who talked about fear is Gerald W. Cormick. In 1973, he and another mediator, Jane McCarthy, once an investment counselor, moved mediation for the first time in U.S. history into the field of environmental affairs, and they became the first formally designated mediators to undertake the settlement of an environmental dispute. They didn't pick an easy one.

For about fifteen years, a conflict had raged in and around Seattle, Washington, over whether a flood-control dam should be built on the Snoqualmie River. The battle involved local, state, and federal agencies; farmers; land developers; and environmentalists. Cormick and McCarthy moved into this caldron. They are currently unofficially involved—although they successfully produced a mediated agreement at the end of 1974 after seven months of intensive negotiation, implementation still appears to be a long way off. The situation has raised questions about the responsibility of mediators with regard to implementation and about whether the right tactics were used in this dispute to insure implementation. There is even the possibility that the mediated agreement may come apart because of the lack of further progress, which would raise still more questions.

Governor Dan Evans appointed Cormick and McCarthy as the official mediators in the dispute. Now president of Evergreen State College in Olympia, Washington, Evans said that if the mediated agreement isn't implemented "it would be a shame; it's the best proposal to come along for solving a very complex problem."

This chapter tells the Snoqualmie story and describes the work of the mediators. Both mediators earned the respect and even the affection of participants in the mediation process and of observers. Cormick, who has been called the "inventor" of environmental mediation, has gone on to mediate other similar disputes and has inspired agencies and organizations to follow his lead. McCarthy received a top reference from George Yount, an environmentalist involved in the Snoqualmie dispute; he described her as a "minor god."

The environment is one of society's most recent concerns. Until Rachel Carson's *Silent Spring* of the early 1960s, land, air, and water were there to be taken and used, most often for commercial purposes. Nature existed to serve humankind. The realization that natural resources had limits and that care should be taken with the balance of nature grew slowly and fitfully, reaching a peak with Earth Day in 1970.

All the while, no weaker forces than business and labor stood side by side against the growing number of environmentalists. On one side was the understandable desire for profit and for jobs; on the other side environmentalists offered cleaner air and water. "We would rather save a man than save a tree," labor leaders scoffed. "Labor would brick over the Grand Canyon if it meant steady work," the environmentalists answered.

Then shortages began to be felt. Utility company executives, who had warned that if they could not build power plants they could not supply power, suddenly sounded less like misanthropes and more like sensible men. The public realized that protecting the environment costs money, and they were less inclined to pay the costs than they had been to cheer for nature. Environmental standards were relaxed by community after community and by the federal government.

Still, the environmental movement successfully lobbied for legislation that embodied many of its goals, and it pressed the courts to enforce the legislation. Significantly, unlike the dissidents in many other disputes—involving racial balance in schools or housing, for example—environmentalists tend not to come from society's oppressed groups. Perhaps more than any other major protest movement of recent years, they draw the bulk of their support from the white middle class. By background, they are comfortable with the process of give and take that is negotiation. Often, their commitment is born of ideology rather than of pressing social or personal economic need. As a result, environmental clashes frequently lack the immediacy of disputes in other arenas. They can go on for years. No answer is required today. What's more, still unlike other disputes, delay favors the dissidents, and they have become skilled in the art of dragging things out.

The Issues

Against this background, politically powerful environmentalists and sportsmen in the Seattle area squared off against farmers and other residents of a fertile agricultural and recreational area thirty miles northeast of Seattle. The farmers and residents had suffered serious periodic flooding by the Snoqualmie River. The Snoqualmie winds its way out of the Cascade Mountians east of Seattle and moves through the agricultural area—the Snohomish River Basin—until it flows into Puget Sound, north of the city. The farmers and other residents wanted flood protection in the form of a dam, but the environmentalists feared that removing the flood threat would lead to heavy commercial development and would spoil one of the few remaining naturally scenic areas readily accessible to Seattle.

The upper portions of the basin form miles of white-water rapids used frequently by sports fishermen and kayakers and highly prized by naturalists. Hikers and others take great pleasure in the adjacent forests of Douglas fir. The environmentalists feared the development and suburbanization of this area if a dam were built on the Middle Fork of the Snoqualmie, as originally proposed in a study by the Army

Corps of Engineers. One contributing factor to the environmentalists' fears was the experience in the nearby Green River Valley. Ed Delanty, one of the key environmentalists and the chairman of the Interim Basin Coordinating Committee attempting to implement the mediated agreement, said: "We had gone through this tremendous experience in the Green River Valley in which . . . a dam provided 100-year flood protection in the lower valley and it went to instant development and cement."

The environmentalists and their supporters were also suspicious of the farmers' motives. They believed that the farmers wanted flood protection not so much to protect their crops, livestock, and homes, but rather to push already escalating land values much higher so that they could sell out at a large profit. Actually, as the mediation process disclosed, the farmers really wanted to remain on the land. They were as much against unrestrained development as were the environmentalists because it made farming uneconomical. One estimate placed the agricultural value of an acre at that time at $800—yet it was selling for $2,000.

Events Leading to Mediation

The formal mediation, which began in May 1974, was aided in successfully reaching a compromise agreement because the various sides had been meeting privately before the mediators entered the dispute. However, although they had agreed among themselves on broad outlines for an eventual settlement, no agreement had emerged from the private talks, and the talks were stalemated. The mediators got all sides talking again, and they suggested the direction in which the negotiations might fruitfully continue. Cormick noted that he and McCarthy took six months prior to coming into the dispute to determine whether the involved parties were ready to compromise and would really give mediation a fair chance. Such careful preparation is necessary, he feels, because mediation is a voluntary process that cannot work if either side is seriously hesitant about participating.

Actually, the damming of the Snoqualmie River had been debated for fifteen years. Yet the dispute was not at a crisis stage when the mediators first arrived on the scene in 1973. In fact, despite serious frustration on all sides, it had never been at a crisis stage, if crisis connotes violence or the threat of violence. There was no confrontation in the streets, and there was not likely to be one. But this is normal for environmental disputes. Although partisans argue heatedly for their points of view, most environmental conflicts have no flash point. Only rarely do the environmentalists sit down in front of bulldozers and invite arrest. To underscore the limited impact of the Snoqualmie conflict on segments of the community at large, a number of the participants readily agreed that many people in Seattle and surrounding areas may never have heard of the controversy.

Although the dispute did not require immediate attention for the sake of public order, it was of vital concern to the residents of the flood plain, whose homes and property were regularly damaged, and it aroused strong emotions among those in the city thirty miles away who were committed to keeping the area free of suburban sprawl.

There was strong pressure on Governor Evans to act. After nearly ten years of confronting the problem, he felt he had to do something. Evans, a civil engineer by profession, agreed with the environmentalists that the Middle Fork dam was ill-advised, and he had twice rejected proposals to build it. In addition to the Corps of Engineers, which is charged with reducing flood damage in the United States, the state's Department of Ecology had also recommended the Middle Fork solution. Evans knew he could not keep saying no in the face of the studies and with the knowledge that sooner or later another flood would devastate the area. He liked the idea of mediation in part because it enabled him to buy more time in which to decide whether to allow construction of the dam.

Furthermore, some development was already going on in the flood plain, regardless of the danger that a major flood might someday wash everything into Puget Sound. The environmentalists realized that they were losing the battle to preserve the valley even without the dam's being built—and they didn't know how much longer they could delay construction. Thus, the indecision was hurting both the environmentalists and the farmers, both of whom saw themselves losing what they wanted. The environmentalists were watching the valley being developed, and the farmers were not getting flood protection. The need for mediation became clear.

The controversy surrounding the Snohomish River Basin, a watershed area of 690 square miles, began in 1959 when a major storm caused severe flooding on the Snoqualmie, Skykomish, and Snohomish rivers, doing $8 million damage to homes, property, and utilities in the largely agricultural region. The following year, the state of Washington requested flood-control assistance from Congress. A series of studies and reports by both King County (which includes Seattle and most of the land in the basin) and by the Army Corps of Engineers led to a proposal by the corps in May 1970 for a flood-control dam and reservoir on the Middle Fork of the Snoqualmie. That recommendation was based on ten years of extensive study. The King County Council approved the plan.

It must be noted that the environmental movement has far greater clout in the Pacific Northwest, with its rivers, forests, and other numerous examples of natural beauty, than in most other areas of the country. Even before the 1970 corps report, representatives of a number of politically powerful environmental groups had expressed concern about the construction of any dam on the Snoqualmie. The Sierra Club, the Mountaineers, the Kayak Club, the Washington Environmental Council, Friends of the Earth, the League of Women Voters, and other groups were strongly opposed to damming the river because of their belief that it would lead to commercial development of the land downstream that would be removed from the flood plain.

With the issues clearly drawn between the residents who wanted flood protection and the environmentalists who wanted land protection, the state's Department of Ecology analyzed the Corps of Engineers' proposal. In November 1970, the department recommended to Governor Evans that the Middle Fork dam not be authorized and that the corps be asked to study alternate methods of flood control. In December 1970, the governor agreed. The corps restudied the situation and concluded again that a dam on the Middle Fork offered the best protection to people living in the flood plain. But in December 1973, Governor Evans again rejected the proposal, calling the Middle Fork project "environmentally disruptive" and "unacceptable to a majority of our people based on today's standards."

In the meantime, although a stalemate seemingly existed, the situation was actually much more fluid. The farmers in the valley shared the environmentalists' desire to keep the land as it was. They did not want to lose their farms to commercial interests who would build tract housing, shopping centers, or industrial complexes.

This shared goal became clear when the environmentalists began meeting informally with the farmers and townspeople during 1973.

Dick Burhans, an architect who lives in the town of North Bend, which gets flooded every time the Snoqualmie overflows its banks, described what happened when a group of mountain climbers—the environmentalists—dropped by his house for a chat:

> We start talking about a dam, we start talking about flood protection. They had no reason to object to flood protection. What they were objecting to was the result of that structure. They were complaining about what happens to land use on down the river. It turns commercial, and you lose the valleys.
>
> I talked to my friends in town and my neighbors. They don't want the land commercial. They want the valley pristine, rural, just like it is. They don't want to lose their farms. These two groups are both saying the same thing.

Burhans, sensing the kernel of agreement, invited the leading farmers and the leading environmentalists to his home to see how far agreement extended and how far it could be pushed. The farmers were in a mood to talk because they thought Governor Evans's opposition to the dam project meant that they were beaten. They wanted to see what could be salvaged. "We drew an outline on what each side wanted," Burhans recalled. "I think there were 10 items on that outline which no one could object to. Flood protection. They had no objection to flood protection. Land protection. We had no objection to land protection."

At the meeting, a clash erupted between a major landowner and one of the most fervent environmentalists, who charged that the only thing the landowner wanted was to increase the value of his property so he could develop it. Among the landowner's holdings was a valuable parcel at the confluence of the three forks of the Snoqualmie River, land that the environmentalists had long sought for a park. To show his good faith, the landowner offered to trade the land for property elsewhere, and the Three Rivers Park eventually became part of the mediated agreement.

The group met twice more, and then sent a letter to the governor saying that a compromise had been struck. "The Governor either didn't see it or didn't believe it," Burhans said. "He didn't pay any attention to it. He just rejected the dam." It was at this point that Cormick and McCarthy entered the picture.

Mediation Begins

In 1973, Cormick, then 32, was director of the Community Crisis Intervention Center at Washington University in St. Louis. He was also an associate professor of sociology and he holds a Ph.D. in business administration. Cormick had mediated community, racial, and labor disputes in the United States and in Canada, where he was born. Prior to going to St. Louis, he worked with the Institute for Mediation and Conflict Resolution in New York. The institute was funded by the Ford Foundation at various levels, ranging from partial to complete, and as early as 1971 Cormick began talking to foundation officers about the possibility of moving mediation into the environmental field. He kept his interest in that concept while in St. Louis and late in 1972 he again talked with a foundation program officer about his interest in the environment. Cormick recalled: "I told him, however, that I was a little reluctant to go exploring this field because of my own lack of experience as to the issues and parties involved. He said, 'We have someone working with us here who might be just the person you need in this exploratory phase.' And that was Jane McCarthy."

McCarthy, then 42, was a consultant to the Ford Foundation and had served in the same position with other social agencies. She had worked in such areas as designing programs in urban environmental management and developing natural resource programs. She had also spent several years working as a counselor for an investment banking firm. She has a degree in labor economics.

One of McCarthy's projects involved work on river basin planning in Seattle, where she made valuable contacts among local, state, and federal officials. She also developed a reputation as someone concerned with environmental affairs—a fact that proved valuable later on.

Once they were introduced, Cormick and McCarthy agreed to search for an environmental dispute that would be suitable for a mediation effort. They looked for seven or eight months before deciding upon Snoqualmie. They realized that it would be an extremely tough assignment, but decided after about six months of study to go ahead. McCarthy described the process this way:

> The tough part was finding somebody who was willing to let you experiment on them. Fortunately, I had built up a very strong relationship, as a result of a grant we had in Seattle, with Sydney Steinborn of

> the Corps of Engineers. [Steinborn was then the corps' chief civilian engineer.] Sydney kept coming to the Snoqualmie issue, and he really desperately wanted to build an enormous dam on the Middle Fork. . . . He didn't understand why the Governor didn't understand that it was so valuable. So Sydney kept coming back to this, and I kept saying, "Sydney, we cannot do that. It is a multimillion dollar dispute; we have to start small. I want to start with something like a local developer and local authorities and sort of grow into something like this. If we do this and botch it, the whole process is in jeopardy and it's really not fair." Well, he kept coming back to it, and I didn't have a dispute so he said, "Come on let's take a look at it." We started talking to the parties and we ended up doing that dispute. That was how we got the dispute. We really got it because it was the only one we could find.

During the entire period of their participation in the mediation process, Cormick maintained his home in St. Louis and McCarthy kept hers in New York. They commuted to Seattle by air—and they feel that such a procedure added a beneficial sense of drama and urgency to the mediation process.

In determining whether mediation would be acceptable to the disputants, Cormick and McCarthy discovered who the key participants were by asking everyone concerned: "Can you name 10 or 12 persons who, if they could agree on something, would have stature and influence enough so that you, who are in disagreement, could reasonably support them and any agreement they might reach?" Those named most often became part of the group that would meet with Cormick and McCarthy to try to work out a compromise. Included in the final selection were Burhans; Delanty, an engineer at the huge Boeing headquarters plant in Seattle; George Yount, a high school teacher and dedicated environmentalist; a dairy farmer and a store owner, both of whom had suffered from past floods; and a realtor who lived in the flood plain. Each was a private citizen representing a view held by a group.

In a crucial decision, Cormick decided to keep out of the mediation sessions elected or appointed government officials who would someday have to implement any compromise agreement. He defends that decision now, even though implementation has stalled due to the reluctance of local officials to take certain actions. Cormick argues that it made no sense and, in fact, would have been counterproductive to have included government people in the Snoqualmie mediation sessions. He firmly believes that officials who have the power to make decisions cannot meet on an equal and effective basis with private citizens who lack such power. "There are a couple of problems," he said.

> One is that if you include them, you end up getting right back into the very same kinds of arguments that you get into at a public hearing. You've got someone in there who you think can make a decision, and you spend your time trying to persuade them that you are right rather than sitting down with your opposite number who disagrees with you and trying to see if you can come up with something jointly that you can take to the government decision makers. We wanted to get some sort of consensus among the citizens so that when they made a decision it was essentially based on some sort of harmony. . . . There is another reason, too. It may well be illegal under the Sunshine Laws out here for elected officials to sit down with selected . . . citizens. I'm convinced there would have been no agreement if they [officials] had been involved.

On this point, Governor Evans, Delanty, and others tended to agree with Cormick, although at times they appeared to waver. Said Evans: "It was probably the best way to go. It gave the people involved a real stake in making the final decision." Evans, Cormick, and others pointed out that although officials did not actually attend the mediation sessions, some were briefed as regularly as possible on developments. Cormick kept King County officials reasonably informed of what was taking place. There was, however, less communication with officials of adjacent Snohomish County, in which part of the river basin lies, and there was virutally none with the fifteen towns in the river basin that would ultimately have to agree to adopt land-use regulations that were being drawn up. Under state law, land-use prerogatives belong to the towns.

One problem that the mediators faced throughout was the need for deadlines. As is well known in labor disputes, people do not like to make decisions in negotiations unless they have to. In labor talks, the deadline is built in: The contract has an expiration date after which, if there is no agreement, there will be a strike. Decisions are made at the last minute because until then each side holds out in the hope of securing better terms. To overcome the problem, the mediators invented deadlines by which time, they said, they had to report to the governor. But the sense of urgency had to be constantly created.

The promising start that the adversaries had made on their own quickly bogged down as each side pressed its presumed advantages in what had reverted to an adversary proceeding. "We had been talking at the level of specifics where it didn't matter and about generalities where it did matter," said Delanty, who is an influential member of the Kayak Club and probably the most persistent of the environmentalists. He has devoted hundreds of hours of his free time and spent a lot of his own money on travel and phone calls to try to settle the dispute as fairly as possible. "Of course, what you need to be doing is speaking of specifics where it matters and generalities where it doesn't," he added.

Although everyone in the mediation group agreed with the Corps of Engineers that the Middle Fork dam offered the best flood protection, the position of the environmental groups had hardened against it to the point that the mediators themselves had to force the discussions toward other alternatives. Every nonstructural flood-control idea was tried and discarded. The only viable alternative was a dam on the North Fork of the Snoqualmie plus an improved system of dikes and levees throughout the flood plain. Although this system offered less flood protection than the Middle Fork dam, it could be sold to the environmentalists because it would cause much less damage to the scenic areas.

"What makes mediation work is that it seeks to protect people from arbitrary change," said Cormick. "The environmentalists had agreed to a dam on the Middle Fork, but the mediators knew they [the environmentalists] couldn't sell it [to their organizations]. The mediators refused to hold any more joint meetings until the environmentalists went back to their constituents and tried it out on them." Delanty recalled:

> I was arguing the case for the Middle Fork because I believed one, that technically it was the best solution, certainly from an engineering standpoint, and two, I thought that a very viable project could be put together on that basis that had a good chance of being implemented.
>
> But the powers in the environmental movement were not so disposed. In fact, they said they would not do that. The only thing they would consider was a program built around the North Fork.

Delanty noted that the Middle Fork dam under consideration by the environmentalists was sharply altered in form and would have caused less environmental damage than the one proposed originally by the corps.

At this point, those in favor of the dam recognized the political problem of the environmentalists and compromised. "We all had to agree on a less-viable compromise, which was the North Fork," said Burhans. "It cost more money, doesn't give as good flood protection, but it was politically sellable." "We could understand that," Burhans added. "We got to the point where they were more concerned about our people and our problems with selling certain things, and we understood their problems on selling theirs. So when that happened, we didn't like it [the need to compromise], nobody liked it, but the North Fork is what had to be done to get the thing sold." "The process gave both sides someone to cry to," Burhans went on.

> Jane and Gerry would say, "We understand, but you've got to understand, ecologists are ecologists" or "local people are local people." They were able to handle it without being fair at all. They were able to handle it as dictators. They had no rules. They didn't have to be fair. What they had to do was get the job done. They could lie to both sides. I know damn well many times we'd ask them to do something and they wouldn't do it. But it was asked, and they came back and gave us a phony answer. They weren't playing by the rules. But it was needed because they kept things moving.
>
> I think their personalities did much for the process. Maybe you need someone in there to make you think you're winning while you're putting the pieces together.

The farmers in the valley were never completely united on what they wanted. Nor are they now. Before and during the mediation, many farmers' voices were raised for the full corps' proposal—the Middle Fork dam—because it would have had a very beneficial effect on flood control in the lower valley, whereas the mediated proposal will have only a minor impact. But the majority of farmers have changed their minds in the last decade; instead of demanding complete flood protection, they realized that land-use planning was the only way that they would be able to keep their farms. They had been exposed to the pressure of taxation and the pressure of industry, including a proposal by the Burlington Northern Railroad to build a large switching yard if the valley could be removed from the flood plain. The farmers came to the conclusion that a certain amount of flooding would have to be put up with in order to keep land values within reason so they could afford to continue farming.

The environmentalists faced a different problem, which is a given in all environmental disputes that seek to prevent something from being built. Unlike labor disputes, where the parties can push a few cents back and forth in an effort to arrive at a final package, it is very difficult to "fine tune" a proposal for a dam. One either builds the dam or one doesn't. You can't build half a dam or three-quarters of a dam as a compromise.

In the Snoqualmie dispute, the compromise was reached by agreeing to a different dam than the one that would give the most flood protection—a dam in a different place, which, while it would afford less flood protection, would also cause less environmental disruption. "Most negotiations don't really happen around the table," Cormick said.

> For every hour we spent in joint session, I suppose Jane and I spent 24 hours each in separate meetings with individuals. Much of the mediation and negotiations occurred within a party rather than between parties.
>
> The mediators cannot bring the extreme party into line. All you can do is create a situation where it becomes very much in the best interests of the moderates to say to the extremists, "Look, we need you on this one. Let's not fight it any more. We'll support you on the next one." That's what the farmers did, that's what the people in the Middle Valley did, that's what the environmentalists did, and they all pulled their supporters into the center. And we had to help with that a certain amount.

Because the participants were relatively new to the negotiation process, the mediators had to instruct them along the way in how to read their opponents' signals and proposals and how to frame their own. Politicians and others skilled in the bargaining process know not to be misled or upset by bombastic rhetoric, but newcomers have to be warned not to be taken in. This training must be done carefully, lest the adversaries get the feeling that the mediator is partial. "In community disputes, it's not enough to want a settlement," said Cormick. "You have a real responsibility to do some training. There's an inverse relationship between the experience of the parties and the responsibility of the mediators." "The environmentalists were the hardest," Cormick continued. "They needed a whole change of perspective from being opposed to things to making proposals. Until they could make a proposal, there was no way to move on. We needed a counterproposal from them, and that was one of the most difficult pieces." At times, Cormick said, the major help he was able to give the negotiations was to have a large supply of coffee and rolls on hand. "We always brought immense amounts of food," he said.

McCarthy, for whom Snoqualmie was the first mediation experience, said that the process was helped when the participants became "captivated by the process—which is one of the differences, I think, between environmental disputes and other kinds of disputes."

> [In environmental conflicts,] the people are process-oriented because most of them are college graduates, and they have a great interest in what's being inflicted on them, and why you are doing what you're doing. They think that's fascinating, and I think they were intrigued by the process partly because it was unusual and because it was the first time that it had been done. Gerry and I were obviously giving it everything we could give it and, in a sense, they built up a loyalty to us and they really, sincerely, wanted to resolve the dispute.

Implementation

Whatever the problems, agreement was reached in a relatively short time on a comprehensive plan for the basin. In September 1974, four months and just six negotiating sessions after the governor appointed Cormick and McCarthy, a tentative agreement was in hand. Reducing it to writing took another two months because it was taken around piecemeal to all of the participants, a tactic that Cormick later said was a mistake. He believes he should have called a joint meeting and hammered out everything with all parties present. Then letters of endorsement were secured from the entire group to transmit the agreement to Governor Evans and to urge him to adopt the proposal. This was a bit of theater, since Evans already knew what the proposals were and had already agreed to them.

Nonetheless, on December 9, 1974, an agreement was signed by the mediation pariticipants incorporating, among other things, the following provisions:

- A single, multipurpose dam would be constructed on the North Fork of the Snoqualmie River. Use of this site would leave the whitewater stretches on the Middle Fork untouched.
- The valley of the Middle Fork would be preserved undeveloped.
- Setback dikes for additional flood protection would be built in certain already developed areas.
- A major park would be established at the confluence of the three forks of the Snoqualmie.
- The lower valley would be preserved as an agricultural green belt.
- Neither quarrying nor development would be allowed on Mount Si, the major mountain in the basin, which hovers over the town of North Bend.
- Land use controls were included to guard against suburbanization of the valley.

The mediated agreement called on the governor to name an Interim Basin Coordinating Committee to make plans for implementing the recommendations through a Snohomish Basin Coordinating Council. Early in 1975, Governor Evans named twenty people to the interim committee, with Delanty as chairman. The committee received technical support from King and Snohomish counties, the state, and the Corps of Engineers. The governor's office provided a liaison officer, Alice Shorett; secretarial help; and a small budget.

Less than a year later, in December 1975, the interim committee made its recommendations on how to implement the agreement. The most controversial recommendation called for King and Snohomish counties and fifteen towns in the basin to commit themselves to a variety of land-use rules in order to monitor development and preserve the undeveloped areas envisioned in the mediated plan. That commitment would take the form of an intergovernmental agreement to establish the council, which would also need federal and state approval. It further called on the Corps of Engineers to do a reconnaissance study of the flood control proposals; the study, which was completed in November 1976, presented other problems, both economic and political.

One key issue, with many ramifications, involved the question of who was going to pay for the whole plan. Who, for example, was going to compensate those who had acquired the development rights in the areas that were to be preserved? The federal government said that it would have nothing to do with that portion, but Delanty argued that prohibiting development in the flood plain would ultimately save the government money in federal flood insurance.

The corps' study included a benefit-cost analysis that found that the North Fork project could be undertaken with about $78 million in federal funds for the dam and $95 million in local money for everything else, $62 million of which would be used to finance the new drinking water supply that the dam would make available.

Water supply is also a bit of a problem. At present, the city of Seattle sells water to all of King County at rates that the rest of the county finds too high. The city of Bellevue, across Lake Washington from Seattle, would very much like to have its own water supply, but whether it would be willing to assume $62 million in debt to do it is a question that has not yet been answered. Said Delanty: "Bellevue is not playing the same cards that I am. My cards are involved in trying to get this mediated plan under way. Bellevue's cards are how they can use this to force the battle over water-rates that's going on with the City of Seattle. If nobody wants to pick up the water, then . . . we're not in good shape from a benefit-cost standpoint." The corps, whose approval was necessary, would not go along with the construction of a dam unless the benefits outweighed the costs under a formula it uses. Bill Bates, a member of the interim committee and publisher of the *Snohomish Tribune*, put it more succinctly. "If we don't find a water user, we don't have a project," he said.

But Delanty and King County officials realized that benefit-cost analyses were not set in stone and that money sought from the non-federal portion could be shifted to the federal portion. Efforts are under way to get the state's congressional delegation to persuade the federal government to assume more of the cost of the project.

Money aside, the major problem of the interim committee's recommendation was political: the proposed intergovernmental agreement among the counties and the towns with regard to land use. "The real problem we have is the structure by which they recommend that the planning and implementation phase of the project be completed," said Keith Artz of the King County Planning Department, who was working full time on the proposal.

> We're having some problems in the wording of their document [the intergovernmental agreement], and legally we are not able to accept it.
>
> The problem is that the committee said in their document that the county *shall* do this and the county *shall* do that; the county *shall* fund certain things or accepts everything as they have said. The county can't do that until it has gone through the process of public hearings.

That's the county's point of view, but Artz believes that eventually everything will be straightened out and the King County Council will approve some modified version of the proposal. The towns in the basin are much less enthusiastic, and they are wary of relinquishing land-use prerogatives to a new regional body. "I expect opposition from people who are opposed on principle to regional concepts of government," said Bill Bates. "They're going to call this a superagency Big Brother project because it requires a linkage of many independent governments. The word 'regional' is a red flag to them."

But if the financial problem can be solved, the towns will have an inducement to come in on the whole project, since the cost to them will be very small. "They'll go for something that isn't going to show up real heavy in their tax statements," Bates said. "If King County and Snohomish County and the State of Washington went into it and none of the towns signed on, the project would still happen," said Artz. "That's where the money's coming from, and they're the ones who have the responsibility for flood control." Bates was not so sure. "I don't think we can lose any of the governments," he said. "If it were just the counties, I don't think that would be enough to pull it across."

In general, King County favored the proposal and Snohomish County, to the north, was more skeptical. George Sherwin, director of the Snohomish County Planning Department, made complaints similar to Artz's. "The issue now comes down to saying who were the mediators and what was their power to mediate," Sherwin said.

> Those people do not have the power to do it. The government can't just accept what they did because they did it. We have to look at the implications. We have to look at the broad public interest, which was not represented at the mediation.
>
> The situation we are now in is that the draft intergovernmental agreement was found to have some inherent flaws, both legal and policywise. I have heard no jurisdiction saying that it disagrees with the

> goal, and with the general findings of the mediated agreement, but the problem has arisen in that there is disagreement over how to put these things in a governmental document meant to be used in setting up the Basin Coordinating Council. Out county commissioners endorsed the last version of the agreement and said we were willing to proceed if others were. King apparently was not.

King County is now apparently asking for significant changes in the intergovenmental agreement.

Sherwin tied current troubles to the failure to have government officials take part in the mediation process.

> Based upon the experience we're going through now, I'd say I probably would have to disagree with the way it was done. Had they selected a limited number of key government officials to participate, the way ahead would have been much better paved for implementation. Although the mediation group came up with a viable solution in the context of those parties who participated, we have had a never ending process of trying to integrate their solution into the political process.

Sherwin also said that he thought there had been a lack of sufficient staff to help push the implementation phase. Actually, Delanty, the chairman, had no paid aides. He did get occasional assistance from Alice Shorett, who is now a successful and highly regarded environmental mediator at the Office of Environmental Mediation situated at the University of Washington in Seattle.

All of the problems have created an enormous strain on the good will of the members of the interim coordinating committee, which has remained in existence to shepherd its proposals through the myriad governments involved. The committee is still trying—more than three years after the mediated agreement was reached—to convince the two counties and fifteen towns to go along with the settlement. Everyone who participated in the mediation agrees that the package must be adopted in toto. It is not a shopping list from which some items can be plucked and others discarded. "These people are being held together—almost psychically—by the mediation experience that they went through," Bates said. "Now they're desperately trying to push this project forward." "It's going to take longer than we thought," he went on. "The completion of the thing could be 10 or 15 years down the pike." Delanty said: "It's not clear to me whether you can ever get 15 incorporated municipalities, two counties, the state and Federal Government all coordinated to the same thing at the same time." "There's something wrong with the way that we picked the whole mediation process," he continued.

> While we got agreement between some *citizens*, we did not have any agreement between the governing agencies.
>
> We didn't intend to have the political power to implement it. That was O.K., because all we were providing was the guidance that said, if you do this, then we believe that you have a viable project that will not seriously be challenged in the public process. But on the other hand, we were terribly naive. We thought we were telling the Federal Government how to create a project: we want some things done, and we recognize that there is a need for some things like flood control, and if you make the following trades we believe it will survive a public hearing. If you fund it.
>
> Well, that isn't the way the thing worked. That's a grand idea, but the trouble is that we've mixed things that are the absolute prerogative of lower government—the lowest level of government—into things that are the prerogative of the Federal Government. We never really have come to a complete understanding as to how you merge those governments. Conceptually, it's easy. But in the arena of the bureaucrats and the elected officials, its' a different world. They jealously guard things like land-use prerogatives. Tell a county commissioner that you're about to deliver a land-use plan from the Federal Government on him, and he's walking on the table, and besides that, stomping on your head.
>
> Let us say that we're getting a hell of a lot smarter as a result of the mediation. As I look over this, I would definitely try to create an endeavor such that at least a certain number of elected officials were cranked into the original mediation process.

Some months later, Delanty changed his mind. "I guess that now, at least with the perspective that I have, I have a feeling that mediation, in environmental disputes, probably has to take place between the factions that are warring. My guess is that it would not be right to include government officials. It was not the governments that were warring."

Cormick does not believe that the Snoqualmie project is in danger of collapse. What would he say if he had to guess when construction would begin on the dam? "In three years," he replied quickly. Would he do anything differently? Cormick recalled that Alice Shorett was assigned by Governor Evans to assist the interim committee that was established when the mediated agreement was concluded. But Cormick noted that Shorett was the only staff provided and that she was assigned on a half-time basis. "One of the things I would change is to have spent more time getting committed funds for two or three years so that we could have hired a couple of full-time staff people to help the Committee."

Some of the implementation delay can be attributed, Cormick believes, to a change in the top staff post at the Corps of Engineers in Seattle and to a change in the statehouse. Governor Evans decided not to seek reelection in November 1976. Evans, a Republican, had served three terms. He was succeeded by Democrat Dixie Lee Ray, who has called for additional studies of the Snoqualmie situation. Regarding the pessimism about implementation of the agreement, Cormick said: "People forget that this thing went 20 years before the mediated agreement. You know, you've still got to go through all the processes. I mean the very notion that the counties are even talking about sharing their great power over land use and planning . . . I mean, that's incredible!"

What are the key qualities a mediator should have? Said Cormick: "One is, not have the answers. Really, being willing to support the voluntary process." He believes that the team approach to mediation is better than one mediator working alone. "It's very difficult for one person to put together all the pieces of a complex dispute," he said. The team approach also allows participants to form different kinds of relationships with the mediators. "The environmentalists thought that they could really talk to Jane, although they trusted me, and industry and farmers thought they could really talk to me. I understood and they trusted me. You've got to have trust."

4
New Faces in the Neighborhood: Mediating the Forest Hills Housing Dispute

Stephen Gillers

Introduction

Mario Cuomo's father typifies the older immigrant:

> He is 77 now and slipping, but at the time of Forest Hills he was fresh as a daisy—illiterate but very smart. He saw in the paper [then] and he heard on the radio, FOREST HILLS, MARIO CUOMO, THE JEWS, THE BLACKS, and he thought, "What's going on?" So, he asked me one day what was happening when it was just about over. And I explained to him as simply as I could.
>
> I said, "Pop, here are all the Jewish people. The black people want to come here."
>
> "How many?" he asked.
>
> "About 840 families," I said.
>
> "And how many do the Jewish people want?" my father responded.
>
> I said, "None."
>
> "Ah, they want 840 and the Jewish people want none."
>
> I said, "That's right."
>
> "And what did you do?"
>
> I said, "I made it [the housing project] three buildings, twelve floors each."
>
> He said, "How many is that?"
>
> I said, "That's about 420."
>
> "That's half."
>
> I said, "That's right."
>
> "Then what took you eight weeks?"

Unfortunately, the mediation of social conflict isn't that easy.

The Problem

The goals are simple and easily understood: a chance for a comfortable life; a chance for as much education as you or your children are capable of absorbing; a chance for decent housing; a chance for a good job; freedom from fear and want; retirement and old age with dignity.

These goals cost money—private money, public money—and the harsh truth is that there are more people who seek them than there are resources available. Some people need not concern themselves with limited resources. They have sufficient access to private wealth to allow them to pursue their goals regardless of what anyone else has or wants. Nor need they be concerned with the effects of the use of public resources because, literally or figuratively, they can simply move if any particular use threatens to interfere with the comfort of their lives.

Others, most of us, do not have these options. To a greater or lesser extent, our lives are affected by the manner in which the government chooses to allocate its resources. For many, public wealth will, at least in part, be needed to get the education, the housing, and the job they want. For others, though they may be able to afford such things on their own, or with the help of only indirect public subsidies, public decisions about resource allocation will nevertheless determine the quality of their education, who lives and works next to them, how safe they feel on the streets or in public transportation, how much "disposable income" remains after taxes, and so on.

Wealthy as the United States may be, it still cannot provide each of its citizens with all of his or her needs. Perhaps that goal is impossible by definition, for as needs are filled, new ones take their place and expectations continue to rise. But the nation, without a sudden shift to strict egalitarian principles, and perhaps even with one, cannot now provide all its people with even the minimum essentials for uneventful lives. There is simply not enough to go around. So tough decisions must be made.

The matter is yet more complicated. In many parts of the nation, the people most in need are racially identifiable. They are black, Hispanic, and Indian, but mainly they are black. This is historically understandable, but emotionally it leads to some predictable but devastating equations. Black equals poverty. Black equals danger. Black equals crime.

In order to get a bigger piece of the economic pie, minority political groups, many of whom obtained their power through the civil rights movement of the 1960s, joined forces with the advocates of civil rights legislation that the movement produced. Also helpful was the Supreme Court's expansive reading of the Constitution's demand for "equal protection of the laws." All of the pressure was aimed at requiring governments—local, state, and federal—to allocate more public resources in ways that would assist poor members of racial minorities. In other words, law and politics combined to favor black and Hispanic access to our (by definition) limited resources.

This situation affects two broad groups of white Americans. It affects those who want but do not get government largesse because a "quota" of blacks and Hispanics do. And it affects those who make no claim to the public funds, but whose lives are "upset" in some other way because of the manner in which the minorities make use of the public money.

The first group of whites—those who are denied a benefit or an advantage because a minority receives it and because there is only so much to go around—sees itself victimized in various ways. Affirmative action is the most obvious and constant plaint. Minorities may get jobs, housing, or education over whites who claim to be more qualified or deserving. Whites charge this is reverse discrimination which is as evil as any other kind. Minorities respond that without some preferential treament, at least for a while, members of their groups will not have a chance to catch up and, eventually, compete equally with the majority. The courts have responded to these disputes with a crazy quilt of rulings that cannot be easily rationalized and that depend, in part, on whether the minority is claiming its rights under the Constitution or under a statute, and whether the specific employer, landlord, or school was guilty of past discrimination. Recently, the U.S. Supreme Court agreed to decide whether the University of California Medical School at Davis could constitutionally have an affirmative action program for the admission of minority group members that was based on rejecting some white applicants who were, in terms of grades at least, better qualified.

The second group of whites affected by government decisions to inject substantial amounts of public funds into the private economy for the benefit of minority group members are not competing for the same public dollar. Rather, they are affected by the way such public money is spent. The most obvious examples occur in housing. Whites in neighborhood X may not be seeking government money to build themselves apartment buildings in neighborhood X; but when the government gives such money to, say, blacks for that purpose, some of the whites perceive that the comfort of their lives is jeopardized. If whites in the first group feel *displaced* by the government's affirmative action programs, whites in the second category feel *invaded*.

An oversimplified version of the displaced white's complaint is: "Why me?" After all, as the white student involved in the University of California case argued: Why should he have to forfeit his medical education to pay for centuries of slavery and discrimination? He did not discriminate against anyone and neither did the school to which he had applied. So why should the burden fall on him?

The invaded whites are not losing anything so directly. Their housing is not being taken away. Their only complaint is that the blacks would not have been able to afford to live in "their" neighborhood, given a free market, had the government not "interfered" by building the housing. The whites contend that the blacks, by moving into the white neighborhood, affect the quality of their lives in ways that, if not as obvious as the affect on the lives of whites actually displaced by affirmative action, are certainly as resented.

The controversy over the construction of three apartment buidings in Forest Hills, New York City, between 1971 and 1973 is an important example, as perceived by some whites, of the problem of black "invasion" of a white neighborhood. All the usual participants were present, plus one. There were the community groups, the city and federal governments, the leaders of the black community, and the groups favoring open housing. There was, in addition, Mario Cuomo, now New York's secretary of state. When the conflict surrounding the construction of the housing became intense and the danger of violence great, John Lindsay, then New York's mayor and a presidential aspirant, asked Cuomo to make an independent assessment of the facts and recommend a solution. Cuomo did. How he did it, the problems he encountered, and the factors he considered in reaching his decision, are the subject of this chapter.

There are several reasons for studying the Forest Hills controversy and Cuomo's response to his assignment. Although the controversy would have been resolved in one or another way without Cuomo, appointment of an independent fact finder or mediator will often be wise, as it was in this case. The courts can only do so much. They are not institutionally equipped to settle complex disputes like the one that arose in Forest Hills. Nor may other government officials or bodies be appropriate. They may be participants in the dispute themselves and therefore not trusted by the other interests to resolve it impartially. They may have low credibility for other reasons or may not be able to provide a fresh perspective. Given, then, the value of independent fact finders (or mediators) from time to time, as one additional tool in dispute resolution, Cuomo's experiences will tell us something of what they can and cannot do, and what the dangers are—how, in short, to use them best.

Forest Hills: The Setting

The Forest Hills controversy actually began in Corona, a less affluent, predominantly Italian neghborhood some two miles from Forest Hills. In 1966, New York City had planned to build low-income housing in Corona for minority families. The housing was to be put up under the city's scatter-site program, which was federally supported and had as its goal meaningful housing integration by locating low-income projects in middle-income neighborhoods. By "scattering" the developments throughout the city, any adverse impact and opposition could supposedly be minimized. The Corona housing was to occupy 4.5 acres, provide 509 apartments, and displace four homes, only one of which was owner-occupied. Pressure from Corona residents, however, altered these plans so that a high school, not housing, was to be built in their community instead. The housing was to be moved across the Long Island Expressway to Forest Hills, the heart of middle-income Queens.

The change from housing to high school presented another, unforeseen, problem to the Corona residents. The high school, with athletic fields, required not 4.5 acres, but 12.5 acres, and would have resulted in the destruction of sixty-nine homes in Corona. Cuomo, a Queens lawyer, was hired to represent the Corona homeowners and, in the eleventh hour, managed to get the plans changed so that the high school could be built without the destruction of any homes, although fourteen of them would have to be moved one block. Most Corona residents were satisfied.

Forest Hills, however, now had a problem. The shift of the scatter-site houses meant that seven apartment buildings would be built on a 8.5 acre tract—one twenty-two-story building, three twelve-story buildings, and three ten-story buildings. The buildings were to contain

828 apartments, over 300 more than had been planned for Corona. In 1969, the plans were changed to three buidings of twenty-four stories each, with a total of 840 apartments. The change was required because the city government had not realized that an underground stream made the soil on which the buildings were to be constructed marshy (private builders had earlier rejected the site for this reason). As a result, the cost of each foundation would be higher than anticipated. If seven buildings were erected, the cost per apartment would have exceeded federal maximums. Since the federal government was paying 90 percent of the bill, the plan had to be changed.

Nothing happened for five years after the switch with Corona. This delay both increased the sense of security in Forest Hills that the "project" would never be built and eventually caused greater feelings of deception when, in 1971, the city belatedly began construction.

The Scatter-Site Theory

The Forest Hills issue would not have occurred before the "theory" of scatter-site housing was developed. It is necessary to understand the theory in order to understand the ensuing controversy and Cuomo's problems as independent fact finder. Scatter-site housing was originally seen as a method of helping small numbers of poor and minority group families to live in middle-class neighborhoods. The alternative—building large "projects" in ghetto neighborhoods like Harlem and Bedford Stuyvesant—may have provided minorities with housing but did not result in true racial and economic integration, and, of course, did nothing to change patterns of the de facto school segregation. Scatter-site housing envisioned moving ghetto residents into white neighborhoods—scattering, as it were, public housing sites throughout the city.

Scatter-site housing became not simply visionary but imperative for local governments seeking federal housing funds—as all do—because in the early 1960s these funds were made more easily available to build housing outside areas of existing minority concentration. Under the guidelines of the U.S. Department of Housing and Urban Development, a local plan that would place subsidized housing for minorities in a neighborhood with few or no minority group members was to be rated *superior,* while a plan that placed the housing in a racially mixed neighborhood would only be *adequate. Superior* plans would get the money before the *adequate* ones.

What about the problem of size? After all, if the idea behind scatter-site housing was to place small numbers of low-income families in wealthier neighborhoods, how does one justify building three twenty-four-story apartment buildings with 240 apartments each in Forest Hills? The buildings were the "highest and largest of the City's scatter-site efforts by a substantial margin, with about twice as many apartments as the runner up," according to Walter Goodman, writing in the *New York Times Magazine*. The explanation for this size flows from two factors: another federal regulation and lack of city planning.

The federal government, understandably, places a dollar per apartment limit on the cost of housing it funds. Although Washington does not actually pay for the apartments, it guarantees principal and interest on Housing Authority bonds and there is a limit to how much it will guarantee. Since the cost of the foundation for the three buildings was comparatively high because of the marshy soil, it was to the city's advantage to make the buildings tall, thereby accommodating more apartments and lowering the cost per unit. Go high enough and the cost would be in accord with the federal requirement. The city government did not realize the implications in the neighborhood when it approved construction on the marshy 8.5 acres. When the city learned how deep local opposition was, the housing had already been approved and it would have been politically difficult to convince the minority community that the city should reduce the size of the project or drop it.

So construction on the project, now fully approved, was underway in 1971 when the pacified residents of Forest Hills, lulled into security for five years as a result of official inaction, suddenly realized what was going on. Almost as fast as a fire spreads through an old wooden building, the community became polarized. Residents organized into opposition groups. Pickets appeared. Violence was threatened and city officials took the threats seriously. National attention focused on Forest Hills.

Enter Cuomo

Cuomo was first approached by former Deputy Mayor Richard Aurelio to assist in resolving a Forest Hills controversy that was fast becoming the Forest Hills crisis. Cuomo had worked with and been helped by Aurelio on the Corona problem. Aurelio's request came on May 6, 1972. Cuomo accepted the next day. Cuomo's role, as he described it, was: "to be a fact-finder who would report back to the mayor, Board of Estimate and other city officials, as soon as possible, with respect to a possible solution. There was to be no staff, no money, no specific instructions and no prior commitments. I was totally free to do as I saw fit and to report precisely what I felt."

This last sentence is important. Cuomo believed that his only real power in the situation—with Mayor Lindsay and with the communities involved—was directly related to his independence, perceived and actual. The commmunity had to view him as an independent power who could influence events and not simply as a functionary whose job was to get the mayor out of a difficult political situation. Cuomo insisted on and received the power to have his report published without change, whether or not Lindsay agreed with him. He expected that if the report was thoughtful and right, it would be hard for the mayor to resist implementing it once it was made public.

But not everyone accepts Cuomo's firm statement that he was acting independently. Simeon Golar, then chairman of the New York City Housing Authority and a staunch supporter of the scatter-site project, recalls the situation in this way: Because of his presidential aspirations, "Mayor Lindsay was trying to regain lost political ground in New York City. In an effort to appease the anger of residents near the Forest Hills site, [the project was changed] and the solution was considerably authored in City Hall. It was not a genuine mediation process; it was a political decision." In response, Cuomo said: "Golar is wrong. As a matter of fact, the truth is . . . that I wrote the final report and City Hall did not like it. And City Hall called me in and tried to change it. I refused [and it remained intact]. I can show him [Golar] the first draft and the comments of the Mayor on it, 'This is Unacceptable.'"

Many of Cuomo's friends and advisers, anticipating the controversies to come, urged him not to take the job or questioned his decision to do so. They argued that there was nothing to gain from it, that he could only come out looking bad in the end. While Cuomo recognized that the mayor's motive for appointing him was to deflect hostility from the mayor himself, he wrote that he nevertheless felt that a dispassionate review of the facts "without foggy rhetoric will help," and he agreed to do it. He declined the title of mediator for the more neutral one of fact finder. He refused money, since he felt it would compromise his credibility, and he rejected a staff as too "cumbersome."

In May 1972, when Cuomo was appointed, the following ten "facts" were among those he would *not* have to "find." They were fairly well accepted.

1. Of the 840 apartments, the city had reserved 40.5 percent, or 340, for the elderly. This was an increase in the number of apartments originally earmarked for the elderly–250, or about 30 percent.

2. The number of apartments for large families was sharply cut. Large families, often without a father present, but with many children, were of particular concern to the Forest Hills residents.

3. There would be a two-story community center, with facilities for the elderly and others, and an early childhood center that could hold two hundred children. Both facilities would be open to residents of the surrounding neighborhood.

4. Density in the new housing would be 310 people per acre. This was high, but not as high as some private developments, such as Lefrak City and Park City. Eighty-five percent of the site would be open space, with additional park space nearby.

5. According to 1960 figures, of the fifty-five thousand people in the immediate area of the proposed housing, only 2 percent were nonwhite and 1 percent Puerto Rican.

6. The total anticipated tenant population, according to the City Housing Authority, was twenty-five hundred to twenty-eight hundred, broken down as follows: 15 percent would be elderly (although elderly people would occupy 40 percent of the apartments, these were the smaller apartments, for one or two people each); occupants of "family apartments" would be drawn from the "working poor," defined as families of four with incomes of less than $8,820 per year (later raised to $9,500). About 10 percent of the total families, more than four hundred people, would be receiving public assistance. Golar contended that this was a lower percentage than existed in any other authority facility. There were to be more whites than blacks and more small families than large ones, mainly as a result of the requirement that the housing population be drawn first from the surrounding Forest Hills community.

7. The extensive and vocal white resistance to the project had been characterized in many ways. Before Cuomo's appointment, various magazine and newspaper articles, written by Roger Starr, Nathan Glazer, Walter Goodman, and others, pointed out that the white resistance should not simplistically be explained in racial terms. At about the same time that the Forest Hills controversy was brewing,

another two-hundred-unit scatter-site project was rejected by the *black* middle-class residents of Baisley Park. The issue was safety, not race, according to Glazer and Goodman. Glazer wrote that, at least in New York City, many whites come to the "dangerous but understandable conclusion . . . that the presence of blacks equals lack of safety." While Glazer believes this equation "wrong," he also concludes that "poor blacks . . . provide a breeding ground for crime—and anyone who values his safety is going to try to distance himself from a tangle of pathology." Furthermore, one "danger" resulting from charges of racism, Glazer suggests, "is that the confusion in the minds of some that black *does* equal crime, which it is in the best interest of all to unravel and straighten out, becomes only deeper. If those who know truly that they search for safety are denounced for being racist, are they not to conclude that the only way *not* to be racist is to accept living with personal danger?" (Glazer's italics)

8. Glazer and Goodman both also wrote of concerns of the large Jewish population of Forest Hills. Goodman quoted one Jewish leader as saying that the Jews "resent the City administration constantly choosing the Jewish population for its experiments in social engineering." Glazer reports that the Jewish population of Forest Hills believed that the mayor would not have tangled with Italians or Slavs or Germans. But the Jews were expected to accept the project without becoming physically violent. "They so rarely did in the face of black residential succession. They simply moved away."

9. One other aspect of the Forest Hills population deserves mention. Many of the residents were only a single generation removed from the indices of poverty and near-poverty that the government was now helping these other minority groups to escape. Forest Hills residents complained that others were getting for free what they struggled to achieve. If opponents of the project could leave the neighborhood without much trouble, the outcry would certainly have been less. But many did not have this economic freedom. So they saw themselves as prisoners or hostages. They had improved their lot by hard work; now the city was about to compromise their advances through "welfare" and there was little they could do to avoid the consequences—except resist on some political or even physical level.

10. Finally, there were the legal realities. They were simple. The project had already been approved by everybody required to do so and was under construction. Although the Forest Hills community would try to challenge the project in the courts, they would ultimately be un-

successful. In short, if no compromise were worked out the three buildings, twenty-four stories each, would be built. Inevitably, this fact had to influence the behavior of those supporting the project and those opposing it.

Without funds, without a staff, with no political base at all, Cuomo entered this fray on May 17, 1972, and promised to issue his report in forty-two days. He would be a little late; it actually took almost five and one-half months for Cuomo to work out a solution.

Cuomo's Role—How He Proceeded

Cuomo does not believe a professional mediator could have succeeded in Forest Hills. It was necessary, he contends, to have someone the community would perceive as an outsider, an "anti-establishment" person, without ties to the government. Even given Cuomo's outside status, many still believed he was agreeing to accept the hopeless task of mediating the dispute in return for some political payoff, that his role, in short, was to "get Lindsay off the hook." For example, Cuomo was charged with "playing some kind of political game with Lindsay," and one woman could not believe he was not getting "paid" in some way.

> Made cynical by years of battling politicians she was convinced that I was getting something "under the table" for my efforts. She arrived at this conclusion because she felt that doing it for nothing was not reasonable. She reminded me that she still believed I had "sold out" the people of Corona, although she had not yet been able to prove what I had received from Mayor Lindsay by way of compensation [Mario Cuomo, *Forest Hills Diary: The Crisis of Low-Income Housing* (New York: Random House, 1974), p. 75].

To the extent that Cuomo was perceived as "the mayor's man," he would be less effective. This problem was further complicated by the fact that Lindsay was not merely perceived as one of the participants in the dispute. He was so distrusted that "it was difficult for them to believe that I could be objective since Lindsay had appointed me."

Cuomo believed that the most important task he could undertake at the outset was to give people a place to "ventilate" their feelings, not only so they would feel they were being heard, but also so they could hear themselves. Cuomo believed that if the participants were permitted to go for a reasonable amount of time in a nonadversary setting—where Cuomo would simply listen and not take a position (*that* would come later)—they would be able to understand the less rational aspects of their arguments. "If you let them talk long enough, it becomes apparent even to them that they are being emotional," Cuomo hoped. So Cuomo listened. He took no notes and had no recorder. But at the end of each day, he dictated his recollections and the result was eventually published as his *Forest Hills Diary*.

Early in his tenure as an intervenor in the Forest Hills controversy, Cuomo recognized the importance of not taking an adversary stance, even though it was sometimes hard to avoid it. Cuomo's trial lawyer experience intuitively led him to take sides. In the course of a discussion with Jerry Birbach, a leading spokesman for those residents opposing the project, Cuomo thought of

> a number of things that I might have ordinarily argued with him about. I didn't. I'll have to resist the temptation to be an advocate so long as I'm in this role. It's much easier being an advocate. The restraint and patience required of the middleman in our situation are hard virtues to cultivate. I'm particularly concerned about my ability to do it on Sunday. The CBS show will be the first—and probably the last—opportunity to establish some credibility on a broad scale, and to do that I'll have to remain objective [Cuomo, *Diary*, p. 30].

Instead of choosing sides, Cuomo picked fact gathering as his primary task: "We must know everything about the history of this project, its relationship to Corona, how it was chosen, why the nature of the site, the construction contracts, the constitutional law, the agency regulations and much more, even before we attempt meaningful discussions. There's no other intelligent way. But it won't be easy" [Cuomo, *Diary*, p. 31]. But as the facts came to be gathered and Cuomo found himself forming an opinion, he also began to be uncertain about his ultimate job: to find the facts and "state" them or to resolve the issues: "But then, is it really for me to say whether the project is good or bad as an absolute? I'm to find 'facts' and display them. I'd rather do more. It's difficult trying to suspend individual judgment—it's easier to make the ultimate decision than to merely 'state.' I'm more and more convinced I'd rather argue than arbitrate" [Cuomo, *Diary*, pp. 41–42].

Looking back at the Forest Hills controversy, Cuomo said:

> When it was all over in Forest Hills, I didn't know whether it was good or bad, whether we could have done better or worse. I was

> satisfied that we had prevented or helped prevent serious racial trouble, but it is very hard to say, particularly when you are that close, whether it is a success or not—as measured against what? As measured against what you might have achieved? Well, then you will never know if it is a success. As measured against what someone else would have achieved? You see, if you are going to do this work you have to be able to recognize the subtleties of problems. If you really recognize all the subtleties, you will never be satisfied. The subtleties are infinite, the possibilities are infinite and you get tired. You settle for things like, "I didn't get hurt. Nobody got hurt." So if you ask me if I enjoyed Forest Hills, I don't know. It was important, important work.

Initially, during the fact-finding process, Cuomo would listen to anyone who wanted to come to the offices he used at the Queens Borough Hall. This was consistent with the notion that the community must be given an opportunity to express itself. But time presented a problem. Cuomo had set a tight deadline for himself. Within a month after his appointment, a change had to be made.

> It is clear now that the burden of trying to talk with all of those who wish to present their position will make it impossible to meet the original six-week deadline. While communication and a measuring of the sentiments of the parties involved was essential, the vast amount of time consumed by the process has made it difficult to do everything else that needs to be done. Beginning next week, we'll be able to see only "leaders." Within the next ten days we must have at least a rough concept of a compromise if there is to be one [Cuomo, *Diary*, p. 67].

Other things changed as the time pressure increased. It must be remembered that while Cuomo proceeded to find facts and go about his mediating function, the buildings were being built. The project—three twenty-four-story buildings—had been approved and there was no legal basis to stop construction. The longer Cuomo took, the more advanced the project and the less room for compromise. So Cuomo realized that he soon had to do more than listen impartially and give others a chance to "ventilate." He had to take various positions in order to more rapidly crystallize the issues and learn if, indeed, there was any middle area within which both sides might compromise.

Here, for example, was how Cuomo responded to a group of lawyers opposing the project. They came to see him toward the end of his first month on the job. Cuomo did not at that time take a substantive position, but he did force the opposition to rethink its flexibility by showing them the limits of their bargaining power:

> The last wave in was perhaps the best equipped of the opponents. Three or four lawyers were included in a group of about twenty or thirty F.H.R.A. [Forest Hills Residents' Association] members. The arguments were the familiar ones, and except for a single person who was willing to consider a project totally for the elderly, the others said the project in any form would be objectionable and they would move. At about midnight, I took this tack with them: "I have been assigned to ascertain whether a compromise can be found that would be reasonably acceptable to both sides. That is the whole of my mandate. If, therefore, the city will not, or cannot, consider killing the project entirely, I am left simply with the alternative of reporting that there is no point in attempting to reduce or alter the project in any way because it would do nothing for the F.H. people." They were distressed at the way I put it and I think they felt it was a threat, but since they had no opportunity to consult with one another, no one was willing to state any reaction. I decided to leave them with the thought and agreed to talk to them again next week [Cuomo, *Diary*, p. 63].

This tactic was used again a few days later with two other groups opposing the project:

> The arguments they made were the traditional ones. In effect, what they said was that low-income people would eventually deteriorate the neighborhood as they had Crown Heights and other Jewish communities. I put to them the flat question whether they wished me to report that unless the entire project was "killed" there would be no acceptable compromise [Cuomo, *Diary*, p. 68].
>
> They swore they would all move out if the project in any form were to be built. "Do you really mean you would want me to report that the project should remain as is unless it could be completely undone?" They softened—but only a bit. The best they would do is to consider all elderly, and at that, the buildings would have to be drastically cut down [Cuomo, *Diary*, pp. 68–69].

Eventually, Cuomo's "devil's advocate" position became a bit more substantive. He began to point out to the opposition its weak negotiating position: (1) the project's proponents could probably win political backing for it in a citywide referendum; (2) the law requires that scatter-site housing be implemented; (3) all legal predicates to completion of the project are concluded—the residents had an opportunity to be heard in the Board of Estimate and elsewhere and had failed; (4) the courts would not help; (5) absolute community control in other scatter-site housing decisions was impossible since no community would vote to accept a project; and (6) there was a recognized moral imperative to improve housing for the poor. The lawyer's "summation" began to work, as Cuomo related:

> When my argument is concluded I haven't convinced any of them, but I think they begin to feel less confident in their "No Project–No Way" stance. Their sense of practicality begins to creep in, and they are less sure that they are willing to gamble on an all-or-nothing-at-all basis. It's too early to be certain, but I feel strongly the repeated body blows through the first ten rounds are beginning to force their guard down, and this is good, because I'm convinced that the only answer here lies somewhere between the polar extremes of both groups [Cuomo, *Diary*, pp. 79–80].

Cuomo even used this approach with some success on Jerry Birbach, perhaps the most vocal and visible opponent:

> I repeatedly stated to Birbach that if I had to report at the present time, I would probably report that all compromise was out of the question because no compromise will suit the people of Forest Hills, and the city might just as well go ahead with the 840 units as designed. He is uncomfortable with this suggestion, particularly since he suspects that I might lay the responsibility for the all-or-nothing-at-all approach at his door [Cuomo, *Diary*, p. 83].

The result of the "are you saying there is no compromise" approach eventually began to pay off. Cuomo was told that he had "been able—by virtue of a persistent 'devil's advocate' approach—to create a 'psychology of compromise.'" Cuomo then began informally to suggest various actual compromises, to be tested by word of mouth in the community. Of Cuomo's style, a participant in some of the fact-gathering sessions characterized it this way: "He kept his cool. He was gentle enough not to exacerbate the situation. I was not quite happy with his compromise at the time—just by cutting a problem in half doesn't solve it." That assessment came from Rabbi Joseph Grunblatt, who opposed the scatter-site concept and still would if it meant putting large numbers of very low-income people, with no hope of advancement, in middle-income areas. "Scatter-site is not workable, it's foolish," the rabbi maintained.

However, Rabbi Grunblatt and others were happy at the way the buildings turned out because the project was transformed into a low-income cooperative—the first of its kind in the United States. Tenants buy their apartments, pay reduced carrying charges, and can sell when they move at the original purchase price. No profit is allowed on a sale because of the government support and the fact that tenants pay no interest charges.

The cooperative idea was not Cuomo's originally. Queens Borough President Donald Manes is generally credited with coming up with the concept following the issuance of Cuomo's report calling for three buildings and 420 families. Cuomo supported the co-op concept, saying it has given the development significant stability.

"The co-op," said Rabbi Grunblatt, a Forest Hills resident, "has tremendous advantages. It gives tenants a sense of ownership, a direct stake in the buildings. And the type of people attracted to it are working people with a sense of upward mobility—that's ideal." A current co-op tenant, Joseph Hennessy, said of the ownership plan: "If you make people feel that they have some responsiblity toward the property, they treat it better than renting. You get the feeling of home ownership." Another tenant, Felix Huggins, said: "It gives a person a sense of ownership." Carrying charges are based on salaries, with no tenant paying more than 25 percent of his or her income in charges. The charges average about $35 per room; purchase price per room averages about $150.

Hennessy, who is white and chairman of the co-op's board of directors, and Huggins, who is black and chairman of the board's finance committee, both said that relations among co-op residents were generally excellent. The residential population breaks down to about 65 percent white, 15 percent black, 15 percent Hispanic, and 5 percent Asian.

Who Speaks for Whom?

Behind the notion of fact-finding or mediating is the assumption that there are two or more interests or sides which, presumably, disagree either on the accuracy of particular facts, the importance of them, the degree to which they imply other facts, and the conclusion such facts permit or compel. Cuomo immediately faced a difficult problem: Who represented which side? Indeed, what sides were there?

These questions were easier to answer for the "lawyers" of project opponents than for its proponents. For the most part, the opponents came from the Forest Hills community. But they were not monolithic. Some were more opposed to the project than others, some were more emotional. Political savvy varied. Finally, some residents actually supported the project in its then current form.

One danger lies in reaching a conclusion that the most vocal are also the most representative. This, of course, is not always so, but at times it is impossible to know, especially if other forces in the community do not come forward to disown the loudest voices. Cuomo had one advantage, however. The leading opponent of the project, Jerry Birbach, decided to try to translate his opposition, and new fame, into political power by challenging the area's state senator in an upcoming political primary. He lost by a four-to-three margin. The "silent majority" had, in a sense, spoken in a way that is often most effective—through the vote—and had also cued Cuomo to its feelings about the extent to which Birbach represented its views.

Aside from the comparatively few residents of the neighborhood willing to come forward in favor of the project, it was difficult to identify the other proponents. It could not be the people who would come to live in the project since they were not yet determined. Cuomo encountered this problem within days after his appointment:

> The other side of the issue has been strongly silent. The quick impression is that there may be no strong feeling in the black community for the project, but that's probably not the fact. One of the difficulties is that the black side of the question is hard to identify. On the Forest Hills side, geography is enough to isolate and mark the adversary—we know who and where they are and that makes communication relatively easy. But unless the Housing Authority is regarded as the other party in interest, it's difficult to say who is. Dealing with the H.A. is, of course, mechanically easy. Presumably, however, the H.A. represents a point of view that is shared by the low income community that would benefit from the development. If that's the fact, it would be good to deal beyond the H.A. with that community itself. I'll have to talk with Golar about this if things don't change after Sunday's "Newsmakers"

show. That exposure might turn things around [Cuomo, *Diary,* pp. 29–30].

Just as the Forest Hills residents initially saw Cuomo as their enemy, someone who was supposed to provide support for the project and save the mayor, Cuomo felt that Golar, Housing Authority chairman, was also in a difficult position and under strong pressure.

> Simeon Golar had come into the mayor's office midway through our meeting. It wasn't difficult to read his displeasure and it was understandable. He had been out front on this issue for months taking the flak for his hard stand. He himself suggested accommodation and compromise of sorts but had been told to stand fast. It wasn't easy for him now to step aside while someone else—an outsider—came in to "set things right." I made no attempt at softening him; I'm not very good at that anyway. I made a simple request for cooperation and he, just as simply and coolly, agreed to give it [Cuomo, *Diary*, pp. 27–28].
>
> I wonder if he thinks that the mayor has arranged something with me that hasn't been disclosed [Cuomo, *Diary*, p. 28].

Cuomo quickly learned Golar's position: He would surrender no low-income housing units without replacing them somewhere in Queens County. Golar felt the correctness of his position morally as well as legally. The city has a commitment to the poor and needy. Cutting back on the project now would be wrong. So Golar was not simply the judicious bureaucrat responsible for determining an official position as accommodating as possible to all sides. Golar was a side. He spoke for the poor and minority interests.

Given this perspective, Cuomo, the trial lawyer, understood Golar's negotiating position: "There is nothing surprising about Golar's position. He is treating this matter as though it were a commercial lawsuit. At the moment, he has "won" 840 units. Unless the Forest Hills' forces prevail in the Court of Appeals, or the Board of Estimate were to decide to reconsider, there is no apparent way in which this number can be reduced, so why give up any units?" [Cuomo, *Diary*, p. 60]. As for the other proponents, Cuomo asked Golar for names. But there was a hitch:

> I talked to Golar today and told him about the failure of communication from the black groups. He's still quite reticent and circumspect with me,

> and I can't blame him. He explained that leaders like Ken Clark and Roy Wilkins would not agree to call me; I would have to call them. I've always beeen impatient with this kind of protocol, but I may do it. Golar promised to have other interest groups who favor the project call me to open lines of communication [Cuomo, *Diary,* pp. 33–34].
>
> Today I received two lists of names from Golar's office with a strong suggestion that I call them, notwithstanding his telling me yesterday he would have them contact me. I'm afraid its more game-playing—this time from the other side—and I don't want to play. While I'd like to speak to as many interested people as I can, I think it would be a mistake to reach out for some at the risk of ignoring others. I'll stay with my announced idea of talking to anyone who contacts me [Cuomo, *Diary*, p. 35].

A few days later, Cuomo had a conversation with a member of the City Planning Commission.

> I pointed out that I had heard from very few blacks or anyone else who would state, let alone articulate in detail, any case for the project. He said the City Planning Commission had regularly been disappointed at the failure of any substantial showing by the low-income community. It still looks like Golar is the only available party "for" [Cuomo, *Diary*, p. 40].

Eventually, some project proponents did meet with Cuomo, mainly people from outside the neighborhood or associated with religious or civic groups; people, in other words, who were touched by the project as a moral issue rather than as something that directly affected their lives. Cuomo noted, after meeting one such group:

> From what I've been able to gather up to this point this group is fairly representative of the groups that support the project. For the most part, they're not residents of the community and aren't immediately affected. It's fair to say that it's easier for these groups to operate from high "moral" precepts. Many of the individuals can recite previous residence in Forest Hills or past personal experiences with projects, but their present platform is from a geographical point sufficiently remote from the site to be free of whatever threat may be inherent in the project [Cuomo, *Diary*, p. 61].

But for the most part, Cuomo's time was spent meeting opponents.

This is understandable given the fact that the project's residents were not yet identified, and also given Cuomo's main role—to convince the residents to accept or acquiesce in a compromise that could also be justified as fair to the future project tenants.

Cuomo was originally appointed because the mayor feared violence. If a project of any size would engender the same strong community reaction, then reducing the scale of the buildings or the nature of the tenancy (e.g., more elderly) would serve no useful purpose. But a reduction in size, or change in tenant composition, or both, could be honestly recommended if they would assure tranquillity; and if the change or changes could also be supported in terms of the other "facts" involved and against some standard of fairness to the as yet unidentified project population. Given this task, the nature and strength of community opposition had to be carefully assessed. The only other alternative—to let the threat of violence give the opponents a veto power over the entire project—was politically impossible.

The Two Issues

In order to determine the depth and breadth of community opposition, Cuomo had to operate on two levels. First, of course, he had to discuss the project on a rational level. What were the articulable negative consequences of the project on the community? This included such issues as the effect on transportation (especially to the city with regard to bus and subway lines), on schools, on play areas, on shopping facilities, and other local resources. It also included understanding the fear that public housing would lead to deterioration of the neighborhood, not because of the great increase in the number of people, but because of the kind of people Forest Hills residents expected the tenants to be. Fear was an articulated reason for opposition and could not be ignored as "emotional." As Glazer wrote in a *New York Times Magazine* article: "The history of neighborhood change is complicated and undoubtedly the simple charge that public housing leads to neighborhood deterioration is too crude. But the unfortunate fact is that no one who is informed on these matters can say it is too crude to be serviceable."

The other level on which Cuomo had to approach issues was an emotional one. People were afraid and angry and when they are, their responses may not always be rationally supportable with articulated reasons. It was this response from fear and anger that Cuomo had to be concerned with because, if frustrated, it could easily lead to violence and it was the fear of violence that had led to Cuomo's appointment. Furthermore, even irrational people try to disguise their oppostion with reasonable explanations, so it would not be as easy to assess the irrational undercurrent in the community as it would to "find facts" on the other issues.

One might wonder why, at this late stage in the project's development, all the groundwork had not already been done. Why hadn't the city assessed the issues, rational and irrational, earlier? The answer is that the people who made the decision to build the project did not do their jobs. Cuomo was needed because the political process had failed. As Walter Goodman pointed out in a *New York Times Magazine* article:

> City officials appear to have assumed or hoped that passions would cool with time and that if they could avoid attracting undue attention, the big buildings would be accepted in the neighborhood as merely another oppressive fact of urban life. Thus, the Housing Authority failed to respond except with polite thank-yous, to the overtures of a friendly community group . . . which had volunteered to give what help it could on such questions as building design and school facilities.

There were other blunders by officialdom, relating to the size of the project, and these will be examined shortly.

The first problem Cuomo had in discussing the issues with the opponents was that they were often just wrong on the facts. Rumors were extensive and believed. Cuomo related a meeting with a group of parents:

> They proposed what they regarded as a perfect solution—move the school from Corona to 108th Street [in Forest Hills] and forget about the project. They were fully armed with the facts and statistics concerning the inefficiency of services. These were four refined, well-intentioned women, none of whom had any firm grasp of the underlying history and actual facts of the present situation. Practically every night one is reminded of how imperfect our system is with regard to communicating facts. Dozens of misconceptions have been generated and are fervently believed and brandished by people involved in this controversy. It's difficult to tell whether this is the result of intellectual

> slippage, the efficacy of the demagogues, or a simple fabrication by the people involved. But if they are fabrications, then I've met some of the best actors in New York City outside of the Broadway stage. I'm more inclined to believe that most of these people are sincere and for some reason have just suspended, in the present context, their normal analytical and intellectual abilities. This is particularly curious, since most of them appear to be skeptical people who would not normally believe anything without hard proof. Perhaps they've simply concluded that politicians are inveterate liars and, therefore, one can safely believe as a fact anything that contradicts a "political" statement. In any event, it's made the dialogue extremely difficult [Cuomo, *Diary*, p. 71].

Cuomo also had to deal with the irrational, some of it nearly bizarre. Examples abound. He wrote:

> The theme generally is that the low-income project results in decay and eventual destruction of the surrounding middle-class community. The evidence for this is usually quite meager. . . . But the conviction is undiminished by the failure of specific proof; I'm inclined to think that no matter what statistics and evidence we're able to marshal, this community's fear will not be totally dissipated. One story of a mugging at a project–whether or not true–will overcome in their minds any array of statistics. The syllogism is simple: Welfare and Blacks are generally responsible for a great deal of crime; there are Welfare and Blacks in projects; there will be a great deal of crime in and around the project [Cuomo, *Diary*, p. 49].

Cuomo reported on the substance of another interview with a resident:

> He tried hard to be coolly professional in his delivery, but before long he was caught up in his own fear and wound up literally screaming at me. There was no devil's advocate role possible with him; any probing question that appeared contradictory of his position was pure "devil" and no advocate. He recited the entire litany of arguments against the project; its ignoble genesis, a borough president who "sold them out," a land "scheme" by Muss, the "phony liberal" concept, the density, and finally, the real issue–crime. There was no shaking his belief that welfare and increased crime are inseparable. He finished up in a crescendo–"My wife will be mugged and raped and you ask me to be reasonable!" He feels–and I'm sure he's sincere–that no project that

> permits any welfare families can be tolerated. He also mentioned the possible depreciation of his property values [Cuomo, *Diary*, p. 57].

Cuomo quickly had to come to terms with the effect this fear could have on his conclusion. On the one hand, was it right to deny low-income people housing because the community was irrationally afraid? On the other hand, was it fair to put low-income people in a neighborhood where they would meet that community response?

> This fear is so ingrained that even if unjustified (and I don't believe it can fairly be said that it is totally unjustified) it must be assuaged somehow. If that can't be done by intellectualizing, then perhaps it should be done by eliminating the source of the fear as much as possible. Is that a "compromise" with principle? Not necessarily. The principle is the validity of serving the need of the low-income segment of our community. But that need is perhaps better served by a project that is acceptable to the community and assured of its cooperation [Cuomo, *Diary*, p. 49].

The question, again, became one of proper balance: Was there a point to which the project could be reduced that would make it both acceptable to the community and fair to the prospective tenants?

The second part of this question required Cuomo to review the correctness of the decision, made long before, to build the project at its then planned height. Cuomo's job would have been much more difficult if he had concluded that, irrespective of the irrational community reaction, the size of the project would not unduly burden the neighborhood. But he concluded otherwise. Based mainly on facts learned from various branches of government itself, his conclusion was that the project was a mistake at the spot it was being built.

In addition to other reasons for the error, there was the simple convergence of the following facts: (1) excavation for the foundation was unduly expensive because a stream ran beneath the site; (2) the federal government would not guarantee its hefty 90 percent of the cost unless the dollar cost per apartment was below a certain amount; (3) in order to keep the per apartment cost below that amount, given the high excavation cost, the building had to be tall. Therefore, it was the desire for federal money that generated the height requirement—not the need for tall buildings in the neighborhood, nor studies showing that the particular height was appropriate or that the neighborhood could withstand the resulting number of new families. This process, obviously, had not produced a decision that was fair to either the current or the expected residents.

Yet, it was also too late to drop the project and build elsewhere. As Cuomo said:

> If one were starting from scratch, the problem would not be so difficult. This is the wrong site–given its cost and all the other various problems–but it would not be reasonable to attempt to undo this whole project at this point. To begin with, the cost would be exorbitant. And perhaps more decisive than the money involved would be the psychological and precedential impact of such a decision. It would mean that no community in the future could reasonably be asked to participate in a dispersal program; all would be able to point to Forest Hills and to demand similar treatment as a matter of fairness [Cuomo, *Diary*, p. 114].

If the project had to be built, given history if not logic, Cuomo had the nearly impossible task of determining what size it should be to sufficiently assuage the residents, but still keep the commitment to the poorly housed low-income tenants who would be moving in.

> The project cannot be left as it is. Not only because the fear must be assuaged, but because the size of the project threatens the potential tenants themselves. As it now stands, this project's dimensions will make it difficult if not impossible to have any kind of meaningful assimilation. Thus, for the sake of the low-income sector who will live in Forest Hills, this project should be reduced. The low-income sector will never accept this proposition nor even believe that it can be sincerely offered, but it is nevertheless clear to me that it's true. So the question becomes: How much smaller and in what composition? [Cuomo, *Diary*, p. 114].

The decision was not an easy one because fear is not easy to quantify and because Cuomo had to risk a potentially sharp reaction from the project's proponents if his proposal resulted in a loss of too many dwellings. No doubt the extensive "lobbying" effort Cuomo had undertaken among the opposition community paid off. The mood of compromise he is credited with creating was important. No doubt, too, his presence as a sounding board, his willingness to listen even to extravagant charges and threats, and his compulsive digging into the legal and construction alternatives also helped.

And so, after much reflection and study and talk, Cuomo concluded that a 50 percent reduction was right. But he had a problem. It sounded as if he just split the total number of apartments in half, when, he maintained, he arrived at this figure in a rational manner. He also had another problem. Should he play all his cards at once? Should he recommend a 50 percent reduction knowing that that was what he believed was right, or should he recommend a less drastic reduction so that there would be negotiating room after issuing his report?

> Three 12's at the present population ratios is the conclusion. There are criteria and I believe it to be reasonable. I think the conclusion could probably be defended against all attacks, but I'm still leery about presenting it. While I think the report can be written persuasively enough to rationalize the conclusion to an intelligent reader, I'm sure that the suggestion of anything like 50 per cent will be regarded by offhand observers as a simple cop-out. . . . On the other side, I'm sure that once the community is told of three 12's they will probably be surprised that this much of a reduction was recommended, but instead of accepting it, their experience as businessmen and bargainers will tell them to demand more. They will no doubt ask for more elderly at least, and probably will demand total elderly [Cuomo, *Diary*, p. 115].

The Outcome: Lessons

The project was built substantially as Cuomo recommended, with the city putting up about $9.8 million because of the loss of federal funds.

The process—dispute, appointment of a fact finder, report, and resolution—can, in the case of Forest Hills, be viewed in two ways. Either it represents the failure of government to use its facilities and resources to prevent the conflict long before Cuomo was called in, or it represents the inability of government even to do what Cuomo did. Cuomo himself believes that, at least at the time he acted, a person seen as part of government could not have been successful. In his book, he speculated that government may often have to be prepared to call on outsiders to solve some kinds of problems.

> In going through my files on Corona tonight, I found some general notes on city government which rang a bell. The present situation and others we've been in, like Corona and Willets Point, were all extraordinary but had a number of elements in common. One thing that strikes me is

> that in each of these cases the eventual solution was basically generated not by government, but by people outside of government. In Corona, it was our compromise plan. In Willets Point, it was our ability to persuade Tom Hoving, who at that time had not yet been appointed parks commissioner. And now in Forest Hills—if there is to be a solution—it will be at least in part the result of this unusual if not unique independent agency [his fact-finding project]. One has to wonder why this needed to be so. Surely government was capable of making these judgments unaided. Perhaps what's needed is some kind of agency or office designed particularly to anticipate, prevent or, if necessary, adjust problems of this type. The ombudsman notion comes as close to any as I can think of offhand, and it's an idea that has been attractive to a lot of people for a long time [Cuomo, *Diary*, p. 111].

Cuomo firmly believes in the value of mediation for settling community disputes. "Of course it is better to do it that way than going to court. The court should be a last resort. It is not a good device for resolving disputes," he said. "The court always leaves one party terribly unhappy. There is a winner and loser." With regard to community disputes, Cuomo feels the courts that are involved in them would be better off trying to extricate themselves by setting up a mediation process. Should that be a formal mediation? There is a place for formal mediation, Cuomo said, but with community disputes "there is a kind of instinct that tells me that to the extent you formalize it you tend to make it more and more like courts. That's been the history."

What is the key element a mediator must bring to the job? "The ability to listen," said Cuomo. "You have to be able to insist on the completeness of the factual presentation. Everything is in the facts. When you get all the facts, solutions recommend themselves. If you are good at gathering facts, you'll be good at solutions because the solution is intrinsic to the facts. The solution is in there somewhere."

Cuomo also played a successful fact-finding role in another major dispute—the forcible takeover in 1974 of land in upstate New York by Mohawk Indians who claimed ownership (see Chapter 1). Would he ever consider heading a large national organization devoted to community mediation efforts? "I mediate every day," Cuomo said. "I have five children." He went on:

> No, I wouldn't want a job like that. It would frustrate me to death because I would assign you to a case and never know if you did it the

way I want to do it. You could do it seven times as well, but I would never know. I don't mind doing it. It's a strain. You can't afford a whole lot of ego in these things either, and you can't want to come out a winner, you will get hurt because that will distort you. You'll start measuring by different criteria—that is, how will this be received by the world out there? That is the worst, trying to make yourself popular. In Forest Hills . . . the one way to gain points was to decide which of the two sides was the stronger politically, or whatever, and then go with them. If you want to make points, you make the wrong decision in Forest Hills. To make the right decision, you had to chance being hurt by both sides and not worry about winning. If, by some misadventure, people say, "Gee, he was objective," that's wonderful, but it's unlikely to happen. What normally would happen is someone saying, "Ah, the bum."

Could Forest Hills happen today?

No. It is inconceivable to me that it would happen. You see, you can't do it. Can you imagine [Mayor] Koch saying to a middle-class Jewish community, considering the few Jewish middle-class people we have left, "I am going to give you a project that is going to be 24 stories high." It would be easier to make an effective case on behalf of neighborhood people today—there is a greater sensitivity to the neighborhoods; there is a greater appreciation of their importance to the City. Neighborhoods are largely middle-class enclaves, and we have so few middle-class people left that they have taken on an importance—an importance that everybody recognizes.

5
Not Without Honor—A Prophet Even in His Own Country: The St. Louis Tenant Strike of 1969

Joel L. Fleishman

Public Housing and Public Policy: The Right Cure, The Wrong Patient

Public housing was originally intended by Congress as shelter for the working poor—those with income to pay rent. The assumption was that the revenue from rents would pay for operating costs and maintenance expenses, with a prudent reserve for repairs, modernization, and replacement. "There are some people we cannot possibly reach," explained the late Robert Wagner, who was the distinguished Senate sponsor of the Housing Act. "I mean those who have no means to pay the rent. Obviously, this bill cannot provide housing for those who cannot pay the rent minus the subsidy allowed."

Public housing was meant to be only transitional shelter for workers who had been dislocated by the depression or other economic forces beyond their control. When the workers had improved their financial position, they were expected to be able to afford private housing, with perhaps some assistance provided by one or another of the housing purchase subsidies enacted as part of the New Deal.

The arrangement designed by Congress for financing public housing reflected this objective. The federal government would indirectly provide municipal authorities with the funds to construct the housing. In actual practice, local housing authorities would sell federally backed bonds in the marketplace to raise the construction money and the federal government would reimburse them for both interest and principal on the loans. In return, the local authorities would agree to manage, maintain, and repair the units out of rental income. With Washington footing the construction and interest costs, which represent the largest component of all rent payments, public housing units could be rented at a level substantially below that of equivalent privately built housing.

Like so many governmental solutions to public problems, the solution remained the same long after the problem had changed. To ensure that public housing actually served the working poor, rather than families with higher incomes, stringent earnings ceilings were imposed on those who resided in public housing. Unfortunately, while incomes during the post–World War II and post–Korean War periods were rising, the public housing income ceilings were allowed to remain close to prewar levels.

By the late fifties and early sixties, the old, unchanged income ceilings were causing an involuntary flow of the working poor out of public housing, creating a substantial number of vacancies, which were quickly occupied by the nonworking poor. At a time that the country was responding to the civil rights movement and the plight of the poor, it was both unconscionable and politically impossible to lift the income ceilings or to raise the rent. Without those alternative means of controlling the socioeconomic mix of the public housing population, empty apartments were occupied by greater numbers of the nonworking poor—the unemployed, the welfare recipients, the elderly struggling to survive only on Social Security, and inevitably, the families burdened with physical, emotional, social, educational, and economic handicaps. At the same time, the remainder of the working poor accelerated their departure from public housing. In the interest of short-run expediency—in this case the need for rent from anyone willing to pay it—the original premise of public housing, to provide decent living quarters for the working poor, was abandoned.

In the forties and fifties, only a minority of public housing tenants were caught in a cycle of dependency. In the sixties, they became the majority. The working poor who had persisted in remaining in public housing faced a radically different living environment, which undermined their efforts to lift themselves out of poverty and into a better life. Sociologists called it the culture of dependency, but it was also a culture of depredation, sweeping with it into the great public housing complexes, and concentrating there, a subculture of crime, narcotics, and vandalism. Bold high-rise complexes, which functioned well enough as temporary shelter for those with self-confidence and hope, became permanent traps for those who were bereft of hope.

The future of public housing seemed bleak. The maintenance and repair emergency was heightened by the inflation generated by the Vietnam War in the late sixties. An 8 percent annual inflation rate between 1965 and 1969 forced most urban public housing authorities to dig even deeper into whatever maintenance reserves they had been fortunate enough to retain. With the depletion of those reserves and with no other source of maintenance funds in sight, approximately one-third of the nation's public housing units were running on an annual deficit. (The 1937 Housing Act insulated the federal government from any claim for operating subsidies, and local governments pleaded no responsibility for anything other than capital investment.) Those responsible for managing public housing had no recourse but to raise rent.

But now most of the tenants, not enjoying the benefits of rising incomes like those of the working poor, simply couldn't afford to absorb the increases. By 1969, between half and three-quarters of the urban public housing residents in the United States existed principally on income provided and fixed by government. It was this single fact that was at the bottom of the St. Louis housing dispute.

Public Housing in St. Louis

In 1968, St. Louis provided a textbook case of the worse aspects of the failure of the national public housing policy. The unmistakable signs of spreading physical and social decay contrasted sharply with the community pride and optimism that had been expressed when these units had been completed a decade earlier. Mayor Alfonso J. Cervantes, in his book *Mr. Mayor,* draws the contrast vividly:

> It was a proud day for St. Louis. The Pruitt-Igoe public housing project was being dedicated. . . . Here on nearly seventy acres of what had been the most miserable slums of the inner city now stood thirty-two shiny, new high-rise buildings, modern homes for nearly ten thousand souls in the lower-income brackets. The whole nation had reason to take heart. . . . Ten years later, Pruitt-Igoe was a shambles. The rows of gleaming windows were mostly dark, jagged-mouth caves now. The thousands of vacant apartments had been stripped by vandals almost

> before their ex-occupants' meager belongings were on the rented truck. Plumbing was ripped out. Pipes were sold for the metal. The public rooms and mail racks were veritable rats' nests. The architectural gem had become a ghost town haunted by muggers [A. J. Cervantes, *Mr. Mayor* (New York: Nash Publishing Corp., 1975), pp. 45–46].

While other developments had not reached Pruitt-Igoe's tragic stage, the pattern of disintegration was alarmingly similar.

As in other cities, the disrepair stemmed from a continuing shortage of sufficient revenues to cover expenses. First, there were occasional deferrals of maintenance, which soon became chronic. St. Louis's housing officials, who were responsible for about eight thousand units dispersed among nine major complexes, housing in all some thirty-two thousand people, reported a 1967–1968 deficit of $533,000. That left the maintenance reserves $2 million short of the minimal federal reserve requirement of $2.3 million. Moreover, the St. Louis Housing Authority had been able to put only $331,000 into nonroutine maintenance that year. Unless other resources could be found, the inflation-swollen deficit for 1968–1969 was projected at $500,000, which spelled bankruptcy for the city's public housing system. It did not appear likely that other resources could be found. There was always the possibility of a rent increase, but rents had already been raised twice in the preceding eighteen months. Neither the state of Missouri nor the city of St. Louis had ever used general revenues to defray public housing operations, and, in any event, neither jurisdiction had any funds to spare.

The federal government had provided other cities with a variety of special maintenance and repair subsidies over time, subsidies which could have helped substantially to ease St. Louis's distress, but Washington was not about to put any money into St. Louis. Officials of the Department of Housing and Urban Development (HUD) had long complained about what they regarded as the utter mismanagement of public housing in St. Louis. They viewed the Housing Authority as politically staffed and fiscally irresponsible and had concluded by 1968 that any additional expenditures in St. Louis amounted to pouring good money after bad. Federal site inspectors recommended that major reforms be adopted before federal aid was provided.

Indeed, Washington's dissatisfaction with St. Louis public housing went back at least ten years. HUD's 1957 criticisms had provoked

Charles L. Farris, then head of the St. Louis Housing and Land Clearance Agency, to increasingly bypass the Federal Housing Administration's Chicago regional office, which until then had been responsible for supervising St. Louis. Using his considerable political influence, he arranged to have St. Louis transferred to the Fort Worth regional office, which had much less experience with urban public housing than the Chicago office. But St. Louis also ran into conflicts with the Fort Worth office and so Farris began dealing directly with Washington. The result of this maneuvering was that no HUD officials were monitoring St. Louis public housing on a continuing basis, and no one in the HUD bureaucracy was particularly eager to help St. Louis when its public housing program came on hard times.

The local Housing Authority was only one division of a comprehensive agency, the St. Louis Housing and Land Clearance Agency, that had responsibility for two separate undertakings: public housing and urban renewal, a relatively new strategy but one that already had a powerful impact on the urban landscape. Urban renewal appealed to city governments as the antidote to slums and was especially favored in St. Louis for making the riverfront and its adjacent business district into a tourist showplace, with its towering Gateway Arch, riverfront parks, new luxury condominium high-rises, gleaming office towers, sports arena, and civic center. Against such glamorous competition, public housing appeared drab and quickly became the city's stepchild.

With no help likely from Washington or from the state government, and with no one committed to fighting for its cause at home, Housing Authority Director Irvin Dagen felt that there was no alternative to another rent increase—the third in two years. Late in October 1968, therefore, a new rent schedule was established that no longer based rents on family income, but on the size of the apartment. The purpose of the new flat-rent schedule was not only to raise additional revenue. It also was designed to attract more working families to public housing and to retain those who still remained. Significantly, it would permit residents with jobs to earn more without paying more in rent, since the income-based rent schedule was to be eliminated.

By 1969, in St. Louis, as in most other large cities, 70 percent of the residents of public housing depended for their income on some form of public assistance. Of that total, nearly half, or twenty-six hundred families, were receiving welfare support under the Aid-to-Families-With-Dependent-Children category, and Missouri's welfare payments were among the lowest in the country. For a family of four, the payment was $124 a month. More than half of the public housing families had incomes of $2,500 or less.

The new flat-rent schedule, which established rents at between sixty and eighty dollars a month depending on the size of the apartment, would force the average family on welfare to pay between 40 percent and 60 percent of its income for rent. (Under the old income-based system, tenants paid between 20 percent and 25 percent of their income.) Faced with these new rents, tenants in St. Louis public housing began to plan for a strike.

Rent Strike

Although the St. Louis Housing Authority delayed announcing the new flat-rent schedule until after the 1968 elections, word of the impending rent increase traveled quickly through the public housing complexes, arousing the deep hostility of the residents. By the middle of November, discussion of a possible "rent strike" was widespread. There was a determination not to pay rent, but no one knew how to organize a rent strike in the massive public housing system of St. Louis. Except for a three-month strike by eighty-nine tenants in the small town of Muskegan Heights, Michigan, earlier in 1968, there had never been a public housing tenant strike anywhere in the United States.

In private housing, such tactics were not rare. Earlier in the 1960s, Jesse Gray's strikes in New York City against upper West Side Manhattan slumlords had attracted national attention. In fact, three or four private housing rent strikes had been called in St. Louis in the preceding three years. Indeed, as pressure was mounting in St. Louis public housing throughout November, a private housing strike, involving thirteen families protesting maintenance conditions in an apartment building, was winding down after the Legal Aid Society had assisted in reaching an agreement.

Now, the public housing tenants turned to Legal Aid for help. They sought out Richard Baron and Phillip Fishman, two young lawyers who had already become known for their skill as well as for their willingness to help the poor with their housing problems. Baron began working in the St. Louis Legal Aid Society shortly after his graduation in June 1968 from the law school at the University of Michigan. He had barely settled in when the Legal Aid director began assigning housing matters to him. "I knew as much about housing when I first came here," he said, "as I did about relativity theory, but like all lawyers I was cocky about being able to get on top of it—or anything else—quickly."

The first protesters who came to him had a minimum of schooling and were inexperienced with bureaucracies. One who was somewhat more experienced was Buck Jones, the son of migrant farmworkers, who had himself grown up in public housing in Tampa, Florida. In 1968, he was twenty-eight years old. He had been ordained a minister at the age of fifteen and, after graduating from the Yale Divinity School, worked as a community organizer both for New Haven's pioneering antipoverty program and among migrant farmworkers on Long Island. He had also taught religion at Florida A.&M. University. Now he was a neighborhood organizer at Plymouth House, a private social service agency serving the twenty-five-year-old Carr Square Village, the first public housing development built in St. Louis, and the nearby Vaughn and Cochran complexes.

Jean King, on the other hand, had no prior involvement with community organization in Darst, the complex where her apartment was located. Eventually, she would lead the tenants there and in the nearby Webbe project, as well as in the Clinton-Peabody developments. Her only community activity had been in the local PTA. King was employed as an admitting officer at Malcolm Bliss Hospital, where she worked the unpopular 11:00 P.M. to 7:00 A.M. shift so that she could be home to keep house for her husband and daughter in the daytime. Bertha Mason, president of the Carr Square Village Tenant Council, owned a flower shop. The other protest leaders were not much different. Loretta Hall, Veapplise Mack, and Mabel Coney all had their jobs, their families, and their routines.

The protestors decided this time not to give up as they had twice before in the preceding eighteen months. While most of the protest leaders themselves were not going to be driven out of their apartments by the new flat-rent schedule—indeed most of them were going to benefit from it—many of their friends and neighbors would surely be out in the streets with no place to live, their lives disrupted, their living standard diminished, and their children even more vulnerable to criminality in the ramshackle private housing to which they would be forced to move.

Baron knew that a successful strike had to be meticulously planned.

Before the public could be informed, the tenants had to be prepared in detail for the strike. For two months, Baron and Fishman met with the would-be strikers. "The most important assistance we gave the strikers," Baron said, "was training them to make precise demands in reasonable language, with the rhetoric serving only as icing instead of the whole cake." One of his most significant recommendations was to advise the strike leaders to pay their rents, so that if the Housing Authority decided to evict striking tenants, the tenants would not be without resident leaders.

On December 2, the threat of a rent strike was made publicly for the first time. Buck Jones announced that he had eight hundred pledges of nonpayment from residents in Carr Square Village and Vaughn, and that there were rent strike committees forming in two other housing developments. While he set no date for the start of the strike, he assured the Housing Authority that one would begin soon unless the authority agreed to limit rents to 25 percent of the tenants' income and to "treat the tenants as people." After waiting two weeks for a formal reply from the Housing Authority, Jones wrote a letter spelling out his two demands. Then he and the representatives of the tenants decided on a strike date of February 1.

By the end of January, two months after a rent strike was threatened, the Housing Authority still had not made any formal response. To his original demands, Jones now added two more. The first was for three-year leases for all public housing tenants (instead of the prevailing one-year standard leases), with no raises to occur during the lease term. The second demand concerned rent reductions for a variety of hardship cases. Jones also announced that picket lines would be established around the rent payment offices in Carr Square Village and Vaughn, and that buses would be provided to transport tenants to designated banks where they could deposit their rents in rent-strike accounts. By the end of January, 300 of Cochran's tenants had pledged to join the strike. Shortly before rent payment day during the first week of February, Darst, Webbe, and Clinton-Peabody also voted to join in the strike with about 250 residents committed to withholding rents. This left Pruitt-Igoe and Blumeyer as the only nonparticipating complexes.

By the end of the first week of the strike, $15,000 had been deposited. The second week saw the total grow to $25,000 and by the end of the month the sum of $60,000 was in the accounts. In some housing complexes, especially Carr Square Village, Cochran, and Vaughn, about half of the tenants were withholding their rents.

The St. Louis Housing Authority Reacts

During the first month of the strike, the Housing Authority employed the carrot-and-stick approach. First the stick. After rents were withheld in the first month, managers of Carr Square Village, Vaughn, and Cochran announced that they were delivering envelopes to all of the residents so that those who did not wish to cross the picket lines could pay their rent directly to the authority. During the next ten days, when it became clear that a substantial number of tenants was withholding rents, the authority took a different tack. On February 10, the manager at Cochran locked a strikers' meeting out of the tenant council room. Three days later, the Housing Authority threatened to evict all tenants who had not paid rent. Later that week it actually filed eviction suits against seventy-three tenants for nonpayment.

At the same time, the authority began to use the carrot. Cochran tenants were amazed to find crews, who had hardly been industrious before the strike, cleaning the grounds. Carpenters, who had rarely responded before to complaints, suddenly began knocking on apartment doors to see if repairs were needed. The tenants, who were not intimidated by the sanctions, interpreted the solicitousness of the authority as evidence of the effectiveness of the strike.

Whatever goodwill might have been produced by the occasional repairs and maintenance was soon dissipated by the authority's not-so-subtle attempt to discredit the strike leaders in the eyes of the tenants. The Housing Authority announced that all of the strike leaders had, in fact, paid their rent. But the tenants knew this was a tactic adopted on Baron's advice, to make sure that the leaders would not be evicted.

Neither inducements nor the threats weakened the determination of the tenants; to the contrary, their effect was to strengthen the strikers' resolve. On February 22, the tenants succeeded in persuading Congressman William Clay to publicly urge the mayor to intervene in the tenants' behalf, as well as to propose an immediate moratorium on evictions. Congressman Clay thereby became the first public official to urge immediate action to avoid violence.

Whether prompted by the congressman's appeal, or by the obvious initial success of the rent strike, or by the growing size of the accounts containing the withheld rent funds, Mayor Cervantes agreed to meet with the strikers on February 23. This was the first time the mayor had taken public notice of the strike, and it was the first indication that he intended to be involved in resolving the dispute. Not much came out of the meeting, however, except the first formal response by the Housing Authority to the strike, undoubtedly at the mayor's insistence.

Buck Jones had presented a list of seven demands to the mayor at the meeting, and, the following day, he threatened to sit in at the Housing Authority offices unless the authority withdrew the seventy-three eviction suits already filed. Irvin Dagen, the executive director of the authority, denied that the number of eviction suits was larger than those usually pending prior to the strike. He defended the flat-rent schedule as a means of increasing the number of working families in public housing and made a series of what can only have been mock proposals: first, to the Board of Commissioners of the Housing and Land Clearance Agency that it might forego rents from welfare recipients if utility companies would forego charges in an equal amount; second, to the Bi-State Transit Authority that it ought to stop charging fares to welfare recipients; third, that Plymouth House, which was Jones's base of operations, ought to pay fair market value rent to the Housing Authority, rather than merely its token one dollar a year; and, finally, that the state government ought to forego sales taxes on welfare recipients. Then, when Jones and the other strike leaders attempted to see Dagen, the latter refused to see anyone but Jones alone, which Jones was unwilling to do.

Just as the Housing Authority's responses increased the tenants' determination to stick with the strike during its early, uncertain phase, Dagen's first sarcastic reply succeeded in bringing the North Side and the South Side strike leaders into a single organization. On February 27, what was to become the City-Wide Rent Strike Committee was established, and Jean King was elected vice-chairman. "So far everybody's been doing their own thing," Terangi Speed, one of the new officers, observed. "So now we've all got to get together." Teamster organizer Frank Boykin, who headed the Tandy Area Council, a new community action agency in the predominantly black Tandy area, now entered the dispute with a call for tenant control of the Board of Commissioners.

Two days later, the Housing Authority counterattacked. On March 1, instead of complying with the strikers' demand that the 73 pending eviction suits be dropped, the Housing Authority filed 175 new eviction suits, with Dagen explaining that dropping eviction suits would be unfair to those tenants who were paying their rents. He also said, "The Housing Authority wants adequate assurances from the strike leaders that the Housing Authority will in fact get the money which is owed to it when the strike is over." The mayor and some of his appointees picked up Dagen's theme, publicly demanding that the strikers establish a "true" escrow fund controlled by an independent third party, rather than bank accounts controlled solely by the strike leaders. Jones called the proposal "totally and clearly unacceptable" and promptly led the rent-strike leaders out of another meeting with the mayor, saying, "The Mayor won't talk about anything but money." The strikers were convinced that control of the withheld funds constituted the most important source of their bargaining power.

Blumeyer, the newest housing complex, which was in relatively good condition after being open only a year, now voted to join the strike, leaving only Pruitt-Igoe not participating. Ten days later, the vacancy-ridden and strife-torn Pruitt-Igoe cast its lot with the strikers. At last, tenants in all the projects were together in the strike.

The participation of Pruitt-Igoe caused the Housing Authority to falter. Dagen had consistently refused to drop any of the eviction suits, despite the demonstrations by the strikers at the Housing Authority offices, but on the day after the Pruitt-Igoe vote, he announced a two-week delay in prosecuting them. He also agreed finally to meet with a delegation of strikers. The following day, the Board of Commissioners also met with the strikers for the first time, one and a half months into the strike and three months after it was first publicly announced.

The fact that they were at last talking with top officials of the Housing Authority gave the strikers some hope that the process of resolving the dispute had begun in earnest. After a two-hour closed meeting, the authority promised not to press the eviction suits, and, in return, the strikers agreed to call off the demonstrations at the Housing Authority offices. Considering the issues at stake, this was hardly an agreement of substance, but in his first optimistic statement since early December, Jones proclaimed "this morning has been a beginning."

But it was a beginning with a quick ending. Two weeks of fruitless sparring led to a stalemate. Then on March 24, Kenneth Brantley, the

Housing Authority's black director of public relations, was fired for announcing his support of the strike. Dismayed and angry, the strikers broke off negotiations that same day in an atmosphere of great hostility. Soon there were calls for disruptive tactics from some strikers and their more militant supporters. Jones threatened to take the withheld funds and invest them in low-income housing if the strikes were not settled by July. Brantley urged the strikers to demand Dagen's dismissal.

Apparently concerned by the changing tone of the strikers, the Housing Authority sought a resumption of negotiations, and another meeting took place on April 2. Again, there was no progress, and the strikers walked out and did not return for nearly two months. Immediately, the Housing Authority resumed the eviction suits and began efforts to gain control of the withheld rent-fund accounts, first by persuasion, and finally, on April 25, by filing a suit in the circuit court to attach the bank accounts.

Raising the Ante: The Strikers Enlarge Their Objectives

As the strike continued into the spring, the strikers increasingly came to believe that a mere rollback of rents would not leave them much better off than they had been before the strike. An agency that could unduly raise rents once could do so again. To prevent hostile policy from being made in the future, the tenants reasoned that they had to gain representation on the Housing Authority. The strikers also wanted to establish nonprofit tenant management corporations (TMCs) for each development with boards of directors elected by the tenants. They also pressed for a tenant affairs board that had some authority rather than a tenant advisory board; they wanted a board that could sit down and discuss problems with the housing commissioners (who had the real policymaking power) rather than with the Housing Authority's staff. In their effort to assume some control over public housing, the strikers were later to add one more demand—which was suggested to them by a HUD team sent out in July. It concerned splitting the combined urban renewal and public housing administration into two separate agencies.

When they failed to persuade the Housing Authority to withdraw the eviction suits, the strikers took part in demonstrations, the first marches of the strike. At the same time, they were fighting the evictions in court. Each of the tenants faced with an eviction suit countered with a claim for physical and emotional damages, which they alleged were caused by the poor sanitary conditions and disrepair of the public housing complexes. These legal actions led to heavy traffic in the courts, including a complicated series of transfers from magistrate to circuit court and back. It took from May until August before the circuit court actually began to consider the validity of the counterclaims. By that time, what the court decided really didn't matter.

The suit brought by the Housing Authority to attach the rent money froze the accounts, which not only prevented the withdrawal of funds, but also precluded the deposit of any additional funds. The strike leaders decided, therefore, that they would no longer deposit withheld rent in any bank. Buck Jones urged his followers in Carr Square Village, Vaughn, and Cochran to take out money orders payable to themselves in the amount of the rent due each month, and turn them over to him for safekeeping in an undisclosed place. Jean King, on the other hand, said, "I don't know what will happen and I really do not care what they [the tenants] do. If they want to keep the rent and spend it, that is O.K. with me." As if in response to these threats, during the first week of May, the Housing Authority made its first policy concession of the strike, announcing that it was now willing to reduce rents in specific cases of hardship and would put such reductions into effect immediately. That didn't help very much because the strikers understood that the authority was still talking about mere exceptions to a flat-rent schedule which they opposed in principle.

Aside from giving the strikers an opportunity to expand their goals and refine their tactics, the Housing Authority's counterattack had one additional effect. It created a united opposition, which had not existed before. From the very beginning of the rent protest, there had been differences among the tenants and among the various strike leaders. Jones had his set of demands, while King had hers. Jones's North Side rent strikers had picket lines around the project rent payment offices; King had none in her South Side complexes. The banks that Jones chose as depositories for his funds were not the same banks that King chose for hers. Jones advised his group of tenants to use self-addressed money orders for the withheld rents, while King told the strikers simply to keep their money and even to spend it. If one leader issued a call for a meeting of strikers, the other failed to show up. These differences had made it extremely difficult for the strikers to form a solid front before May. Indeed, their internal conflicts caused Legal Aid Society attorneys Fishman and Baron to publicly complain about the disagreements and infighting.

Dagen succeeded, however, in forging, for the time being at least, the unity that even the persistent pleas of the Legal Aid lawyers had not been able to achieve. The first objective on which the strikers managed to agree was a demand that the mayor fire Dagen. Had Dagen acted differently, he might have defused the controversy in a variety of ways. He was regarded by those who knew him as a liberal, stongly committed to organizations and programs that helped the poor and disadvantaged, as well as dedicated to efforts aimed at achieving racial justice. But something about the rent strike apparently unsettled him, and he did not respond to the striking tenants as his reputation would have led one to expect. For the strikers, he became the villain of the piece. As Mayor Cervantes said, "Dagen was not the most diplomatic of men. His bluntness caused many people to call him an abrasive personality." [Cervantes, *Mr. Mayor,* p. 56].

The authority's decision to counterattack instead of negotiate had one other consequence. It gave the strikers the time they needed to develop widespread community support. Early in January, the strikers had asked the St. Louis Health and Welfare Council, a sixty-year-old voluntary citizens' organization for planning in health and social services, to help resolve their differences with the Housing Authority. Dan McDonald, the council executive director, was eager to try, as was council President Richard S. Jones. The council had met separately first with Housing Authority Chairman Leo Flotron and Dagen, and, a week later, with the strike leaders. Those two meetings were followed by a third, also closed to the press, which brought all major parties together for the first time. After these discussions and a meeting among its members alone, the council came out against any evictions at that time. The council formed a coalition of nineteen community organizations aimed at obtaining a moratorium on eviction suits and getting strikers together for negotiations with the Housing Authority.

The involvement of the Health and Welfare Council in turn led to separate attempts by business leaders to mediate the strike. Some of those who had attended the council sessions decided to bring the strikers' grievances to the attention of Civic Progress, Inc. (CPI), an organization composed of St. Louis's business and financial leaders. For several months thereafter, CPI members met from time to time with strikers and their attorneys, with black community leaders, and with representatives of the Housing Authority, but never with any substantial progress toward settlement.

During the spring, the strikers began to get the support of many of the social welfare organizations represented on the council, especially the religious community. Representatives of the Interreligious Council for Metropolitan Affairs, the Interreligious Center for Urban Affairs, and the Administrative Committee of the Metropolitan Church Federation declared on March 3 their "concern for the financial dilemma faced by both the Housing Authority and the rent strikers." In the middle of April, the Metropolitan Church Federation proposed the establishment of a committee of five thousand members to raise funds to support the strikers and followed immediately by writing letters to over five hundred ministers seeking donations to the strike fund. A month later, in an unprecedented action, Cardinal John J. Carberry put the Archdiocese of St. Louis firmly on record in support of the rent strikers. His example was followed in three weeks by Episcopal Bishop Cadigan. Dagen's caustic response to church support for the strikers was to urge that the churches themselves ought to undertake to run St. Louis public housing.

The strikers also received the editorial support of the conservative *Globe-Democrat*, as well as the liberal *St. Louis Post Dispatch*. In calling for the appointment of a mediator, the latter editorialized on March 12:

> While the issues in the rent strike against the St. Louis Housing Authority are both important and familiar ones, they are also very nearly irreconcilable. It is for this reason that the tenants and representatives of the Authority now find themselves at an impasse. Tenants clearly cannot afford to pay 60 to 70 per cent of their income for rent, as some do; equally obviously, the Authority cannot continue to function, as by law it must, on a formula that requires it to meet operating expenses out of rent revenues, which fail to keep pace with rising costs. . . . Prolonging the strike can only exacerbate the already dismal realities of public housing.

On the political front, Congressman Clay was the first prominent politician to side with the strikers, but because of the influence of Mayor Cervantes, it was four months before any other major politicians announced their support.

Looking back on the evolution of the tenant demands, one cannot help but note that the outcome of the strike would surely have been different, and far less significant for national public housing management, had any of the winter or spring settlement attempts succeeded. The strikers might well have won the battle over a rent rollback, but they would surely have lost the underlying war for tenant participation in Housing Authority decision making, for that conflict was not joined until early summer.

The Role of the Political Establishment

A week after the authority's rent increase had been announced, the Board of Aldermen, at the initiative of Mrs. Ernestine Hinton who represented a district where one of the public housing complexes was situated, voted to have its Housing and Urban Development Committee "investigate the proposed rent increases," because, as Mrs. Hinton put it, they had "greatly disturbed the tenants." A day after Buck Jones backed up his public call for a strike with eight hundred signed pledges, the aldermen spent most of their meeting listening to complaining public housing residents. It was not until six months later, however, that the Board of Aldermen was able to muster a majority behind a proposal to attempt to find a solution to the rent strike, and still another two months before it made a small financial contribution to easing the Housing Authority's fiscal plight.

Mayor Cervantes, who had appointed both Dagen and the members of the Board of Commissioners of the Housing and Land Clearance Agency, was the natural target of the strikers. They expected him to act to settle the dispute. That he failed to do so in any substantial way for nearly nine months is puzzling. Cervantes, who had taken office in 1965, was highly regarded, both in St. Louis and in urban centers throughout the country. He had launched a massive Challenge of the Seventies goal-setting plan for St. Louis, headed by a leading Republican in the city and involving extensive participation by business and community leaders. He was a pioneer in urban redevelopment, first with La Salle Park, a joint effort of city government and the Ralston-

Purina Company, and then with LaClede Town, a racially mixed, middle-income housing development.

When a disturbance broke out in minority areas, he would be quick to intervene personally. After becoming mayor, he would usually rush to the scene of a disturbance and seek to calm it. For example, the night Martin Luther King was assassinated, he left a dinner party for Spain's Minister of Tourism and Information at his own home. He traveled from one television station to another, taping his personal statements of grief at each. At 2:30 A.M., he ended up, uninvited, in the heart of the ghetto at a tense gathering of blacks, who were trying to figure out an appropriate response of their own to the tragedy. Although 125 other cities in twenty-nine states had riots of some nature that night, there was none in St. Louis, then or later. By and large, Cervantes was popular in the black community. He had appointed a large number of blacks to positions in his administration, including two top-level posts – commissioner of Community Services and director of the Model Cities Program. He had also named St. Louis's first black judge. He had gone out of his way to get federal money for programs of special interest to the black community – summer jobs, Headstart, job training – and he usually made a point of appearing personally to announce these grants to the interested groups.

Here, then, was a mayor who had always tried to deal quickly, firmly, and positively with protest as soon as it surfaced. But, for some still unexplained reason, his response to the rent strike was different. Cervantes chose, first, to ignore it; next, to paper it over with words and promises; and finally, to put the responsibility on someone else. By failing to speak out on the tenants' behalf or even to meet with them until nearly four months after the rent increase was announced, Mayor Cervantes led the tenants to believe that he didn't care about their grievances. When, in late February, he finally did agree to meet with them, he spoke only in generalities. The tenants began to wonder if perhaps the Housing Authority's position was *his* in the first place, with the authority advancing it at the mayor's direction. Most strikers came increasingly to believe that Dagen was simply carrying out the mayor's orders and that it was the mayor himself who was their chief opponent.

At the end of April, six months after the public housing rent increase, the mayor tried to shift responsibility to George Romney, secretary of HUD. If it were true, as Cervantes claimed, that the public housing financial crisis in St. Louis could be solved only through federal action, why postpone for six months any attempt to bring the federal government into the conflict? To the tenants, that seemed to be avoiding responsibility for reaching a solution. By the time the mayor did try to invoke HUD's aid, relations among the strikers, the Housing Authority, and the mayor's office had so badly deteriorated that Romney and Lawrence Cox, the assistant secretary for renewal and housing assistance, could argue with some justification that the dispute was a local problem.

Other politicians were more responsive than the mayor. Sarkis J. Webbe, a candidate for the Democratic nomination for president of the Board of Aldermen, called for greater tenant participation in management. Congressman Clay, who had publicly asked Mayor Cervantes to intervene on behalf of the tenants, later introduced in the U.S. House of Representatives a bill to prohibit public housing rents from exceeding 25 percent of tenant income. Back in February, several St. Louis representatives in the Missouri legislature had introduced bills that would have provided a statewide subsidy to needy tenants in public housing. The St. Louis legislators fought hard for that legislation throughout the session, but it was defeated decisively in both state houses.

July: Federal Officials Take Center Stage

The mayor joined a CPI delegation of civic and business leaders to see Secretary Romney at the end of April, but all they received was a general promise that HUD officials would consider the matter and, perhaps, send a team out to conduct a review of the Housing Authority's operations. Actually, two and a half months passed before the HUD team arrived.

In the interim, however, Mayor Cervantes and the Housing Authority prepared a 1969–1970 fiscal year budget for public housing that reflected all of the tenant demands, including rent reduction; but the budget also resulted in a sizable deficit, which the Housing Authority said it expected to make up by seeking federal, state, and city subsidies. The strikers responded cautiously to this proposal. The promised rent reduction would not take effect until the following October, if then, and the authority said nothing about lowering the rents retroactive to the preceding November when the new schedule had first been instituted. Most important, the strikers knew that, before the new budget could go into effect, it had to be approved by HUD, which already provided an annual subsidy of $5.5 million for St. Louis public housing. According to a Fort Worth regional office spokesman, HUD had never before approved a deficit budget for public housing anywhere. Dagen said, "If HUD withholds the annual contribution, that is something for our bondholders to worry about, not the tenants."

The Board of Aldermen decided on July 13 to reduce by half, from $240,000 to $120,000 a year, the annual payment made by the Housing Authority to the city in lieu of property taxes on the public housing units. Because that was the first tangible contribution to solving public housing's financial problem by either the state or the city government, it was expected to have some impact on HUD's decision. To the dismay of both the city government and the strikers, it did not.

On July 20, HUD Assistant Secretary Cox wrote the mayor that HUD could not legally approve a deficit budget. Cox did not rest his position solely on legal limitations that precluded HUD assistance. "We are convinced that your community is not without the resources and capacity to deal with the problem in a responsible and effective manner," he explained. "There appears to be a mistaken impression held by some officials and citizens that if the Housing Authority does become bankrupt, the federal government will have to take over its operation. This definitely is not the case." Mayor Cervantes on the same day responded that "our public housing program was . . . federally conceived, federally designed, federally financed, and federally controlled. Their control is indicated in the very letter that states what they will and won't do. . . . We don't know of any solutions available here. I wish they would get explicit and give us some solutions rather than talking in general terms."

The HUD task force, led by Edgar M. Ewing, a retired black public official from Baltimore with a distinguished national record in public housing, then arrived in St. Louis. After spending a week investigating the housing conflict, Ewing said, "The community has not been sensitive enough to the problem. The public housing projects here are badly deteriorated, and that's an understatement. All one has to do is to go and look at them. I have never seen a more critical situation than the one existing here, and I've been to nearly every state in the Union."

In a private report to the mayor, the federal team found that the strikers were fully justified in their complaints and endorsed virtually every one of the strikers' demands, including (1) the division of the St. Louis Housing and Land Clearance Agency into two separate agencies, one exclusively for public housing; (2) replacement of Housing Authority Executive Director Dagen; (3) the appointment of at least one tenant to the Board of Commissioners; (4) the creation of a tenant affairs board with real power; and (5) reduction of rents to a maximum of 25 percent of family income. But the task force went even further than the strikers' demands by insisting that there be an immediate fiscal, management, and engineering audit of the Housing Authority to be performed by private, independent firms. It also proposed that the Housing Authority promptly institute an effective preventive maintenance program and that HUD withhold all operating and modernization funds pending the implementation of the other recommendations.

While the mayor and, perhaps, Dagen were informed of these recommendations, the public as a whole was not. But what the public learned very soon after the departure of the task force, on July 30, was symbolically as important as the task force's support of the strikers' demands. The task force had concluded that the Housing Authority's new rent schedule was apparently illegal because the HUD regional office had never given its express approval, as required by HUD regulations and the terms of the annual contributions contract between HUD and the Housing Authority. These findings gave added legitimacy to the strike. In effect, the task force had found that the rent increases were illegal.

The task force made another significant contribution to the resolution of the strike. It involved Father Kirk Walsh, a Jesuit priest who was serving as an unpaid special assistant to the undersecretary of HUD. Romney had designated him as the principal troubleshooter for St. Louis. Walsh came out to St. Louis for the first time with the task force and remained there until the end of the strike. He became deeply committed to helping the strikers resolve the differences among themselves and win their battle with the Housing Authority.

Dangerous August Doldrums

With the rent increase judged illegal and Cervantes himself under attack by the federal government, the mayor tried to deflect the criticism he knew would follow public disclosure of the HUD findings by coming out publicly for most of the recommendations. On August 1, he offered to remove Dagen if his dismissal would lead to an end of the strike. In addition, he revealed that he was considering separating the housing and land clearance functions. He asked HUD to furnish assistance in mediating or arbitrating the dispute and requested that agency to send in one or more representatives to do a fiscal and management audit of the Housing Authority.

When those concessions failed to impress the strike leaders, the mayor went further. On August 5, he offered to satisfy all of the eighteen demands of the citywide rent-strike committee if the strikers in turn would agree to turn over all withheld rents to the Housing Authority by midnight. The rent-strike committee rejected the mayor's offer because they did not believe the mayor was leveling with them. As Jean King stated, "He is still only promising so that he can get his hands on the money. He will not say how or when he would meet our demands. Cervantes is still trying to make donkeys out of the tenants."

The mayor reacted angrily the following day. "Where is the money," he asked, "which the poor tenants have turned over to the strike leaders? The strike leaders have a moral and legal obligation to these poor families to make a complete public accounting of all the money they have received." By the end of July, the outstanding rents had reached $466,000. Both Jean King and Buck Jones remained firm. King had already said that she had no money, having returned it all to the South Side tenants. Jones, in turn, retorted that he would rather go to jail than tell the mayor where the money was, unless his followers told him to reveal it. "Moreover," he added, "the Mayor's statement was aimed at discrediting us in the eyes of the tenants."

The charges and countercharges became very bitter. Robert Curtis, one of the lawyers working with the strikers, urged the strike leaders not to answer Mayor Cervante's questions, but instead to insist that the mayor make public his income tax returns since becoming mayor in 1965, along with an accounting of how he had accumulated his wealth. The mayor in turn asked: "Are their neighbors paying into a rent strike fund which will eventually be used to pay the back rent? Are they paying into a strike fund which will not be used to serve the purpose for which it was intended? Or, are they not paying at all, while responsible families work and save to pay their rent each month?"

Increasingly, the strike leaders believed that nothing, not the justice of their position, not the support of the newspapers or the churches, and not even the backing of the federal government, could force the Housing Authority, the mayor, and the St. Louis establishment to deliver on their promises. Some thought that it was time for an expression of protest not unlike what had taken place in Newark, Watts, and Detroit. Certainly, the makings of a similar blowup were present in St. Louis in August of 1969: massive public housing complexes, populated overwhelmingly by poor and despondent blacks who had little to lose. Even their occupancy of public housing was threatened by the pending eviction suits. The local courts had become impatient with the strike lawyers' delaying tactics. And Housing Authority lawyers repeatedly called the judges' attention to their responsibility for the growing likelihood of bankruptcy for the Housing Authority. Many tenants were armed and angry. Indeed, a number of constables who had been sent in to serve eviction papers had been mugged. It was rumored that the mayor had persuaded the governor to alert the National Guard.

Early in the last week of August, the strikers somehow obtained a copy of the HUD Task Force report and released it to the press. The mayor was now being frontally attacked for being "unwilling to end the strike and for being negligent in running and maintaining the housing developments." The Housing Authority was castigated for ineptitude and characterized as being staffed by incompetent political hacks. The last vestiges of the mayor's credibility on this issue had been destroyed.

Enter the Mediator

"The Teamsters are behind you 100 per cent!" said Jake McCarthy, jumping to his feet and taking the microphone, obviously moved by the tenants who packed a meeting that was called and chaired by Mayor Cervantes in June. McCarthy was administrative assistant to Harold Gibbons, the Teamster leader in St. Louis who was to play the central role in mediating the rent strike dispute. McCarthy had gone to several meetings of the rent strikers to see whether the union could give them modest support. "I was scared as hell," he says, "because Gibbons had not yet said anything publicly about either his or the Teamster's position on the rent strike. Harold was traveling and I couldn't even talk to him."

When Mayor Cervantes wrote Gibbons in June requesting him to form a committee to raise a million dollars in order to end the strike, the mayor's emphasis on money as the sole solution convinced Gibbons that Cervantes really didn't understand what the strike was all about. So he turned the mayor down privately and publicly left the letter unanswered. The Housing Authority also tried to get him to agree to mediate the dispute, but again he refused. As he observed later, "You've got to both talk and listen before you negotiate, and neither the Mayor nor the Housing Authority was willing to listen seriously to the striking tenants."

Over a twenty-year period, Gibbons had gradually overcome some of the hostility that businessmen often feel for union leaders. He had negotiated contracts with many of St. Louis's corporate executives, and they knew him to be both a tough bargainer and a man of his word. As one of them put it, "When you shake hands with Harold Gibbons, you've got yourself a deal you can bank on." One of his admirers in the city's business establishment was Duncan Bauman, publisher of the conservative *Globe-Democrat.* They had known one another for years. In 1959, the Newspaper Guild struck the *Globe-Democrat* for three months, but after Gibbons entered the negotiations, the strike was settled in two days. Another indication of St. Louis businessmen's high regard for Gibbons was the 1964 agreement by the conservative banks to loan Gibbons's union several million dollars to constuct Council Plaza, a housing development for lower-income and elderly Teamster members, long one of Gibbons's dreams.

Gibbons had also earned the confidence of St. Louis blacks. He began working in St. Louis in the 1940s, when racial segregation was deeply entrenched. When blacks complained of police brutality, Gibbons supported them. He was the first, and for a long time the only, St. Louis labor leader who *insisted* that there be no racial segregation in the work places he organized. He led the way in organizing the black taxi drivers, who had been ignored by the other local unions that represented the white cabbies. Even in the forties, his local had black members and officers. As far as blacks were concerned, in McCarthy's words, "Gibbons had clearly paid his dues."

Gibbons's influence extended far beyond St. Louis. At the time of the strike, he was executive director of the Central Conference of Teamsters, the largest and strongest Teamster regional division, as well as an international vice-president of the Teamsters.

By August, Richard Baron and Jean King began to feel that they were running out of time. Despite receiving public support from the federal government and winning over public opinion, the newpapers, and the civic leadership, they thought they had delayed the eviction suits for as long as they could. At that point, King asked Baron to set up an appointment for her with Gibbons. Neither King nor Baron had ever met Gibbons, but, as King noted, "I knew he was the only person in St. Louis who could get us a decent settlement, and I felt that he wouldn't have the heart to turn us down if I asked him personally."

Gibbons did not accept her invitation on the spot. He had been giving a good deal of thought to possible strategies for ending the strike ever since Mayor Cervantes first asked him to help in June. He had spent time talking with a variety of people, including Father Kirk Walsh. With the striking tenants increasingly impatient, the federal government and a substantial body of public opinion behind the strikers, Gibbons felt for the first time that perhaps the dispute was open to resolution. But he had one more step to take before entering the negotiations. He implied to King that he would do it, but, as he said, "How a negotiator gets asked to mediate a dispute is even more important than the skill or other assets he brings with him." He knew that no resolution could stand without the solid support of the mayor. He needed more leverage with him than with the strikers, whose confidence he had already earned. He invited Mayor Cervantes to breakfast at his apartment and immediately told him, "You've got 45 days to get an agreement or the lights are going out in public housing. If that happens, you're going to have the biggest riot any city has ever had, and I personally will lead the blacks out to Clayton and Ladue."

Gibbons then asked Cervantes whether he was still limiting Gibbons's involvement to raising private funds, or whether the mayor would propose alternative roles for him in the dispute. The mayor replied that Gibbons had carte blanche and that he would agree to any terms he recommended. Gibbons answered that he had two terms in mind. First, said Gibbons, "I want your tacit support for an effort to mobilize a broadly based citizens organization to oversee the implementation of the agreement." That first condition wouldn't cost the mayor anything, so he readily agreed. Aware that any settlement he obtained could be undermined by a hostile Board of Commissioners, Gibbons went on, "I want you to get the resignations of all five commissioners, and then replace them with five persons of my choosing." Cervantes was somewhat taken aback, but he had known that Gibbons was a tough bargainer. He agreed to both proposals. With a handshake, Gibbons accepted the mayor's offer to mediate the dispute.

Reaching an Agreement and Enforcing It

Gibbons set out to mobilize community leadership for an agreement between the strikers and the Housing Authority. While the mayor had in fact committed himself to support whatever agreement Gibbons recommended, Gibbons had doubts. He said,

> I was certain that if I walked away from the signed agreement, congratulating myself on a job well done, it would all sour within two weeks, because neither the Mayor nor the Housing Authority could be counted on to implement it faithfully, and the strikers by themselves didn't have enough leverage to force faithful performance. I had to bring in the people with enough clout to make the Mayor and the Housing Authority do what the heat of the strike had forced them to agree to do.

He decided that it would be necessary to create a private blue-ribbon organization, which could in fact guarantee the settlement and perhaps take part in its implementation. He immediately set about recruiting some of the most powerful citizens of the city. He asked his long-time friend, Duncan Bauman, a member and formerly three-term chairman of the St. Louis Health and Welfare Council, "to introduce me to St. Louis leadership with the integrity required to give a settlement instant acceptance." Bauman agreed and set up a meeting between the labor leader and General Leif Sverdrup, one of Bauman's close friends and head of Sverdrup and Parcel, a worldwide engineering firm headquartered in St. Louis.

Bauman introduced Gibbons to Sverdrup at the exclusive downtown Noonday Club. Gibbons's message was direct: "You've got to do something about the rent strike or it will blow the town to pieces." Sverdrup agreed to help, and they decided to broaden the group by adding such civic leaders as Maurice Chambers, chairman of Interco, Inc.; Harold Thayer, president of Mallincrodt Chemical Corporation; and others. Because they all respected Sverdrup, who, in turn trusted Gibbons, they agreed to do whatever he asked.

About the same time, Gibbons decided to go directly to beer executive August A. Busch, Jr., perhaps the most prominent and influential business leader in St. Louis. Gibbons was no stranger to Busch, since the two had been on opposite sides of the bargaining table in a recent brewery strike. Gibbons repeated his message, but, instead of merely asking Busch for help, he requested that Busch take on principal leadership in raising funds to support the new organization. Busch, too, signed on, and his participation made Gibbons's job much easier.

Harold Thayer helped to convince some of Gibbons's long time adversaries to join the new organization. Thayer himself had been one of those adversaries when, several years earlier, Gibbons had tried unsuccessfully to unionize Mallincrodt Chemical Corporation. With Sverdrup, Busch, Thayer, and Gibbons taking the lead, they brought together at several luncheons and dinners during September most of the principal business, financial, professional, religious, and political leaders of St. Louis. By October 10, when the new organization met for the first time and was named the St. Louis Civic Alliance for Housing, Gibbons had many of St. Louis's leaders on hand to make common cause with the city's most destitute citizens.

While Gibbons spent the days recruiting for the Civic Alliance, he devoted the nights to the harder task of negotiating the agreement the alliance was intended to enforce. As his principal aides in the negotiations, he brought in Terry McCormack and Arthur Klein, two staff members of the Teamsters Local 688, who worked principally on Teamster-sponsored housing projects. Klein was an expert on the subject. McCormack's main assets were, as Richard Baron (now his partner in a consulting firm) put it, "his quickness of mind, absolute reliability, enthusiasm and infectious Boston-Irish humor."

When the formal negotiating sessions began, the mayor was not there; one of his assistants, David Meeker, attended periodically, but played no active role in the bargaining. Cervantes appeared willing to forego any personal involvement in the negotiations. Moreover, he didn't even try to influence the recommendations. Gibbons was probably pleased that the mayor did not attend, because of the bitter feelings that existed between the strikers and the city administration. The negotiating sessions occupied two to three nights a week between late August and early October. Gibbons would keep the participants going until two or three in the morning, first in hard bargaining and later in relaxation over drinks. If one or another striker needed cajoling or reassurance, Gibbons would detain him or her for another hour of private conversation.

At his first meeting with the strikers, Gibbons agreed with them that the 25 percent-of-income rent ceiling was absolutely essential to the agreement. While he agreed that none of the rent funds already collected should be paid until an agreement was reached and implemented, he insisted to the strikers from the beginning that all the rent owed to the Housing Authority had to be repaid, or that he would not attempt to work out a solution. He believed that without that provision, the business establishment would not support an agreement. The strikers went along with this stipulation.

Gibbons insisted that negotiations include all parties because he wanted both to avoid later accusations of secret deals to make sure there would be no dissenters who might provide the mayor with a pretext to back out after negotiations were concluded. The settlement did not come easy. The hardest job was forming a unified position among the strikers themselves. Baron took on the difficult assignment of getting the divided strike leaders to agree on a single negotiating committee. While Baron had earned their trust—by advising and representing them during the past year—many of the strike leaders, with the exception of Jean King, were suspicious of Gibbons as well as of the other whites trying to facilitate a negotiated settlement. "Who," asked one strike leader, "do these dudes think they are, moving in on us, trying to take our strike away from us?"

Gibbons would chair the full meetings of the negotiating sessions, but there had to be frequent recesses so that the united front that Baron had carefully and patiently cultivated among the strikers could be reinforced every time it began to unravel. Then Gibbons would sometimes take them aside and give them a lesson in union-management bargaining. He received important assistance from King.

The toughest issues to be resolved were tenant representation on the Board of Commissioners and repayment of back rents. Neither the mayor nor the Housing Authority particularly wanted tenants as commissioners. It was widely believed that the mayor had been instrumental in getting State Attorney General John Danforth to rule that it was conflict of interest under Missouri law for public housing tenants to serve as commissioners. But the tenants insisted that, whatever the attorney general's opinion on the legality of the issue, they were right as a matter of policy and would worry about the legal technicalities later. While the HUD task force had recommended one tenant on the five-member board, the strike leaders wanted three. The final compromise was for two.

The more complex issue was the matter of repayment of rents: How much was to be repaid, and how long would the tenants have to repay it? It was a complicated issue for several reasons. First, which rent schedule determined how much was owed? The original schedule, or the one that provoked the strike, or the one that was to govern the housing units as part of the strike settlement? Second, no one involved in the negotiations knew how much rent any of the tenants had either paid to the Housing Authority, deposited to the rent-strike account, or simply failed to pay at all. Unable to specify the amounts as part of the settlement agreement, the negotiators had to develop instead a set of guidelines to be used later in auditing each of the tenants' rent accounts, as well as various contingencies that governed repayment schedules. "These issues," said Gibbons, "were as complicated as any cost-of-living wage provisions or fringe benefit demands I had ever before confronted."

Nor was what the strikers wanted from the city very simple—a total reorganization of decision-making authority on public housing in St. Louis. There was the matter of the tenant affairs board, and how much power it was to have. There were the proposed tenant management corporations for each of the housing complexes, as well as a variety of other issues. One was the question of who was to replace Dagen, who had already resigned under pressure from the mayor. At Gibbons's request, Thomas Costello, who was an auditor in the finance division of the Housing Authority, was asked to take the job of acting executive director. Costello accepted, and it is a tribute to Gibbons's judgment that nine years later he is still in the job.

Gibbons helped the strikers to agree on exactly what they wanted. They had general grievances; he embodied them in specific language. Their grievances implied solutions; he formulated them. His years of labor bargaining came in very handy. Dispute resolution, when the parties *wish* to settle their conflict, often requires finding new terminology, a formula which can perhaps present an idea in new language acceptable to all. That takes imagination and skill, as well as resourcefulness, all of which Gibbons had. It also takes a good sense of timing and sound judgment about the people involved.

While the inventive Gibbons found the right words to embody a solution, Richard Baron was equally vital to the settlement process. The strikers trusted him, and he helped them frame their complaints. Baron assisted the strikers to say precisely what they felt and meant.

By the end of September, the parties had substantially agreed on the terms of a resolution. The agreement created a separate and independent housing authority; replaced all existing members of the Board of

Commissioners with commissioners approved by Gibbons, including two tenants; established a strong tenant affairs board; required the strikers to repay all rents owed to the Housing Authority; and set up a committee to which disputes and hardship cases would be referred.

The agreement also included the establishment of the Civic Alliance for Housing. During the period of the negotiations, Gibbons had been actively recruiting St. Louis's most powerful citizens for membership in the alliance. By the terms of the agreement, the alliance would be a nonprofit, nongovernmental organization that would operate the public housing units in something like receivership for a period after the strike. He wanted the new organization to take over from the Housing Authority, by legal contract, the actual administration and management of the public housing units. With the power of St. Louis's actual community leadership behind such an organization, it could function as an administratively effective surrogate for the Housing Authority and insulate the housing program from politics. Gibbons also felt that if privately raised money were needed to bail out the Housing Authority in the short run, an independent organization was the only way both to raise it and to guarantee that the funds would be used effectively.

Gibbons later said that the negotiations were as grueling as any he had ever been involved with. Previously he had always been an adversary, now for the first time he had mediated a dispute between others. He was, as Baron later said, "an incredibly graceful negotiator."

At the first meeting of the Civic Alliance for Housing on October 10, 1969, the bargain that had been struck was given formal sanction.

Making the Agreement Stick: The Civic Alliance Goes Public

Aside from ensuring that the mayor and Housing Authority lived up to the agreement, Gibbons had three other goals for the Civic Alliance. First, he envisioned that the group would "act as a kind of cloak or umbrella around the operations of the Housing Authority in order to prevent any kind of political interference with an efficient operation." Second, he proposed that the citizens organization itself take over from the Housing Authority all major decision making about public housing in St. Louis. This would reduce the Housing Authority to an entity with only formal, legal authority. The legally constituted Board of Commissioners would, by contract with the Civic Alliance, delegate all policymaking and day-to-day decision making to the alliance. As events turned out, that departure from the conventional practices of government accountability proved to be unnecessary.

Gibbons's third major goal for the Civic Alliance was to influence the federal government in two quite different ways. One was to change the image of St. Louis's inefficient, politically motivated, and hostile administration of public housing to a cooperative and thoroughly competent housing agency. "We want," he said, "to bring into the situation some trained people who have had to balance budgets every day of their life, and we want them to help us take a good, hard look at the efficiencies or inefficiencies of the current Housing Authority so that, if there is a wasted dollar there, it can be saved and it can be utilized for better improvement of the physical condition of the housing projects."

If St. Louis succeeded in this improvement and thereby convinced HUD of the sincerity of the city's attempts to solve its housing problem, that would increase the likelihood of more generous HUD appropriations. Gibbons also believed that the Civic Alliance could help persuade the House of Representatives to enact legislation sponsored by Senator Edward Brooke, requiring a 25 percent-of-income rent ceiling, which had already been approved by the Senate. Because the rent ceiling would provide local authorities with an operating subsidy amounting to the difference between the rent ceiling and a rent schedule calculated on the basis of actual operating costs, it was the only realistic basis for achieving housing solvency in St. Louis.

At the October 10 meeting when the Civic Alliance was formed, the chief executive officers of nearly every bank, insurance company, and major corporation headquartered in St. Louis were present, along with a host of prominent local businessmen, the board chairmen of both newspapers, the president of the Danforth Foundation, and the chancellor of Washington University. As might be expected because of Gibbons's involvement and connections, the heads of every major St. Louis labor union were also there. Present, too, were the leaders of the black professional and business communities, whom Gibbons had taken special pains to recruit.

The religious leaders were also there in force. While the Episcopal bishop of St. Louis, George Cadigar, had been visible in a number of social causes, the Catholic prelate, Cardinal John Carberry, had not. Knowing that there were many more Catholics than Episcopalians in

St. Louis, Gibbons was determined to involve the cardinal in the settlement. Together with Father Walsh and his own aide, Jake McCarthy, Gibbons had an audience with the cardinal to impress upon him the urgency of the strike. He was only part way through his plea when Carberry turned to his subordinate, Bishop McNicholas, and said, "Cancel all my appointments on October 10; I'm going to Mr. Gibbons's meeting." He gave more help later by gaining support of the agreement among the church's parishioners and clergy.

The meeting also included substantial representation from the striking housing tenants, some of whom were on Gibbons's slate for board of directors. The contrast between the high and mighty on the one hand, and the lowly and powerless on the other, was striking. Indeed, it moved one of the participants to comment: "I'm Jerome Williams. I was just wondering and going over the list of the Board of Trustees, that there really seem to be two extremes—the extremely eminent persons and those of the rent strikers who do not fall in that category. I don't see but perhaps one that would be in the category of in between and that is Dr. Suggs. I'm wondering if that is going to be a conflicting group. I'm just wondering."

The main business of the meeting was a consideration and ratification of the agreement which Gibbons had already worked out with the strikers. The agreement included the following provisions, which would have to be implemented before rent payments would be resumed: (1) the Civic Alliance, the mayor, and HUD were to formally agree to implement the "proposed program for low-income housing developments of St. Louis"; (2) HUD was to approve the 25 percent-of-income rent ceiling; (3) the present members of the Board of Commissioners were to be replaced by five alliance-approved commissioners; (4) a tenant affairs board was to be instituted; (5) all parties were to agree that at a later date tenants would be encouraged to establish a tenant management corporation; (6) when the above five conditions were met, a firm of certified public accountants would audit the finances of the strikers and submit a report to the commissioners and to the coalition; and (7) the rent charged to the tenants in excess of the established schedule and paid by them was to be returned through rent credits.

Gibbons had Jim Pace, one of his staffers, explain each condition in detail and then he himself took the floor. He said:

> Now as I have talked to representatives I see sitting here today, I have stressed that there cannot be any solution to the low cost housing problem on anything like a permanent basis unless we get the deepest kind of involvement among the tenants, and, looking down the road, we envision training—they will take those buildings and have their own contract for management and operation purposes and, even further down the road, changing into co-ops, and they will be able to purchase their own apartments, but the concept of the tenant being involved is basic to all our thinking.

Gibbons wanted to be certain that the right housing commissioners were appointed by the mayor. That was one of the conditions that had to be met before the strikers were to start paying rent again and turning over their back rents. So he had the alliance choose a nominating committee for selection of the five commissioners, whom they expected the mayor to appoint. Gibbons also insisted that each candidate for commissioner write an undated letter of resignation to facilitate his departure if he was unable to fulfill his responsibilities.

He went on to outline how he expected the new commissioners to delegate to the Civic Alliance operating responsibility for public housing. He wanted particularly to neutralize the possible objections of the mayor, particularly that the binding contract between the Housing Authority and the Civic Alliance for Housing was invalid because the Housing Authority could not legally contract away its mandated responsibilities. Arthur Klein, the Teamster housing finance specialist, said that

> while it is true . . . that municipal bodies or the Mayor's office cannot contract away authority that is designated under statutes, we can prepare a memorandum of understanding which sets forth all of the things that we would ask of the Mayor's office for now, for then, and for the foreseeable future, so it's crystal clear between the coalition and the Mayor's office who is the operative head of that authority, just what the plans, purposes and goals are, and the Mayor's office will be required to participate and cooperate.

Preston Estep, board chairman of the Bank of St. Louis, then asked about assurances from the federal government. "Do we have any kind of commitment?" asked Estep. "I don't want to be kidded, I'm sure the strikers don't want to be kidded, and I'm sure the public doesn't want to be kidded!" Father Walsh, who was attending the meeting as the representative of HUD Secretary Romney, responded to Estep. About $11 million in already approved federal modernization funds would be available once St. Louis public housing was being properly managed. If the alliance worked as envisioned, he said, it would provide the desired quality of management. Walsh also urged the group to press members of the House of Representatives to enact the Brooke Amendment, already passed by the Senate.

Members of the coalition unanimously ratified the proposed plan of the settlement and elected Gibbons as president and chief executive officer, along with a board of directors of fifteen persons. The board of directors then created an executive committee that included August Busch, Jr., General Leif Sverdrup, and a representative to be designated by the tenants. The board also set up a committee under Gibbons's chairmanship to embody the strike agreement in precise language.

It took about two weeks to put the agreement in final form, and then a press conference was scheduled for the morning of October 28. When Gibbons arrived at the mayor's office, the television cameras had already been set up and reporters were present. With Gibbons came most of the members of the board of directors of the Civic Alliance, as well as the rent strike leaders who were going to sign the document on behalf of the strikers.

The mayor signaled to Gibbons that he wanted to talk privately with Gibbons in his office. Cervantes told him that he had gotten four of the five commissioners' resignations, but that one member–Julian Thompson–was refusing to resign, and the mayor didn't know what to do about it. Moreover, Cervantes cautioned Gibbons that he was unwilling to promise the Civic Alliance a veto over future appointments to the Board of Commissioners. Gibbons told the mayor, "You'd better get Thompson's resignation, or the whole deal is off." He went out to the assembled dignitaries and strike leaders, told them that problems had developed and led them out of city hall.

Gibbons says that Cervantes later called him to ask for help in getting the needed resignation. He told the mayor he would do it if the latter would agree to promise to consult fully with the Civic Alliance on naming any future members to the Board of Commissioners, which was somewhat less than Gibbons had asked for in the first place. The mayor agreed, and Gibbons managed to secure the resignation from the only holdout on the board.

The Alliance Goes to Work

Now Gibbons had the mayor's agreement to the terms of the settlement, and five new members had been appointed to the Board of Commissioners. Three days after the mayor gave his approval, Gibbons led the principal alliance officials and the new housing commissioners to the Housing Authority offices, where they met with the entire Housing Authority staff to explain the new system of operating St. Louis's public housing. He was especially eager for the authority staff to understand that policy and major decisions would be made by the alliance and carried out by the authority staff.

The following day, on November 3, the alliance staff began preparing the various studies called for under the settlement agreement. Each was done under the supervision of tenant representatives, representatives of the Housing Authority, the alliance board of directors or executive staff, and HUD. There were committees charged with a management and financial audit of the Housing Authority's operation; an exploration of the social goals in housing complexes; an audit of the rent strike funds; and development of policies on back rent collection, eviction, and new rent schedules.

Although Gibbons had told the Civic Alliance that he did not envision any major need for funds and would not use privately raised funds for actually solving the problems of the Housing Authority, he did explain that some administrative costs would be incurred by the operation of the Civic Alliance for Housing itself, and that it would be neither fair nor possible for the Teamsters to foot these costs alone. A one-year budget of $350,000 was needed. Busch, the chairman of the finance committee, asked his fellow business leaders to call a special meeting of Civic Progress, Inc., the organization of St. Louis's business and financial leaders. Busch invited Gibbons in to speak to the assembled executives, and after Gibbons repeated the appeal with which he had persuaded many of them to join the Civic Alliance for Housing a month earlier, he withdrew from the room. At the end of the meeting Busch told Gibbons that he had raised about $250,000. To this amount, Gibbons added $91,000 from the Alliance for Labor Action and the Pipe Fitters Union. He raised most of that by conferring with Walter Reuther at the United Automobile Workers' health camp in Black Lake, Michigan.

In a month's time, Busch and Gibbons together had raised $350,000 for the first year of the alliance. Terry McCormack, a Teamster staff member who was an expert on housing, was installed as executive director of the Civic Alliance. Looking back, McCormack says: "Never have I seen anything happen so fast. Once the leading members of the community decided to act, there was no stopping them. What in any other circumstances should have taken months to accomplish happened overnight." The alliance was also able to persuade HUD to release the already committed, but long-blocked, $11.5 million in federal funds for various purposes in St. Louis, including $5 million for modernization of the housing units. Father Kirk Walsh not only managed to free the money in Washington, but also flew to Fort Worth and obtained the HUD regional officer's approval of the new St. Louis Housing Authority budget. Walsh was also prominent in efforts to persuade Nixon administration officials to support the Brooke Amendment after passage by the Senate.

By November, the House had still failed to act on its version of the amendment. The ranking member of the housing subcommittee was Congressman Leonor K. Sullivan of St. Louis, who was opposed to the 25 percent-of-income ceiling and had been blocking it in the subcommittee. Because of the direct financial interest which St. Louis had in this subsidy, Gibbons took a delegation of the alliance leadership with him to Washington and succeeded in persuading Congressman Sullivan to send the housing amendments to the floor of the House. Gibbons himself, together with a number of the prominent alliance members, lobbied other congressmen. The House passed the entire bill, including the ceiling provision. At least partially due to alliance lobbying, President Nixon was able to sign the ceiling into law on December 24, 1969.

By the year's end, too, the audit of the rent-strike funds had been completed, as had the audit of the Housing Authority rent accounts. Other alliance projects also made progress. The Committee on Modernization and Consolidation, which Gibbons himself chaired, had completed its occupancy audit, finding that approximately one quarter of all of the 8,036 units were vacant. It recommended consolidating tenants in some projects and closing excess units. The Housing Authority Operations report recommended an entirely new organizational arrangement for the Housing Authority headquarters staff, which would yield a reduction of the personnel budget in the amount of $902,000 annually. Gibbons contributed also to implementing these recommendations. He persuaded the Building Trades Council of St. Louis to support the reductions in force, and, on February 6, 105 Housing Authority staff people were laid off, including 36 office staffers, 40 maintenance personnel, and 29 custodial workers.

The Tenant Affairs Board (TAB) was organized early in 1970 and a group of highly qualified specialists were constituted as the Tenant Affairs Team. The alliance agreed to defray the organizational expenses of the TAB, including modest salaries for the members. The TAB hired Richard Baron as a consultant.

In addition, the alliance commissioned a crime and security specialist at the University of Missouri at St. Louis to do a study of the security needs of the housing projects. The study, which was completed by May, led to a program to train residents as security personnel in courses offered by the Police Academy.

By January 1971, the board of directors of the alliance noted that the Housing Authority had reduced its monthly deficit from $125,000 to $35,000. It was clear then that the continuing deficit was caused principally by the persistently high vacancy rate attributable to the slowness of the modernization efforts. Pruitt-Igoe, for example, was discovered to have a $1.7 million deficit in its operating budget alone. This huge deficit was largely responsible for preventing other units from modernizing. That discovery started the chain of events that lead to the total demolition of Pruitt-Igoe three years later.

In the first year of its existence, the TAB had become very familiar with all phases of the Housing Authority operations. More important, it was working with tenants in keeping rent accounts current and had even supported the authority in eviction suits, where necessary. Its members also spent much time counseling and generally assisting the tenants.

By September 1971, the alliance's coffers were empty, which meant that there was no money left to pay the TAB members' salaries. Gibbons decided, therefore, to go back to the business community for $50,000 for that purpose. At his request, General Sverdrup convened a number of businessmen at his home. This time, however, despite a federal offer to provide $5 million for new units and the need for continued TAB support, the businessmen refused Gibbon's request. Maurice Chambers, chairman of Interco, said:

> I don't know how you can do this. When we were scared out of our minds because the city was on the brink of riot, burning, and looting, you turned to Harold Gibbons to help us out. Now he's done everything we asked, he has solved the problem and he has come back to get enough money to see the effort through. But now you're not scared anymore. The pressure's off, and you know it won't explode, so you're not afraid to turn him down. I don't know how he did it, but here he has a chance to get St. Louis $5,000,000 if we raise a measly $50,000, and you turn him down. That's a hell of a note.

After being turned down by the businessmen, Gibbons and McCormack approached HUD for $50,000 to pay the TAB members, but were rejected. Walter Kloetzli, HUD's assistant regional administrator, suggested that the alliance approach the Ford Foundation for support and went with alliance officials to meet foundation representatives in New York. Several months later, the foundation approved a proposal for a $130,000 grant to cover the training and technical assistance costs involved in the establishment of tenant management corporations (TMCs) in two of the St. Louis public housing complexes. In addition to moving the TMCs ahead, that 1972 grant had the incidental effect of freeing Housing Authority funds, which could then be used to pay the salaries of the TAB members.

With Ford Foundation and HUD support, the TMCs thrived. The initial foundation grant in March 1973 provided for the establishment of two TMCs, one in Carr Square Village, where the rent strike began slightly over four years earlier under the prodding of Buck Jones, and the other in Darst, where Jean King had lived while leading the strike. Tom Costello, the executive director of the Housing Authority, was not impressed with the idea of TMCs in the beginning and, indeed, was openly skeptical. But he was willing to try the idea because of his respect for Gibbons, Baron, and McCormack. The success of the TMCs, however, soon won him over. Because of the obvious success of the St. Louis TMCs after a year of experimentation, the foundation made an additional grant to extend the TMC idea to Webbe and Clinton-Peabody. By 1978, the Housing Authority had contracted out all of its management functions—some to TMCs, some to nonprofit sponsors, and some to private, for-profit real estate corporations. The Housing Authority is no longer directly managing individual sites.

After the initial meetings and the very important task force reports in late 1969 and early 1970, the elaborate alliance structure of sixteen subcommittees and task forces never really functioned. It was obviously designed more to impress the mayor and HUD with St. Louis's seriousness of purpose—and to force the Housing Authority to start doing what had to be done—than to function effectively over a long period of time.

The new commissioners Gibbons chose for the mayor to appoint, and the new executive director similarly selected, were so cooperative that the new Housing Authority itself undertook most of the projects that Gibbons had originally assigned to the Civic Alliance.

The most important accomplishment of the alliance was making sure that the mayor lived up to his agreement. On a more mundane, but equally important, level, the existence of a separate entity such as the Civic Alliance for Housing outside the governmental bureaucracy provided an entity for receiving federal funds that probably never would have been given directly to the city government at that time. The existence of the alliance also gave Gibbons and Costello a measure of freedom and flexibility in making and implementing decisions. It was an organization that served its purpose well. When the circumstances changed, its leaders disbanded the alliance. They could do so with confidence because their organization had already established the policies that were to serve as the next generation's way of dealing with the problems of public housing, not only in St. Louis but throughout the entire United States.

The Consequences of the St. Louis Strike

Without asserting an explicit cause-and-effect relationship, one can probably attribute several national housing innovations to the resolution of the St. Louis housing conflict. The following summary cites nationwide developments that apparently stemmed from a local rent strike.

The Brooke Amendment

The congressional decision to establish a 25 percent-of-income ceiling on public housing rent was influenced, in substantial part, by the rent strike. St. Louis gave focus to an obvious national need that had yet to be defined. Moreover, while tenant and civil rights groups elsewhere in the nation were pushing for the ceiling, only the St. Louis group included businessmen lobbying for the provision.

Tenant Membership on Public Housing Governing Boards

St. Louis strikers demanded that public housing residents be represented on the policy board governing the Housing Authority, and two residents were appointed to the five-member board. Because it is one of the nation's largest metropolitan areas, St. Louis, according to housing professionals, gave national impetus to tenant representation on authority boards.

Tenant Affairs Boards

The St. Louis strikers wanted not only formal, and to some extent symbolic, representation on the housing policy board, but also an ongoing, elected mechanism by which they could articulate and resolve grievances. The establishment of a tenant affairs board in St. Louis, with members elected by the residents themselves and salaried by the public, has led to the acceptance of similar bodies in other cities. The value of full-time tenant representatives has become evident to the Housing Authority and to others working with public housing in St. Louis. Tenant morale improved, manifesting itself in less vandalism, better security, more community activity, and higher occupancy rates. Most observers credit the TAB and its elected members with the improvement. TAB members attended all meetings of the Board of Commissioners and worked on a daily basis with Executive Director Thomas Costello and his staff. The mutual confidence that developed as a consequence of the TAB members' extensive involvement with all phases of public housing yielded many benefits: new rental and occupancy policies, and a new standard lease, a procedure for dealing with tenant grievances, a new rent collection procedure, hardship rules for stretching or deferring rent payments, a security program, a social services program, physical modernization programs, a new system for the preparation of annual budgets, and, most important, a tenant management program, which merits much longer discussion. What is clear, however, is that the TAB, first established in St. Louis, is nationally significant in its own right, whether or not it institutionally evolves to the next stage of tenant management corporations.

Tenant Management Corporations

Each TMC is a separate, not-for-profit corporation, with a five-member board of directors elected by the residents themselves. The corporations then enter into binding agreements with the Housing Authority, with each contract allocating responsibilities between the Housing Authority and the TMC. The TMC receives from the Housing Authority a management fee, out of which it hires and pays a general manager and all other management personnel employed in the particular project. In addition, the TMC chairman and manager supervise all maintenance, custodial, and utility personnel, whose salaries are paid by the Housing Authority. The Housing Authority, in turn, receives the rent, does the accounting, and furnishes the TMC with bimonthly delinquency reports, as well as a variety of other reports on such matters as family income ranges and vacancy rates. Generally, the Housing Authority serves as a monitor of contract performance and an agent of fiscal oversight.

The fee paid by the Housing Authority to the TMC, and all other contract managers, includes penalty and bonus incentives based on the TMC's timely and effective performance of its obligations under the contract. The faster the rent delinquencies are cleared up, or the fewer the vacancies in the project, or the higher the maintenance ratings, the larger the TMC's fee. The larger the TMC's fee, the more programming the TMC can afford. In other words, the relationship between the Housing Authority and the TMCs is based on arm's-length transaction. What the TMC can do is based on a budget agreed to with the Housing Authority and depends on how well it performs its contractual obligations. All of the reports and analyses generated by the Housing Authority are designed to aid the TMCs and contract managers to stay within their budgets.

But if all the TMCs did was to manage the units, in the long run they would be insufficient to deal with the larger problem: the lack of productive jobs for housing residents. What the TMCs do best, however, is to use their housing management role as a base on which to build other job-producing efforts, either directly, or instrumentally through education (such as by having a junior college on the housing unit site).

St. Louis's success in pioneering a new and more effective way of managing public housing invited duplication. The Ford Foundation persuaded HUD in 1975 to launch a $21 million National Tenant Management Demonstration Program. At the present time, there are TMCs operating under this program in six cities: Jersey City, New Jersey; Louisville, Kentucky; New Haven, Connecticut; New Orleans, Louisiana; Oklahoma City, Oklahoma; and Rochester, New York.

St. Louis: Tenant Service Corporations

While these major St. Louis innovations are gradually making their way into housing policy and management around the country, St. Louis continues to adopt other innovations. Richard Baron has proposed that the TMCs provide a base for managing and training tenants to provide similar services for pay *outside* the housing projects that they now provide within their own projects.

Currently there are several TMC subsidiary service corporations, which contract to perform a variety of services outside the housing projects. For example, some maintenance and janitorial work in St. Louis's downtown central business district is performed by a public housing tenant-run corporation. Other corporations prepare and deliver meals to the elderly and operate day care centers that are under contract with the city and federal agencies. The Carr Square Village and Cochran TMCs are engaged in planning and building one hundred new public units under a grant from HUD's Urban Development Action Grant Program, the first time public housing tenants have themselves been the sponsors and builders of new housing.

Conclusion

The St. Louis Housing Authority is no longer in the housing management business, and the tenants are becoming increasingly productive citizens. That was the principal goal that Harold Gibbons had set forth in creating the Civic Alliance for Housing. That tenants ended up managing their housing, instead of having it managed for them by the Civic Alliance, is perhaps the most eloquent tribute that can be paid to Gibbons. He had the vision to see that an impersonal municipal bureaucracy was inadequate to manage public housing in a way that would provide maximum benefits to residents. And he also acknowledged that once free of the city's bureaucracy, the units were more likely to be effectively managed by the tenants themselves than under the direction of a group of business leaders.

6

The Real Against the Ideal—Making the Solution Fit the Problem: The Atlanta Public School Agreement of 1973

Joel L. Fleishman

Introduction: Change in Atlanta

In 1958, Vivian Calhoun and eight other parents of black school-age children sued to compel the desegregation of Atlanta's public school system. For the next fourteen years the legal struggle between the plaintiffs, represented by the National Association for the Advancement of Colored People (NAACP) and the Atlanta Board of Education, kept the suit in the federal courts, and the policies of the board kept the schools almost as segregated as they were in 1958. On October 6, 1972, the federal appeals court, meeting in New Orleans, ordered the board to submit a comprehensive integration plan within a month. The court insisted on the integration of the city school system by the start of its second six-week school term on November 27.

When Calhoun went to court, the issues had seemed pretty clear-cut—integration versus segregation, racism versus justice. But in 1972, when the court set a final deadline for integration, the attitudes of both the black leadership and white establishment of Atlanta toward desegregation had changed significantly. Those who had fought to establish the legal principle of integration remained committed to it, but now they balanced it against other vital concerns. For its part, the Board of Education had softened its resistance and was open to some compromise resolution of this long drawn-out conflict. Overall, the social climate of the city was very different from what it had been in

1958 when Atlanta was perceived as another unyielding bastion of southern intolerance. To understand how the biracial leadership of the city finally reached agreement in 1972 on a plan to integrate the schools, one must first understand how Atlanta had changed.

One important indicator of change was the establishment of the Atlanta Action Forum. In the past, prominent blacks felt aggrieved that there was no vehicle for ongoing discussion with the white leadership of the city's racial problems. For many blacks, the absence of such an institution signified a lack of acceptance by white civic leaders. When a problem with racial implications arose in the city, members of the white establishment conferred among themselves, agreed on a solution, and implemented it before anyone else could respond. The leaders of Atlanta's rising black middle-class and upper middle-class communities felt they had been excluded from this informal but highly influential decision-making apparatus. In early 1972, William Callaway, one of Atlanta's most successful black realtors, decided to change the situation. He contacted Mills Lane, chairman of the Citizens' and Southern Bank, Atlanta's largest, and the preeminent white establishment leader. Together they organized the Action Forum, an interracial organization of community leaders that met periodically.

A few days after the court order was handed down, the forum met to discuss the integration conflict. The guest speaker at this meeting was U.S. Circuit Judge Griffin Bell. Among those present were thirty members of Atlanta's establishment, both black and white, and they included Lonnie King, president of the Atlanta branch of the NAACP; Lyndon Wade, executive director of the Atlanta Urban League; and two school board members, William Van Landingham, executive vice-president of the Citizens' and Southern Bank, and Frank Smith, president of a large computer firm in Atlanta. Judge Bell began by observing that "our school dispute has been in continuous litigation over a period of fourteen years with never an end and never a final decision, creating uncertainty and instability as well as probably causing a decline in the white student population." Then he added: "My advice is to do what black and white leaders in other cities in the South have done, to get together and recognize the fact that school desegregation is not something to be left only to lawyers but that it is the responsibility of the parties and the community to be resolved without delay." To the audience's surprise, similar advice was offered by Elliot

Goldstein, a well-known Atlanta attorney. "If you really want to get rid of the suit," he said, "you have to take it out of the hands of the lawyers."

Judge Bell was emphatic on another point. He told his listeners that it was highly unlikely that the federal courts would permit any further delay in submitting a plan. In April of 1972, the American Civil Liberties Union (ACLU) had brought action seeking desegregation in the entire metropolitan area. Now the two school board members, Van Landingham and Smith, asked Judge Bell whether the board would join as plaintiffs in the ACLU suit because a metropolitan areawide plan seemed a preferable alternative to a solution that was limited to the city of Atlanta with its predominantly black student population. Moreover, they thought that this new legal initiative might result in an extension of the court deadline, now only a few weeks away. But Judge Bell discouraged them. He said he doubted that the court would grant a further delay and, again, he urged them to try to negotiate an out-of-court settlement. When Bell finished speaking, many of the blacks present felt that he had exerted pressure on the city's white leadership to settle the suit. Many of the whites, however, felt that the judge had been just as insistent that the blacks direct their efforts to achieve a settlement.

Responding to Judge Bell's advice, King and Van Landingham convened the first mediation-planning session the following Tuesday, October 17, to consider how they ought to proceed. With Lyndon Wade and Frank Smith joining them, and after consultation with Board of Education President Benjamin Mays who was the black president of Morehouse College in Atlanta and perhaps the senior black educator in the South, they agreed to expand their number for their first day-long meeting to discuss the substantive issues at stake.

Dr. Mays's position as president of the board was another important indication of how the racial climate had changed in the city. By filing appeal after appeal, the board had managed to delay for all those years a binding court order to integrate. At the same time, the board had devised different educational strategies to keep integration to a minimum. In the 1972–1973 school year, 106 of the 153 schools in the city system were virtually totally segregated. Of those 106, 81 had operated continuously as more than 90 percent black or 90 percent white, since the Georgia law that compelled segregation had been enacted. Only 47 schools in the entire system enrolled more than 10 percent of the minority race at those schools, and few were significantly above the 10 percent level.

Until 1961, all of the board members had been white. During the 1960s, there was only one black member. But by 1972, three prominent blacks had been elected. They were Dr. Mays; J. H. Middleton, president of Morris Brown College; and Asa G. Yancey, M.D., medical director of Grady Memorial Hospital, the largest in Atlanta. Their election, however, had only limited impact on the pattern of segregation. Partly, this was because of the influence wielded by two men—former board President A. C. Latimer and School Superintendent John Letson. Latimer's power derived in part from his long tenure on the board and his close associations with other members. After completing his service on the board, he was appointed counsel, and in that position he continued to influence the board's policy.

In 1972, Latimer died and left Letson as the prime architect of resistance to large-scale integration of the schools. Much of the black community was determined to remove Letson from his policymaking position. Their view increasingly came to be shared by a number of board members, including some of Atlanta's most prominent business leaders. (Among those who had served on the board were Thomas Beebe, president of Delta Airlines; Smith; Van Landingham; and Jerry Luxemberger, an attorney with close ties to the business community.) When Letson's contract came up for renewal in January 1972, it was evident that his support on the board had eroded. A majority of the members agreed to renew the contract *only* after obtaining his written stipulation that he would not serve out a full term.

A number of Atlanta's leading black activists were recruited for the first substantive negotiating session on Saturday, October 21, one week after the Action Forum meeting. In addition to King, Wade, and Mays, they included:

- Jesse Hill, president of the city's leading black insurance company, who had provided financial support to civil rights organizations for a decade
- Dr. Vivian Henderson, president of Clark College, chairman of the integrationist Southern Regional Council, and a director of the Citizens' and Southern Bank, the Bendix Corporation, and the Ford Foundation

- Ruby Hurley, southeastern regional director of the NAACP
- Dr. Wiley Bolden, longtime professor at Georgia State University
- Jondelle Johnson, executive director of the Atlanta NAACP

At that first negotiating session, the white participants, school board members Van Landingham, Smith, and Luxemberger, together with Trust Company of Georgia President A. H. (Billy) Stern, were startled to find that the black activists were unenthusiastic about the prospect of massive busing to achieve school integration. They had not expected this response from the black leaders who had long been active in the movement to integrate all public institutions, ranging from government-sponsored housing to the schools. Why weren't they pressing now for citywide busing? At least part of the answer can be found in the shifting status of Atlanta's black middle class. As representatives of that group, the participants had shared in the general prosperity and development of the South's most dynamic city. They had made their influence felt in virtually every area of urban life and, notably, in the political arena. Their political force would soon be demonstrated in the election of a black congressman and the first black mayor of a major southern city. As their involvement in the city's policymaking process grew, their enthusiasm for integration at any cost waned. The swelling black pride, which they all shared, brought with it the realization that mixing black students with whites was not the only way for black children to receive a superior education. The attitudes of these black leaders seemed to reflect the feeling of the larger black community that it was important to preserve the neighborhood school concept. At this meeting, the black representatives emphasized that black parents, as much as white parents, wanted their children to be able to walk to school. They regarded their schools as a symbol of their community, the center of social and recreational activity, as well as a place to teach children.

Perhaps the most important reason for seeking an alternative to massive busing was pragmatism. Realistically, it was no longer possible to fully integrate all of Atlanta's public schools. The demography of the student population pointed to one conclusion: Atlanta's schools were becoming a largely black system. In 1959, 42 percent of the student body (40,000 students) was black and 58 percent (55,000 students) was white. By 1972, the black student enrollment had increased to 77 percent or 74,400 students, while the percentage of white students had declined to 23 percent or 21,600 students.

In Atlanta, as in so many other cities, whites were moving to the suburbs in increasingly large numbers. In 1940, 43 percent of all the students in the metropolitan area were enrolled in the city school system; in 1970, it was 30 percent. During the same period, the number of students enrolled in suburban systems had nearly doubled. Atlanta's suburbs were heavily white and the city was heavily black. Whites leaving the city to settle in the suburbs outnumbered blacks three-to-one. Blacks leaving outlying parts of the metropolitan area to live within the city outnumbered whites three-to-one. The shift of white students to suburban schools was one major change that complicated efforts to integrate the city school system. Another factor was the rise in enrollment at private schools. From an insignificant number in 1961, private school enrollment had increased to 20,000 by 1972. So whatever plan the negotiators devised had to confront this one inescapable reality: Busing would not integrate a system that was already 77 percent black.

The biracial leadership of Atlanta, charged with drafting an integration plan in the next thirty days, had to consider all of the changes that had taken place in the city during the past decade: the declining influence of School Superintendent John Letson; the white flight to the suburbs and the black concentration within the city; the rise in private school enrollment among whites; a developing sense of common interest and a new cooperative spirit among the black and white leaders; a heightened black pride and confidence which subordinated the goal of integration to the quest for quality education; and the apparent attachment of many black parents to their community schools.

The Conflict Resolution Process Begins

The principal negotiators, William Van Landingham, Lyndon Wade, and Lonnie King, were aware of these changes that had taken place in Atlanta. Van Landingham knew that he could probably count on the three black members of the school board to support any reasonable solution that he and Frank Smith reached, and he was optimistic about persuading one of the other five white members to join them in making up a majority. Wade, in addition to his Urban League role, had been appointed two years earlier as chairman of the district court's special advisory committee on Atlanta's school desegregation problems. Because of his stature in the community and his role in that committee, he would clearly be in a key role to help design an acceptable solution. Of the three men, perhaps the most important person in the mediation process was King. He had assumed his NAACP office in 1969, and as each year passed without any substantial progress in integrating the Atlanta schools, he became more and more convinced that some new approach had to be tried.

King had experience in the complexities of school desegregation. He had worked in the Department of Health, Education, and Welfare's (HEW) Office of Civil Rights for several years drawing up Title VI school plans for cities and towns all over the South. In 1960, while still a student at Atlanta's prestigious black liberal arts Morehouse College, he had headed the Student Coalition for Human Rights, which led the drive to desegregate Atlanta's lunch counters, hotels, restaurants, movie theaters, and other public places. As a founder of the Student Nonviolent Coordinating Committee (SNCC), he had participated in demonstrations all over the South in the early sixties. Later in that decade, he had taken part in the drive to get more jobs for blacks in white-owned businesses.

Based on his experience with HEW, he had set up his own consulting firm which received various assignments from the federal, state, and local governments. Through his business, he became familiar with several of the leading members of Atlanta's black business establishment, and he already enjoyed a close relationship with most of Atlanta's black businessmen, as well as with a good part of the general black population of Atlanta. With these contacts, King believed that if he could draft the elements of an acceptable plan, he could muster support from NAACP members, Atlanta's black leaders, and the city's white establishment.

King was convinced that the school system must accede to demands to hire more black teachers, supervisors, and administrators. But how many should be hired? He knew there had to be more student integration. But how much and how? The NAACP lawyers who had led the legal effort had told him that nothing short of massive busing would be sufficient to reach the goal of 80:20 integration in each school to reflect the overall racial balance in the school system. But he also recognized that with only 20,000 white students left in the system, massive busing could not be the basis for a compromise. It would only accelerate white migration to the suburbs, increase enrollment in private schools, and frustrate those black parents who wished to retain community-centered schools.

The first negotiating session was a promising beginning, although it almost went off the track when NAACP's Legal Defense Fund (LDF) Assistant Director James Nabrit III, who had been invited by King, arrived with a tape recorder intending to tape the entire proceedings. Van Landingham left the room and refused to participate until the recorder was turned off. Nabrit did not participate in any subsequent negotiating sessions. While not significant in itself, the tape recorder incident suggests the difficulty created by publicity to the negotiating stages of dispute resolution. Moreover, in the earliest stages, sensitivities are so high that fear of a trivial slip can be a major barrier to discussions among antagonists. Despite the shaky start, the first meeting went well. In Wade's words, it "produced a fantastic openness on the part of all concerned," even if no specific decisions had been reached.

Some sense of where the negotiators were heading, however, was evident when the Board of Education met two days later. With more than a hundred white parents in attendance, board member Ann Woodward declared to resounding applause, that she would be willing to go to jail "for the children." Another member, Howard Klein, warned that "if we wreck our public school system, we wreck our city, [a] city [which] is in utter chaos with various segments distrusting the others." The board was not swayed by the rhetoric. It calmly adopted a set of guidelines to aid the board staff in preparing a specific plan. Frank Smith, one of the two white negotiators, suggested that the first priority was to encourage and facilitate the voluntary transfer of students under the majority-to-minority plan. The plan provided that a student who is assigned to a school in which his or her race is in the majority is permitted to transfer to another school where that race is in the minority. He also suggested that those schools in which neither race makes up more than 90 percent of the students should be exempt from the plan. His last suggestion was that attendance zones be redrawn, and schools near each other be grouped and paired, some other schools closed, and some nonadjacent schools grouped and paired. But reassignment, he said, should be limited to the school nearest a student's home or to the next nearest school. Under Smith's proposal, schools that had once been segregated and then integrated, but which had become resegregated, would not be affected by this plan.

By the time the negotiators met the following Wednesday, October 25, the school board had been refused a stay by the Fifth Circuit Court, just as Judge Bell had predicted, and the board had sent Warren Fortson, its attorney, to Washington to seek a stay from Supreme Court Justice Lewis F. Powell. The negotiators, however, continued their discussions, considering the various elements of a possible plan. There seemed to be substantial agreement on the broad outline suggested by Smith, and they began to examine the consequences for particular schools. It seemed to all the participants that a great deal of progress was being made. Indeed, the attitude was so optimistic that when the Board of Education met again the following Monday, October 30, it refused to consider Superintendent Letson's own plan, which called for busing between one thousand and two thousand students, because it didn't want to prejudice the negotiations then in progress. Instead, it approved a progress report to the Fifth Circuit Court, detailing the board's belief that a solution was in the making. Two days later, the *Atlanta Constitution* praised the negotiations that were under way. "We believe," the editorial writer said, "one of the more encouraging things happening is that members of the school board and spokesmen for the NAACP side of the present law suit have been meeting in frank discussion sessions to see if both sides can't agree on a reasonable approach."

On November 1, HEW criticized the school board for failing to live up to a 1970 court order requiring the integration of teachers in the system. At the time of the court order, 57 percent of Atlanta's school teachers were black and 43 percent were white, and the court required the Board of Education to transfer teachers to achieve those racial ratios in each school in the system. The next fall the ratios had changed, with blacks increasing and whites decreasing, and still the board hadn't adjusted teacher assignments accordingly. By the fall of 1972, the disparity was even greater, 62 percent black and 38 percent white, and no adjustments had yet been made. At their next meeting, the negotiators considered the issue of teacher assignment, but decided that the matter of student desegregation was what was really uppermost in the court's mind and had to be resolved first. They therefore decided to focus their attention exclusively on student desegregation.

During the next week, the negotiators met almost daily, early in the morning in the Citizens' and Southern Bank's ninth floor conference room. The following Tuesday, November 7, the U.S. Supreme Court refused the stay that the board had been seeking, and the Fifth Circuit Court told the board that it had to submit its school integration plan within one week.

Prodded by this new court deadline, the negotiators met the following Saturday, November 11, for sixteen hours. They had pretty much worked out the details of the plan, which was not substantially different from the one proposed by Smith. They then brought in their attorneys to put the proposal in writing. Elizabeth Rindskopf and Howard Moore represented the NAACP Legal Defense Fund, and Warren Fortson, the Board of Education. Rindskopf and Moore did not appear eager to accept the negotiated plan. Both of them had been advocating for some time a plan that would have required massive busing to redistribute students in each school in the Atlanta system in accordance with the racial proportions in the system as a whole.

The negotiators decided that, although Rindskopf, Moore, and Nabrit objected to the plan, they would proceed. They discussed specific details, focusing particularly on ironing out "snags on certain schools." They were now down to dotting i's and crossing t's, but the pact had not yet been formally sealed. One of the items that had not yet been resolved was the question of whether schools with no more than 90 percent of one race should be exempted from a pairing and busing plan. Another point of disagreement was what was to be done with the resegregated schools.

When the Board of Education met later that Tuesday, November 14, it again withheld any action on a specific plan to give the negotiators more time. Van Landingham, Smith, and Mays reported to the board that an agreement was near. The president of the board, Dr. Mays, said that "there is increasing hope that a plan can be agreed to with the plaintiffs, but such an out of court settlement is not yet guaranteed."

In fact, the negotiators *had* reached agreement, but they were still unsuccessful in selling it to the LDF attorneys. They had essentially agreed on a fleshed-out version of the plan offered by Smith. School zones would be redrawn in order to increase the extent of desegregation, and schools in adjacent zones would be paired. Some schools would be closed, their students assigned to other schools. Schools not in adjacent zones would also be paired. Finally, more students would be encouraged to use the majority-to-minority program. In all, it was estimated that the agreement would require the busing of approximately five thousand to six thousand students.

The next day, Wednesday, the negotiators met again in the late afternoon and kept trying to persuade the LDF attorneys to agree to their plan. As Elizabeth Rindskopf left the meeting about 10 P.M., she told a *Constitution* reporter, "There is not an agreement. As far as I am concerned, there is no change." The conflict, which had seemed so close to resolution, was at an impasse again.

Negotiations: The Second Round

> *The Legal Defense Fund is and has been indefatigable in its efforts to desegregate schools. In Atlanta it was pushing for a plan which would have left the school system with virtually all black children. That is not an integrated system.*
>
> –*Atlanta Constitution*, November 24, 1972

With the negotiations floundering, most board members felt that they had no choice other than to go forward with the plan prepared by Letson and his staff, which would have required busing only about fourteen hundred students. However, the plan represented such a minimal integration effort that Dr. Mays was concerned that the Fifth Circuit Court

> might feel that we are playing with them. . . . There are 95,000 students in the Atlanta system. The court has asked us for further desegregation. Now, we have before us and have discussed a plan which would have moved 30,000 students, a plan which would have moved 13,000, a plan which would have moved 6,800. But we adopted a plan which the court may think is minimal. The plan calling for moving 30,000 students is before the court, and I am afraid they may stick that one on us and it would be the most disruptive thing that could happen to our school system.

The next board meeting was stormy. There were between one hundred and two hundred angry white parents, many carrying placards proclaiming "Busing is Unfair" or "Quality Education–Yes, Busing That's a No-No." Indeed, some parents urged the board to do nothing and let itself be in contempt of court. The heated attacks on the board finally led Charles Carnes, a defeated state legislator, who had later won a seat on the board, to say: "I'd like to say what you want to hear. I'm against busing. This [plan] is the least amount of disruption of the school system. We on the board are not your enemies. This has been forced upon us. . . . We are going to do the minimum." Carnes did not help the situation, however, by adding that, if busing were required, he would send his son to a private school next year. That prompted one of the protesting white parents to respond, "What about us who can't afford private schools?"

As far as Lonnie King was concerned, the reason for the breakdown in negotiations was that the LDF lawyers were still controlling the plaintiffs' position, which was exactly what direct negotiations by the laymen had been designed to avoid. As long as Elizabeth Rindskopf, Howard Moore, and James Nabrit III believed *they* had a veto over any proposed plan, agreement would be difficult. Indeed, Nabrit told the Board of Education on November 16 that he would have to approve any agreement before it became final. King quickly came to realize that he had no attorney to assert his position and that situation had to be remedied quickly. He decided to try to get Nabrit removed as attorney. The board of directors of the Atlanta NAACP unanimously approved King's recommendation that LDF attorney Nabrit be removed as their counsel in the case.

Now that the Atlanta NAACP had made it clear that it did not regard Nabrit as its attorney, it had to find one. King knew that it was going to be difficult to find a competent attorney willing to take the case. Lawyers with established reputations in the civil rights field might shy away, since the matter was controversial and there *was* a good deal of solidarity among civil rights lawyers. He first approached Elliott Goldstein, the attorney who had suggested negotiation of the conflict without lawyers. Goldstein declined on the ground that his firm had earlier represented the Board of Education. "Even if that didn't absolutely disqualify me," Goldstein said later, "it was a sufficient reason to turn down the assignment, especially since I was convinced that the role required a black attorney." King then tried to persuade Howard Moore, one of the leading black civil rights attorneys in Atlanta to sever his association with the LDF and to join the Atlanta NAACP. Moore, however, also declined. Finally, at the suggestion of then Vice Mayor Maynard Jackson (later elected mayor), King asked Ben Spaulding, a young lawyer who had moved to Atlanta from

Michigan in 1971, if he would be willing to take the case. Before going into private practice, however, Spaulding was a staff lawyer of the Atlanta Legal Aid and had worked on occasion with Peter and Elizabeth Rindskopf, who, along with Moore, were also LDF attorneys. Because of his prior relationship with Elizabeth Rindskopf, it was only natural for Spaulding to inform her of his decision to take the case. She urged him *not* to do so because he was being used as a pawn and would surely suffer some disrepute in civil rights circles if he did. Spaulding, however, thought that King was on the right track in his approach and decided to take the case, despite Rindskopf's advice. Two days later, it was announced that the Atlanta NAACP had discharged Nabrit and Rindskopf, and, shortly thereafter, Spaulding was hired.

Before he could succeed in his effort, King knew that he had to solve one more major procedural problem. Although he was considered the leading black negotiator, the LDF lawyers did not have to go along with King's plan because he was in fact not a party to the case. The parties were Vivian Calhoun along with eight other named black plaintiffs claiming to act on behalf of the class of all black parents with children in the Atlanta city schools. And *their* attorneys were Rindskopf, Nabrit, and Moore.

In his present legal status, King could only function as a "friend of the court." The only way he could exert his leadership was to become a party to the action. To do that, he had to acquire powers of attorney from as many of the original plaintiffs as he could. With their powers of attorney in hand, in effect he would become the client, and he had every intention of being a client who not only knew exactly what he wanted but who made his lawyers do what he told them. Working very quickly, he managed to acquire absolute powers of attorney from eight of the original nine "named" plaintiffs, from all but Vivian Calhoun herself. And what would later prove to be just as important, he obtained these powers in his own personal, individual capacity and not as president of the Atlanta branch of the NAACP. He took special pains on that point, because, he later said, he was worried then about the kind of pressure which the LDF would be able to bring on the NAACP in New York. Now he was in a position directly to influence the case, if not in fact to control it.

While white parents were attempting to organize an antibusing boycott of the schools for November 27, when the new term was to start, and while Lieutenant Governor Lester Maddox was declaiming that busing was "ungodly, unconstitutional, and communistic," King and Spaulding were moving ahead forcefully. Two days before a scheduled hearing by the Fifth Circuit Court, King and Spaulding met for five hours in Van Landingham's office with the three-member Board of Education negotiating committee. Having earlier resolved the differences between the Atlanta blacks and the school board on the matter of student desegregation, they now turned their attention to the other two principal issues to be resolved—teacher desegregation and administrative staff desegregation.

On the former, there was little disagreement. The district court had ruled in 1970 that in order for the Atlanta system to be regarded as "desegregated," the racial proportions among teachers in each school had to represent the racial proportions in the Atlanta city school system as a whole. The only question was whether these assignments had to be made annually. The negotiators agreed that it would be made one time only, during the following fall.

The administrative desegregation issue, however, was much stickier. Teachers can be moved from one school to another, so long as they are teaching the same subject matter and at the same grade level. Because few changes had been made in the racial composition of the school administration during the period that the schools themselves were becoming predominantly black, the central administration of the school system was almost totally white. There were a number of black administrators, but all were concentrated either in the individual black schools or as district superintendents for groups of black schools. To accomplish substantial desegregation of the school administration, the white administrators would either have to be demoted to field positions, or a number of new jobs costing a great deal of money would have to be created in the central administration.

But King was insistent on the point of administrative desegregation. Even if black parents were as unenthusiastic about busing as white parents, King knew he was open to charges of selling out because many blacks would believe that he and his fellow negotiators had acceded to white opposition to busing. If the blacks yielded on the question of busing, they had to receive something that would be perceived as being of equal value to what the public thought they were giving up.

What the blacks wanted in return for yielding on the question of busing was black administrative control of the school system. A major difference between blacks in Atlanta and blacks in other large cities was that Atlanta had a very large and well-knit black middle class. It was confident of its capacity to run a school system of superior quality, just as it already ran outstanding colleges, hospitals, banks, life insurance companies, and other businesses. A lot of black middle-class parents knew that one of the most pernicious aspects of segregation was the documented disparity in the quality of equipment, textbooks, and facilities. If black administrators were in control of the system, however, black parents could be certain of equity in the distribution of resources among the schools. As Dr. Asa Yancey, member of the Board of Education and perhaps the principal architect of the administrative desegregation plan, was later to assert, "If you have racial balance in administration from the superintendent at the top right on down through all personnel who deal with students, then there *can't* be any racial discrimination against any child." Indeed, a full year before the negotiations, Yancey had urged making the administration "colorless" as a way out of Atlanta's dilemma.

There was another important reason to desegregate the school administration. King believed that the future responsiveness of the schools to court orders depended on an integrated administration. "In other cities," he said, "the NAACP had fought the school superintendents in court, and after the court decision, the same people were left in charge of implementing an order which they had opposed; we *had* to change the administration if any future court order was to be implemented sympathetically."

In addition to insisting that the superintendent be black, King considered two approaches to administrative integration. First was that racial proportions in the school administration be equivalent to racial proportions then existing in the entire city school administration as a whole. That formula might work for teachers, but it would either require the firing or transfer of many existing white administrators, or the creation of new "black" administrative positions at substantial added cost for the city. The alternative he chose called for racial parity among the *top* administrative and supervisory personnel of the school system. If he could get the schoool board negotiating committee to agree to that principle, he could later sit down with them and work out which positions were to be filled by whites and which by blacks. Van Landingham and his white co-negotiators believed that absolute parity would be tough to sell to their colleagues on the board, but they also knew that they might be able to encourage flexibility when they reached the point of deciding which positions were to be filled by blacks. Besides, there was also the possibility of stipulating that the changes be spread over a period of years. At the end of a long night's discussion, the white negotiators decided to go along with King, although Smith continued to object to the stipulation that the new superintendent *had* to be black. Now the negotiators reported to the school board that they had reached an agreement. After a frequently heated public discussion, the Board of Education approved the compromise plan over the dissenting votes of two board members. "That was the scariest meeting I've ever attended," remembered Smith, "with a half dozen school policemen on duty to keep order and prevent violence."

The agreement approved by the board called for the transfer of about four thousand students; the closing of four elementary schools; the pairing, both by rezoning and by transfering students, of other schools; and the creation of between nine and twelve middle schools. Pupil reassignment would be carried out at the start of the third school quarter, beginning January 1. The administrative desegregation and teacher desegregation plans were approved in the form the negotiators presented them.

On Wednesday morning, Spaulding and Fortson, respectively representing King and the school board, flew to New Orleans to report the good news to the Fifth Circuit Court, taking with them a brief in support of the plan, written entirely by nonlawyer Smith and embodying Dr. Mays's arguments. But they were not the only lawyers in the court when the hearing commenced. Legal Defense Fund lawyers Moore, Nabrit, and Rindskopf were also present.

Instead of a united front, the court was faced with the always unfortunate dilemma of different lawyers claiming to represent the same parties. Nabrit contended that the board's plan would result in approximately two-thirds of Atlanta's black elementary school children remaining in schools 90 percent or more black. Moore attacked the compromise plan as representing "a slave auctioning himself off more or less . . . literally selling out the rights of our children." He told the court that it was wrong "to trade off the constitutional rights of Negro pupils for the constitutional rights of Negro administrators." Both of the LDF lawyers vigorously urged the court to disregard the compromise and impose a plan of its own, preferably the LDF plan requiring the busing of thirty thousand students. Spaulding and Fortson defended the compromise, claiming that it would help "prevent a conscious discriminatory pattern from developing in its administration of the school program," as well as advance the cause of integration. Moreover, they said, if the court would withhold an immediate desegregation order and thereby allow more time for the negotiations to continue, they had hopes of reconciling the differences among the competing lawyers. The antagonism that divided the plaintiffs' attorneys was underscored by the arrival in the courtroom of a busload of placard-bearing black school children who had been brought to New Orleans by an Episcopal minister to protest the compromise.

Judge Charles Clark, a member of the three-judge panel, declared, "I despair at the present moment." He said that the "good spirit" in Atlanta had earlier created "a favorable climate in the court's mind that the case could be settled by compromise." But now, he added, "It looks like we are going to have to lay a court edict on Atlanta." The three-judge panel sent the lawyers back to Atlanta and promised them a prompt answer to their questions.

Back in Atlanta, there was a good deal of confusion. Many people believed that the matter had been substantially settled once the Atlanta NAACP and the school board had worked out an agreement, and the school board had approved it. Now the issue seemed far from settled.

By Friday, the impasse was eased when the Fifth Circuit Court announced that it had sent the case back to the district court in Atlanta and ordered it to determine which of the two factions, represented by different lawyers, was acting for all the black parents and children in the schools. Lyndon Wade, chairman of the district courts' advisory committee, was obviously speaking not only for his fellow negotiators but also for a substantial portion of the public when he said, "The court has given us one more chance to work out an equitable solution—they realize there are good sports and reasonable people on both sides of the table."

During the next ten days, King mobilized Atlanta's black leaders to support his position publicly. Congressman Andrew Young, among the first to speak out, declared, "I think if Howard Moore had been around the community for the last year or so, he would have understood what Lonnie King and others were trying to do and he would have supported their plan." Ruby Hurley, southeastern regional director of the

NAACP, and one of the members of the negotiating committee, said that the LDF lawyers, "don't understand that they should be in communication with the agency which is most directly concerned with school desegregation in the city of Atlanta and which has been most concerned all along." King, himself, confined his public comments to the busing issue, attempting to convince the public that his substantive position was the right one. "A school bus," he declared, "is no solution to racial problems where 77 per cent of the pupils are black. I think there will be substantial desegregation–by substantial I mean as much as you can get when you're trying to integrate 77 per cent of the pupils into 23 per cent."

King also asked members of Atlanta's black establishment to support him in a private meeting with Jack Greenberg, national director of the LDF, and his associates, Nabrit and Moore, to demonstrate that Atlanta's black community was solidly behind King's efforts. King knew that despite everything he had done to become a party to the suit, to get his own lawyer, and to reach agreement with the school board, the LDF and its lawyers were still capable of preventing a successful resolution of the conflict by objecting in court to the terms of any proposed agreement. The only sure way of preventing them from doing so, King believed, was by persuading the LDF lawyers to join with him, under his and Spaulding's leadership, in any representations to the court.

An important step toward persuading the LDF lawyers to join with King took place at a meeting on Saturday, December 1. In addition to King, the participants included Congressman Young; businessmen Jesse Hill and William Callaway; educators Vivian Henderson, Dr. Mays, and Wiley Bolden; Atlanta Urban League Executive Director Lyndon Wade; Southern Christian Leadership Conference Chairman J. E. Lowery; and others. After the meeting, a diplomatic statement was issued: "The participants agreed to work cooperatively in a spirit of give-and-take to formulate a plan of desegregation which will give expression to the highest aspirations of all interested parties and concerned citizens and to accommodate their worst apprehensions." The participants had also agreed on the need to "sponsor workshops, community meetings, and field trips to acquaint the community with the plan, in an effort to win wide acceptance, understanding and cooperation from all citizens in the implementation of a final plan."

News of the outcome of the meeting elicited the following editorial comment from the *Atlanta Constitution*:

> We admire King for facing up to the difficult side of working out real issues affecting real people. What some of the New York lawyers involved in this case . . . would like apparently is an impressive legal ruling going up through the U.S. Supreme Court, one that would bus children all over Atlanta so that you had roughly 23 per cent white children in each individual school. The trouble with that approach is, if history means anything in such matters, most white parents would simply pull their children out of the public schools. No law or court decision can prevent parents from moving across the county line or putting children in private schools. . . . We think Lonnie King is among those talking sense on a difficult issue.

Negotiations: Round Three

On Monday, December 4, King notified all participants in the negotiations—the same individuals as before with the addition of Elizabeth Rindskopf—that the discussions would resume the following night. He also told school board President Mays that the plaintiffs would try to work out a common position with the hope of presenting it to the school board for consideration the following week. At the first negotiating session, the participants discovered that there were a lot of things on which they could agree. Rindskopf, however, was not as optimistic as King about the possibility of an early settlement. "Some of us," she said, "seem to feel we can arrive at a plan more quickly than others. . . . I think it's premature to say when we're going to finish."

Although the negotiating sessions were private, King continued his campaign to gain public support for his framework for a settlement. At a major speech to the predominantly white Atlanta PTA Council, King claimed that the NAACP won its 1954 *Brown* Supreme Court decision because "we found that hundreds of thousands of black kids were being bused past all-white schools to black shacks, and that white kids were being bused past the shacks to their all-white schools. Now somewhere between busing and no busing, there has to be some common ground, and we are trying to find that common ground." When asked whether so many whites had left the Atlanta school system because of "successful integration," King said that it couldn't possibly have been "because of desegregation, because we haven't had that much. We refuse to take the responsibility for white people running out of Atlanta." At that same meeting, he made a strong appeal for putting blacks in the top central school administrative positions, claiming that this would result in a "change—maybe subtle, but a change—in the overall thrust for school desegregation in America."

Following his talk, Sue Yocum, whose first attempts at a school boycott had failed, called for another boycott and attacked the biracial negotiating committee. The PTA Council, however, passed the same resolution condemning busing in general that had been approved a week earlier by the predominantly black City-Wide PTA Council.

The black PTAs were only the first of many black groups to take strong antibusing stands. When the school board met the following week, with the plaintiffs still not having reached agreement, more than two hundred parents were on hand, many of them black, and most of them wearing yellow bus-shaped paper badges proclaiming "No Forced Busing." Moreover, in the first formal statement by black parents to the board on this topic, one black mother said, "I am opposed to busing, I was opposed to busing when I was bused by a school to a school, and I still hold that same position. We must not repeat history."

Black groups were not the only vocal critics of school busing. To no one's surprise, the Atlanta Real Estate Board attacked the desegregation suit itself, claiming that it would not only harm thousands of school children but "will ultimately cause considerable damage to the whole city of Atlanta, and the entire metropolitan area." The board continued:

> It has already been proved that most parents will not tolerate school busing. . . . All those who can afford to will enroll their children in private schools or will move to one of the adjoining counties. . . . This white exodus would leave the Atlanta school system made up predominantly of children in lower-income brackets. . . . It is obvious that the NAACP feels that institutions which are mixed black and white are much better than institutions which are either all black or all white. . . . If the Atlanta Board of Education and the school system were left alone, and were allowed to concern itself with the education of the children instead of lawsuits, the result would be a good, healthy, integrated school system which offered an excellent education to the children enrolled.

The following day, the *Atlanta Constitution* reported that many white parents who actually lived in Atlanta were establishing false residences in suburban counties to qualify their children for schools there. The practice was thought to be so widespread that some counties, especially Fulton County, were requiring that all transfer applications be accompanied by affidavits from the school system from which the students were leaving and that the home addresses be verified by administrators or teachers.

At the next school board meeting, King conceded that the talks were going more slowly than he had expected and that he could not predict how long it would take the plaintiffs to reach an agreement. That was not the only disappointing news the board members received that evening. Frank Smith, who had spent many long hours that fall as one of the three school board negotiators, declared that his other personal and business obligations forced him to resign from the board. Because vacancies on the board were filled by the board itself, this meant the board would have to make another difficult decision affecting its desegregation posture.

With the plaintiffs taking more time to reach agreement than had been expected, some Atlanta citizens began to think about the possibility of a metropolitan solution. Periodically, since she had first filed the ACLU's metropolitan integration suit in April, Margie Pitts Hames had been attempting to move the suit forward through the district court. In October, however, the district court judges had decided to stay the suit, pending the outcome of negotiations on the Atlanta-only suit. With no agreement near, Hames once again petitioned the court to consider a metropolitan solution. The court took her request under advisement.

On Friday, December 15, the plaintiffs continued to struggle toward agreement, and once again, an unnamed participant was reported to have said that the group might, indeed, have a plan ready for the Board of Education meeting the following Monday. Once again, however, they did not. Instead, the Board of Education set up public meetings for both Monday and Tuesday nights to review the metropolitan desegregation suit involving Richmond, Virginia, still pending before the U.S. Supreme Court, and to explore generally the Supreme Court's policy nationally with respect to school integration. Both meetings were poorly attended, without even a quorum of board members present.

The day after Christmas, LDF attorney Howard Moore, who had been out of town and therefore did not join in most of the negotiations, discussed progress. In the first public comment by one of the participants, Moore talked of the plaintiffs' commitment to "quality education," and their attempt to develop "a model plan with flexibilities that can be adjusted to reflect realities, minimize political resistance and encourage widespread acceptance by the public." He declared that, if School Superintendent Letson resigned and if the school system administration were reorganized, a student integration plan "can be far more flexible than it can be otherwise."

On January 4, the district court judges refused Margie Pitts Hames's request for lifting the stay on the metropolitan integration suit that she had brought. That same day, Federal Judges Albert Henderson, Jr., and Sydney Smith announced that the Board of Education would have only thirty days to respond to the plaintiffs' plan, once it was submitted to the court.

Most important to later developments, the two judges, in response to a written request from both Moore and Spaulding, certified Moore, Spaulding, and Elizabeth Rindskopf as "joint and several" attorneys for all the parties. This meant, in effect, that any one of the three lawyers for the plaintiffs could legally enter into an agreement binding *all* of the plaintiffs, both named and unnamed. As a consequence, while Spaulding was in fact only the attorney for King and those plaintiffs whose powers of attorney King held, he was now empowered to speak and act for all the named as well as the unnamed plaintiffs of the class action suit.

It took until January 16 for the different lawyers to agree on a plan. King had achieved a number of his objectives—administrative desegregation, teacher assignment, and the establishment of a school for talented children. But he had lost out on the issue of student desegregation. The new plan was to require the busing of between ten thousand and thirty thousand students. On the issue of student integration, it now appeared that the LDF had prevailed.

Lonnie King's Strategy

When queried informally by the press, eight of the ten school board members said flatly that they disapproved of this plan. All of them reserved final judgment until after they had had a chance to examine the school board staff analysis of the plan, which was to be completed shortly. "On the basis of the staff's data," said Board President Mays, "we would be in better position to make a decision as to whether we will seek negotiation, accept the plan or reject it. We want to do some negotiations in good faith; if we fail, we fail—but we'll try."

That weekend, the school board also made a point of releasing figures documenting the continuing exodus of students from the Atlanta school system. In the period since the beginning of November, nearly 1,200 white students had withdrawn from school. That was nearly 8 percent of the total white enrollment at the beginning of the year. The decline in white enrollment was not very surprising. What did surprise many, however, was the fact that during the same period, 450 black students had left the system—a larger number than anyone expected—with the decline occurring during approximately the same period that the plaintiffs were stuggling over the busing issue.

The staff analysis of the plaintiffs' proposal was highly critical. Earlier estimates of the number of students likely to be bused under the plan were right on target—eighteen thousand students, of whom fourteen thousand were black. If the plaintiffs' plan was carried out, the school staff concluded that 156 new buses would be required with an annual operating expenditure of between $1.5 million and $3 million, depending on how the routes were laid out.

Superintendent Letson used the next board meeting to object to the plaintiffs' administrative reorganization plan, which called for creating, by July 1973, twenty-two new positions in the top five levels of the central school administration and for hiring a black superintendent and two associate superintendents—one black and one white. Of the twelve highest positions, seven were to be black. Of the remaining positions in the top five levels of the administration, fifty-two were to be filled by blacks and twenty-three by whites. The plan, Letson said, was "a ridiculous proposal, and under no circumstances should it be approved." That outburst by the superintendent prompted board member Van Landingham and Chairman Wade to appeal to the other members of the board for an end to "inflammatory statements."

Board President Mays named a new five-member committee to negotiate with the plaintiffs. All members of the school board were to be invited to the meetings, but those members specifically charged with negotiation were (in addition to Van Landingham and Dr. Yancey) June Cofer, Charles Carnes, and Richard Hodges, the Chamber of

Commerce's Education Committee chairman, who had been elected by the board without any controversy to fill the vacancy created by Frank Smith's resignation.

With the criticism of the plaintiffs' plan mounting daily, Lonnie King counterattacked the critics. In a round of speeches obviously intended to solidify his reputation as an advocate of integration, he criticized white opponents of busing as having "racist motives." Then, referring to a newspaper report that the plaintiffs' plan would force a substantial tax rate increase, he said, "The Atlanta newspapers and other defenders of white supremacy run up the flag of fiscal economy whenever there is a question of human rights."

Next, he took on the Board of Education, characterizing its staff analysis as "a twenty-four page dictum of deception and half-truths," which made it seem to him "clear that the framers of this document cannot read or have deliberately played with the truth for propaganda purposes." Then, he focused on Letson who, King said, "Came to Atlanta with one charge—officially or unofficially—to make sure that integration doesn't happen in Atlanta." "He has done well," King added, "but his day is about over." King used the same speeches to defend the plaintiffs in the suit, whom he described as "not black Atlanta's richest or finest, but plain people," people who aren't very active in community life "because so many are in somebody's kitchen working from can't to can't." ("Can't to can't" refers to working long hours, from when you can't see in the morning to when you can't see at night.)

The Atlanta newspapers were stung by King's criticism, even if it was intended only as a tactical maneuver. They continued to laud King's efforts, but also praised Superintendent Letson, whom they described as an integrationist. The *Atlanta Constitution* editorial writer concluded: "Just two months ago, members of the Atlanta School Board believed that they and NAACP spokesmen were pretty close to an agreement. But when the NAACP submitted their new detailed proposal to the School Board last week, it involved far more busing or school pairing than the Atlanta school officials thought they had all but agreed on with the NAACP."

The same day the editorial appeared, 240 white Northside High School parents met to protest the plan. One was quoted as saying: "It sounds like somebody's got some marbles loose somewhere when they talk about shipping the kids around to different schools. . . . I have schools five blocks from my house in three directions, and they are going to send my kids all across town. Somebody's crazy."

A few days later, King gave a long interview to the *Atlanta Constitution.* In that interview, he spelled out at length what he saw as the delicate balancing act circumstances had forced upon him:

> I guess you could say I became the man in the middle when I took the position that we ought to put more emphasis on desegregating top-level staff people who are responsible for implementing from day to day whatever plan is finally adopted.
>
> There is no way that I, Lonnie King, can come out of this thing a winner. We have a problem here that has existed for 15 years. I have been one of the very few persons who have tried to hammer out a settlement in this case so we could get out of court and move on to the more important issue of educating kids. Both black and white leadership in Atlanta felt we ought to sit down and negotiate. I just happened to be president of the Atlanta [NAACP] branch at this moment in history. It could have been anyone else at another time.
>
> You can't just close your eyes to the goals of the NAACP and everything we have stood for since our inception. I recognize there is a strain in the black community that says, "If white folks don't want us around, we don't want to be around." But we started these cases because the bulk of the tax dollar historically followed the white child. The white community escaped the 1954 Supreme court decision by building what we call "Supreme Court Schools," these big modern schools in the black community . . . to perpetuate segregation. So we are faced with a school system which has had 15 years to come up with the bricks and mortar with which to make it virtually impossible to desegregate the schools.
>
> Atlanta has to desegregate its schools—period. I operated on the premise that the only way we could eliminate the racial identity of all the black and white schools would be to cut the white population up. . . . If you really sit down and look at this plan, there have been some strong concessions to the white community's feelings. There have also been some strong concessions to the black community's feelings.
>
> But there are 80,000 blacks and 20,000 whites in the school system. The white schools are all smaller and the big schools are in the inner-city. To split the whites up into groups of ten and send them out to the black schools is just ridiculous. There just aren't enough white folks to go around.

> Whites are opposed to the plan to bus 2,000 students. They were opposed to the "Tom" plan [the way King's black opponents referred to the plan he had negotiated with the school board earlier] and they were opposed to the Stolee Plan [a plan to bus many more students].
>
> That could only lead me to the conclusion that any plan that meaningfully desegregates the Atlanta schools will find opposition from the white folks in this town. And they are the ones that have kept the Atlanta school board from doing what they had to do for the last fifteen years. I tried to be mindful of the concerns of the majority of the people. If not this, then a variation of this plan is what's going into effect. That's my honest opinion [*Atlanta Constitution,* January 28, 1973, p. 8].

At the end of the interview, King said he fully expected to see in the newspaper one day a headline that said "King Betrays Whites," followed by a story the next day, with the headline, "King Betrays Blacks."

Even while King was publicly supporting the plaintiffs' entire package, wide opposition to busing continued to break into the open, especially on Atlanta's south side. Theresa Dortch, student body president at the black Douglass High School, had this to say: "It's unfair to us as students. They are not thinking about us at all. When they say they're going to take many of us and send us across town to maintain some kind of racial balance, it's unfair to the students. We're the ones who will . . . sit in the classrooms, but nobody's asking us anything about it." The president of the PTA at Douglass High School, Alfred Knox, spoke from the parents' point of view: "Since we were not involved with causing segregation, I don't think we should be inconvenienced in any way in correcting it. A lot of these black mothers work and they are very upset about their children going off to school. They want them closer to home so they'll know where they are."

When the Board of Education met on Monday, February 6, most of the observers were black. In addition to hearing from two individual school PTAs, the board heard a long and impassioned presentation by Reverend O. L. Blackshear, pastor of the Mount Pleasant Baptist Church, who was representing three black community groups. He told the board that these organizations represented thousands of blacks on the south side of Atlanta who were unalterably opposed to busing and who believed that the schools should worry about improving the education they offered, "rather than trying to figure out whether or not a black boy and a white girl are going to be able to sit in the same classroom together." Other speakers that evening were perhaps not as unalterably opposed to busing as Reverend Blackshear, but were certainly opposed. One black father said, "Philosophically, I'm for busing because I know what has happened with school systems in the South. But there are a lot of practical reasons that prevent me from wholeheartedly wanting to send my child from here to there."

At the conclusion of the meeting, Dr. Yancey, chairman of the negotiating committee appointed by the board, reported that he had asked Superintendent Letson and the staff to prepare a Board of Education plan for busing about six thousand students, including those already participating in the volunteer majority-to-minority transfer program, just in case negotiations with the plaintiffs failed. When the board's negotiating committee had its second session on Saturday, February 10, the committee decided to make the staff plan prepared under the direction of Superintendent Letson its basis for negotiation with the plaintiffs. Under Letson's plan, no students would be bused. Most of the members of the committee were unhappy with the thought of ending up with that plan, but they figured that it was a negotiating position that could be modified.

The plaintiffs had been ready with their negotiating plan for that month. The school board was now ready with its counterproposals. The issue was joined, and the long-recessed negotiations between the school board and the plaintiffs were ready to resume in earnest.

Negotiating the Details

On February 12, after the first session of this round of negotiations, Lyndon Wade told the press he was pleased with the favorable tone of the negotiations. Most of the negotiators felt, however, that the Board of Education conference room was not conducive to the kind of confidential discussions they thought would be necessary. Wade, therefore, proposed to move the negotiations to another location where secrecy could be assured, but was forced to obtain a court order permitting him to do so, as secret public meetings were violations of Georgia's "sunshine" law. Accordingly, when the negotiators met on Tuesday night, they were around a conference table high up in the Trust Company of Georgia Building, a brand new steel-and-glass tower with an unobstructed view of all of southeast Atlanta. "I think," said Wade, "that the attitude and mood of the first discussion continued and prevailed; the group made significant progress and essentially defined the route it is going to travel." Dr. Mays also said he was "encouraged."

Under the authority of his court order, Wade barred all reporters from the meeting, explaining that, "I want to avoid any extraneous discussions at this point. I've got an assignment [and] I've got to try to get it completed. I want to get it done before the deadline." The deadline, fixed over five weeks by the court, was three days away.

While plainclothes guards patrolled the ground-floor lobby, barring all unauthorized persons from entering the meeting, the negotiators on the eleventh floor began their first substantive discussion—desegregation of the Board of Education's administrative staff. The plaintiffs had come in with a plan calling for the top administration (the top five levels) to be 63 percent black. The school board negotiators were pushing for less, but made it clear that they would be willing to compromise on a 50:50 desegregation pattern in return for substantial concessions by the plaintiffs on the matter of student desegregation. Most participants felt that the plaintiffs would accept such an outcome, if they could all subsequently agree on some substantial student integration. For five hours that evening, they considered not only what the black and white percentages ought to be, but which jobs should be specified with a racial qualification. (It was a foregone conclusion that the superintendent's position would be held by a black.) Tagging specific positions as either black or white undoubtedly bothered some of the participants, but it was an idea that they had gotten used to, since it had been discussed at some length in the fall. There were a number of other issues to be resolved, such as whether positions once filled on the basis of race would continue to be designated as "black" or "white" positions when they subsequently became vacant. There were also the questions of whether the percentage of black-filled jobs had to be reached at once or could be spread over several years, whether new jobs would be created or existing white jobholders replaced, and whether whites must necessarily be fired or could be replaced by attrition over a period of time. All in all, the participants felt that they were not dealing with intractable issues. They believed that it would not be difficult to bridge their differences.

Their optimism about agreement even permitted the participants to joke a little, which, in turn, undoubtedly facilitated further agreement. As they were going over specific jobs, the discussion began to lag. Lonnie King was about to give up demanding that a particular deputy comptroller's job be filled by a black. With the twinkle that was always brightly flashing in his eyes, Vivian Henderson leaned over to King, and, in a stage whisper, said, "Take the deputy comptroller's job! That's where the money is! Take it!" The late Vivian Henderson was the unsung hero of the negotiations.

The endurance of Tuesday night's agreement, however, would obviously depend on whether an agreement could be reached on the question of student desegregation. That was the topic for Wednesday night's session, which started at 5:00 P.M. Many of the members expected that the session could be over and done with in time for a late dinner, at which they hoped to be able to celebrate the crossing of the toughest hurdle. The issue of how much busing was to be required, however, proved to be a tough hurdle indeed, one not willing to yield to so summary a treatment. The plaintiffs initially insisted that there had to be enough busing to raise the percentage of black students in every school to at least 50 percent. The Board of Education negotiators refused to budge. Back and forth the discussion went, with no one willing to yield on the point of principle and everyone eager to explain why he or she was absolutely right.

As the evening grew later, the talkers grew hungrier. At 9:15 P.M., they sent out for several buckets of fried chicken and a crate of Pepsi Cola. Their appetites were obviously as ravenous as their capacity for talk was great. Only an hour later, they sent out for more buckets of chicken and another crate of Pepsi.

The meeting lasted until 12:30 A.M., but they had still not reached an agreement on the question of student desegregation. They were clearly at an impasse. They had met, talked, munched chicken, and guzzled Pepsi for seven and one-half hours with nothing to show for it.

While the negotiators were arguing heatedly in the Trust Company of Georgia Building, parents—both black and white—were publicly expressing their opposition to forced busing. Simultaneous meetings occurred at the black Price High School and the white Dykes High School, with about three hundred parents protesting at each school. Each meeting voted with near unanimity to intervene in the class action suit to oppose any widespread busing. In addition, a brand new organization, the Quality Education Council, was formed for the express purpose of waging a court battle against substantial integration efforts. The busing issue managed to bring together the city's black and white PTAs in a coalition for the same pupose. The Quality Education Council was even more explicit about its aim to intervene in the suit to challenge the plaintiffs' claim to represent the position of all black parents. Southside black leader Reverend Blackshear was fulfilling his promise to organize massive resistance to busing. "We could find ourselves working with segregationists opposed to busing," he said, "[but] if they want to join us to follow along and work under our leadership that's okay, but we're leading the movement—we're spearheading it!"

Blackshear was not alone. Two state representatives—one white and one black—were also opposing substantial busing. Dr. John Savage, the white, said, "We're in this ballgame together." Billy McKinney, the black, said: "Sixteen years ago, I was for busing because I felt it was necessary for quality education. At that time, we were 30 percent of the population. Now, we're over 80 per cent of it and we have to go out and find some white folks to be integrated with. I say to hell with it. . . . Fire Letson, and the Board of Education comes up for election in a few months. Get your own Board of Education." He, too, was strongly for intervening in the court suit. Even State Republican Party Chairman Robert J. Shaw made the rounds and said, "It's time we told the school board we're tired of this monkeying around and that we want our system like it is." After covering the protest meetings and checking with his sources among the negotiators, a *Constitution* reporter noted that "there was 'a feeling' that both sides want an agreement. . . . Plaintiffs have been 'catching hell' from both whites and blacks for their efforts to have the school system, whose enrollment is 78 per cent black, desegregated further."

After two difficult meetings, Wade was convinced that not even a miracle could produce agreement in time for the scheduled appearance in court. Back he went to the judges, told them "much progress has been made," and requested another extension in which to continue negotiating. Obviously hopeful for the first time since the fall, the judges gave the mediators five more days, until Wednesday, February 21.

At a seven-and-a-half-hour meeting on Thursday night, the plaintiffs, to overcome the impasse, reduced their demands and asked only for sufficient busing, pairing, and rezoning to assure that at least 30 percent of the students in every school would be black. In the same conciliatory tone, the Board of Education now offered a plan that would assure that no school would be less than 20 percent black. To determine the impact of each approach, the Board of Education negotiators asked their staff to run projections of how the two plans would affect specific schools. The Board of Education was obviously continuing to cover itself with a fall-back position, because the staff was also working diligently on plans to implement the minimalist position approved earlier by the board.

If the school board negotiators were in fact willing, as the papers said, to think about a 20 percent black percentage in all schools, there was bound to be some busing. But on "Sweet Auburn" Avenue and Hunter Street, where Atlanta's black businesses are concentrated, there was speculation that if the plaintiffs accepted even a 30 percent goal for black student integration, there would be "one hell of a fight" between the LDF and the Atlanta NAACP. Howard Moore told a newspaper reporter that the 30 percent figure represented "tokenism" and was "not legal." He continued to doubt whether an agreement would emerge, he said, since he was going to have to approve whatever the negotiators came up with.

When the negotiators met on the Friday before the court deadline, reporters were excluded even from the lobby of the Trust Company of Georgia Building. Upstairs, the negotiators examined the two sets of projections that the school board staff had produced. They wrangled over them for about three hours, when King suggested that the parties agree on a 30 percent target for most schools, but permit any school that was at least 20 percent black and had stabilized at that level for several years, to be excluded from the 30 percent goal. This proposal provided the basis for a solution. From then on, it was only a question of filling in the details. They agreed to meet again on Saturday to go over the entire agreement point by point and to hold a Board of Education meeting on Monday.

At the Saturday session, it took about six hours to flesh out the details of the prior agreements. Neither June Cofer nor Charles Carnes attended, because both felt pretty much that they had lost out to a plan that would considerably disadvantage the schools in the area they represented in south Atlanta.

The school board members left the meeting fifteen to twenty

minutes before the NAACP negotiators, leading the press to wonder whether new differences had developed. Wade denied that there was any problem at all and said that those who remained at the meeting were "caucusing." When King addressed a public hearing at Allen Temple A.M.E. Church the next day, he said that the major problems had been resolved. He urged everyone to "take away your picket signs and take away your demonstrations for at least the next 96 hours to allow people of goodwill on both sides of this issue to work out an agreement that will satisfy all of you who are reasonable people. If you knew what has been tentatively agreed," he said, "you would not be as upset as some of you have been in the last few days." King noted that the plan would require a moderate amount of busing, but that the longest bus ride would be seven miles. He noted that there would also be some school closings. But that was all he said.

It was obvious that King did not entirely reassure the audience. State Representative McKinney was applauded when he told the same audience, "Whenever the NAACP and the school board make any decisions affecting our schools, they should consult us and this they haven't done. For the NAACP to continue to negotiate without finding out how black people feel is a mistake." He ended by chiding King, "I am happy you are meeting here with us but you should have done that before you met with the white PTA president at Buckhead." McKinney nonetheless supported the agreement and helped persuade others of its wisdom.

The negotiators spent three and one-half hours Sunday evening, starting at six o'clock, going over the agreement in detail and ended up by ratifying it. They came out looking relaxed and optimistic, with some of them joking and smiling. Wade explained to a reporter that they were "extremely tired" and had "come to know each other better." The entire process, he said, was "a very elusive thing. You think that you're coming to agreement on a specific point, only to have someone raise a concern about it later and then things are unsettled."

One portent of unsettlement was immediately reported. Howard Moore again criticized the plan: "The agreement is wrong for Atlanta." He went on: "If it is approved by the court, it will abort the transition of the Atlanta school system from a dual to a unitary one. The hopes and dreams of black people for equal education and equal educational opportunities will have been betrayed." But he didn't say he would oppose it in court, and King said that Moore had told him explicitly he would not do so.

The Public Reaction

When the school board met on Monday, February 20, the plan was described in detail. (See Table 6.1 for a comparison of all the proposed plans.) "Moderate busing" meant three thousand to four thousand students would be bused in order to achieve a 30 percent minimum enrollment of black students in all schools with the 20 percent exception for stable schools. Because of the two thousand black students already participating in the majority-to-minority program, the plan would require compulsory busing of only two thousand more students. The basic intent of the plan was to desegregate the twenty all-white schools remaining in the system. "Some school closings" meant six elementary schools and two high schools, which would be converted to middle schools. There was to be a black superintendent with 50:50 white-black staffing, although appointments to the new positions would be by attrition and there would be no firings. Teacher and administrative reassignment was to be on a one-time basis and thereafter solely on the basis of merit.

School board members Howard Klein and Anne Woodward were known to oppose this plan. They had opposed negotiations with the plaintiffs all along. Charles Carnes and June Cofer had felt the plan would damage the south side schools they represented. They had stopped attending meetings after the school board negotiators outvoted them three to two.

No one in the audience of 125 people seemed disposed to attack the plan, even after Woodward remarked, "It seems to me there has been a lot of horsetrading going on, and the tragedy is that we're not talking about horses—we're talking about students." Balanced against her objection was the endorsement of Dr. Mays. He said the plan would "do much to stabilize this community," and perhaps even reverse white flight. The board voted eight-to-two to approve the plan.

This was the outcome that the negotiators had expected. Indeed, Van Landingham and Hodges were so confident of approval that they had arranged a breakfast meeting with the board of directors of the Atlanta Chamber of Commerce before the Board of Education met. Together with Dr. Mays, they presented the plan to the assembled businessmen and sought their support for its implementation. In response, the chamber passed a resolution in support of the compromise plan, which it described as "negotiated in good faith on the part of dedicated leadership." "Now the uncertainty that has existed

TABLE 6.1 The Plans Proposed in the Atlanta Integration Dispute

	Number of Students in Integrated Schools	*Percentage of Students in Integrated Schools*[a]	*Number of Integrated Schools*[a]	*Number of Segregated Black Schools*[b]	*Number of Segregated White Schools*	*Number of Students in All-Black Schools*	*Number of Students in All-White Schools*	*Number of Students Transferred*	*Number of Students Bused*
Beginning of school, September 1972	27,239		47	86	20	59,826	7,728		2,200
Board's November 17 plan	35,179	44	64	79	6	56,252	3,362	2,860	1,400
Atlanta NAACP plan I								4,325	
Atlanta NAACP plan II	48,555	53	90	59	0	42,074	0	20,438	18,395
Legal Defense Fund plan	All	100	153	0	0	0	0		30,000
Board's February 10 plan	34,953	37						15,127	0
Final compromise plan	38,718	40	64	83	0	59,000	0		2,761

[a] Schools with at least 30 percent of the race in the minority at that school, except for one school with at least 20 percent.
[b] Schools at least 90 percent black.

for so long has been removed and we are grateful," the resolution read. In addition, Van Landingham arranged for the Citizens' and Southern Bank's *Public Affairs Bulletin*, which he directed, to send out a special issue explaining the plan in detail. The bank also set up an Education Action Line, a telephone number that interested citizens could call for detailed information. The *Atlanta Constitution* endorsed the compromise and encouraged the district court to approve it. Congressman Andrew Young also praised the plan that same day and promised to help obtain federal funds to defray the additional costs arising from the plan.

The plan received very little criticism. When the Congress of Racial Equality (CORE) attacked it and even tried formally to intervene in the suit, no one was particularly surprised. CORE had been opposed to any busing all along and had publicly backed King because it was thought he was holding out against all busing. Now that it appeared that he had compromised, CORE attacked him as "trading off quality education for a few big jobs for a few big Negroes." CORE's basic position continued to be "respect for neighborhoods" and neighborhood schools. A week later, the judges summarily denied CORE's petition for intervention.

The absence of public criticism of the compromise for the first ten days was deceptive. The first sign of trouble came the following Friday when Elizabeth Rindskopf, who had participated in all of the negotiating sessions, did not sign the petition in which the board and the plaintiffs asked the court to enforce the agreement they had reached. Rindskopf's name was typed on the face of the petition, with a line where she was to sign. For two days, the judges had held the petition waiting for her to come by to sign it. When they queried her as to why she had not signed, she explained, "I didn't think I needed to [because] Spaulding has the power to sign for everyone.'" But she insisted that she would not object to the plan. Spaulding alone, therefore, signed for the plaintiffs, while Dr. Yancey and Fortson did so for the Board of Education.

Both the *New York Times* and the *Washington Post* ran substantial stories about the agreement on the same day. The *Times* led off its story by declaring that "The National Association for the Advancement of Colored People, in a major departure, consented this week to a desegregation plan for Atlanta's public schools that accepts a minimum of integrated classrooms in exchange for a maximum of integrated administrative positions." In addition, national NAACP Executive Director Roy Wilkins was quoted as explaining that "the achievement of quality education for black children is a more important goal than putting blacks and whites in classrooms together."

The reports in those two papers, circulated nationally by their syndicates, drew considerable attention to the Atlanta school compromise agreement. For the next several days, both Roy Wilkins and Jack Greenberg, executive director of the LDF, received protests from many civil rights activists around the country. These civil rights leaders seemed convinced that the Atlanta compromise plan would seriously undermine the efforts of blacks in other cities to attain integrated public education.

Against this background Wilkins summoned King, Spaulding, and Ruby Hurley, southeastern regional director of the NAACP, to a meeting in New York with him and with Bishop Stephen G. Spottswood, chairman of the NAACP board. That meeting, on Thursday, March 1, was inconclusive. The same day, Wilkins and Spottswood sent a telegram to the Atlanta branch ordering it to "reverse its approval" of the compromise plan. They raised the possibility of "lifting its charter" if it failed to heed the national directive.

The next day, both Wilkins and Greenberg vigorously attacked the plan. Wilkins declared that "The National Affairs Office of the NAACP repudiates the so-called agreement," and Greenberg, after declaring that the LDF's position was identical with that of the national NAACP, went on to say, "We think the plan is illegal, but what we're going to do about it and how we're going to do it is a matter of some discussion among us." Despite Rindskopf's statement to the court that she did not intend to oppose the plan, Greenberg refused to exclude the possibility that the LDF would oppose it. Wilkins went on to say:

> The stories that appeared in the *New York Times* and the *Washington Post* gave the appearance that the Atlanta branch has made a major break with national policy. This is not the case at all. We remain of the same opinion.
>
> But there is only one choice in equalizing the school system—that is instant equality for black schools or wholesale busing. Those are the only choices. We can't ask the kids to wait ten years. They are eleven years old only once.

> If you can't give black children equal education by tomorrow, then bus them to where the education is.
>
> But the picture that has been given to the rest of the country is that Atlanta is advancing a plan which trades the busing of children for jobs. That may be their way, I don't know, but it's not my way. The *New York Times* and the *Washington Post* said that in so many words the local NAACP had exchanged administrative posts and what we think we will get for so much power and in return we agreed not to bus.
>
> I don't know what it was, I am trying to find out. What's come out of Atlanta is an unholy mess of hopes and fears.

Publicly, Lonnie King expressed confidence that he would be able to change the position of the national officers. Privately, he was stunned. "Roy Wilkins," he said later, "was consulted in detail ahead of time, and approved the terms. . . . Moreover, all of the elements of the plan were developed in meetings at the home of Ruby Hurley, southeastern regional director of the national NAACP."

Hurley was clearly pained by the unraveling of the relationships that she had nurtured so carefully ever since she had organized the southeastern NAACP office in 1951. Her tenure with the NAACP was longer than anyone's except Wilkins himself. While she accepted some of the blame by conceding that she may not have kept the national office sufficiently well informed, she said, "For the life of me, I do not see how this plan is in violation of NAACP policy." On Sunday afternoon, March 4, the executive committee of the Atlanta NAACP branch defied Wilkins and voted unanimously to continue supporting the compromise plan.

Black Georgia State Representative McKinney wrote Wilkins that, "We must challenge the idea of a few outside so-called leaders with no compassion for our local situation, passing judgement on how we operate our schools in the community." He added that "Taxpaying citizens . . . demand that these so-called class action suits really represent the wishes and desires of the class. Black parents and students of Atlanta *are* the class, and mass busing should not be forced on them against their wishes by any outside agency."

On Tuesday, March 6, the Atlanta black leaders met again in New York with Wilkins, Spottswood, and NAACP Assistant Executive Director John Morrell. The day after the meeting, Jack Greenberg informed Judges Henderson and Smith that the LDF would in fact oppose the settlement plan. That same day, King confirmed that he had not succeeded in turning the national officers around, but said he was "hopeful" that he could settle the disagreement. In any event, he said that "the Atlanta black leadership is not backing down on the plan."

On Thursday, March 8, Wilkins suspended King and all the Atlanta NAACP officers and executive committee members—forty people in all—pending a hearing by the national NAACP. King responded to the suspension in a tone of reluctant submission, explaining he had "promised the national office that we would come to court, and would do nothing overtly to push the plan or fight the plan." It was obvious that King was trying to abide by Wilkins's order, which said, "By this action, you are hereby prohibited and enjoined from acting in behalf of or in the name of the NAACP and of the Atlanta Branch with respect to the school desegregation plan pending before the United States District Court and on any other matters."

The suspension came the same day Judges Smith and Henderson had scheduled the first court hearing on the plan. The question was, with King's suspension, who was going to fight for the compromise settlement that had been so painstakingly negotiated over the last year?

The Court Responds

The plan was in the hands of federal Judges Henderson and Smith—and with their approval, it would be implemented. If the judges disapproved, no one knew what would happen next.

LDF attorneys Howard Moore and Elizabeth Rindskopf led off the attack against the plan in a twelve-page petition challenging it substantively as "unfair, unreasonable, inequitable, and unconstitutional." They claimed that the plan would leave most of the white schools "disproportionately white," and, because virtually all of the busing involved moving black students to previously white or integrated schools, would have the effect of inconveniencing mainly poor blacks and poor whites. Finally, the LDF claimed that "its lawyers have been in communication with a number of named plaintiffs and with various other members of the plaintiffs' class who have stated their objection to the proposed settlement and urged that counsel oppose the settlement in their behalf." Contradicting what Rindskopf had told the court only a week earlier, the LDF challenged Ben Spaulding's authority to act for all the plaintiffs.

Judge Smith reminded the LDF attorneys that they had told him at a hearing only three months earlier that they had joined with the Atlanta branch of the NAACP. That assurance, Judge Smith told them, had spared the court in December from the necessity of deciding which lawyers represented which clients. Smith said, "We may have to end up polling the class to resolve some of the differences that have appeared here today."

The court was not content to let the matter rest there. Judge Smith pressed Rindskopf, both on her earlier statement to the court that she "did not intend to object to the proposed settlement," and also on her assurance to the court that the LDF regarded Spaulding as being capable of speaking for all members of the class. Claiming to have made the statements "based on a conversation with leading counsel," referring either to Moore or Greenberg, she defended herself by saying that her authority had subsequently been withdrawn. Her attempt to explain the inconsistency shifted the blame and the ire of the judges to Moore, who was also present in court. "You don't have the authority to withdraw the authority from her," Judge Smith said to Moore. "I can't help it if you don't tend to your business and failed to look at the plan!"

While the LDF lawyers argued that the plan did not go far enough, informal statements that the court solicited from some of those attending the hearing that day attacked the plan for going too far. Both Howard Klein and Anne Woodward, the two members of the Board of Education who had voted against the plan, appeared in court that day to press their opposition. Representatives of CORE were there for similar purposes. However, most of the sentiments expressed that day in court strongly supported the plan.

The task of determining the truth from among so many conflicting positions required the court to delay its decision. Before adjourning the March 8 hearing, Judges Smith and Henderson promised a new hearing in about three weeks on March 29. The court also ordered the Board of Education to make the details of the plan available throughout the city schools so that parents and the public would have a chance to familiarize themselves with it.

Prior to the court hearing, Lonnie King had restrained himself from responding to the criticism directed toward him by the LDF and the NAACP. He was so angered, however, by the position which the LDF lawyers took in court, that he decided to counterattack. After touching base with a number of his friends and supporters in Atlanta, he charged that the LDF had "sabotaged all efforts to reach a settlement" and claimed that both Moore and Greenberg had been informed of all of the details of the plan and had promised him that they would not oppose the settlement. "To come back now and say they are going to oppose the plan," he declared, "smacks to me of double-dealing. Legal Defense Fund attorneys sat with us through the negotiations, they drafted the language for at least two-thirds of the agreement, and then they promised they would not oppose the plan."

Moreover, King said that it was the LDF and not local branches of the NAACP that had pressured Roy Wilkins to retract his endorsement of the compromise, repudiate the plan, and suspend the Atlanta branch officers. "And then they moved aggressively at the national level," King said, "to try and create the impression that there was a massive sell-out in Atlanta, Georgia, which precipitated all of the reverberations which made Mr. Wilkins take the precipitous action that he took." LDF attorneys Rindskopf and Nabrit immediately denied that they were responsible. Nabrit denied any knowledge of LDF efforts to change Wilkins's position, but Rindskopf went further, claiming that the pressure really came from within the NAACP. "I don't say that we weren't pleased to see it," she said, "but we certainly had nothing to do with it."

Before the day was out, CORE had called a press conference and had launched its own attack on Wilkins. Describing Wilkins as "an extremist—a radical," Associate National Executive Director Victor Solomon declared, "He is extremely committed to a solution he insists on forcing down the throats of everybody."

King had other concerns apart from the actions of the national NAACP. A report began circulating in Atlanta that the school board intended to continue the services of Superintendent John Letson as a special consultant, once he was replaced as superintendent. King knew he had to protect himself from charges of "sell-out" on an issue that might get him into difficulty with his black supporters, even if they saw eye to eye with him on the busing issue. He said:

> If the board does that, I will convene the persons who have been supporting this side of the law suit. My inclination is that this is a sign of bad faith and we ought to seriously consider whether we ought to continue to support the plan. . . . It seems that on the one hand, they are

> going to bring in a new black superintendent, but on the other hand, they are going to keep a white superintendent over whom the new man would have no control.

That statement did precisely what it was intended to do. It produced an answer by board President Mays explaining that Letson's "special consultancy" was the board's way of buying out the remainder of his contract and would continue only until Letson got another job. In no event, Dr. Mays assured the public, was Letson to have any authority over the school system or over the new superintendent.

King's statement was criticized by June Cofer, who had never enthusiastically supported the compromise: "It's just a political scheme on the part of Lonnie King. The board was awfully naive to accept the plan. They should have suspected something like this all along."

Backed by a nonpartisan analysis of the plan, the *Atlanta Constitution* unreservedly endorsed it on March 19. The paper also told interested parents where they could inspect the plan and urged everyone to do so. The same day, the *Washington Daily News and Evening Star* also supported the plan.

> The Atlanta agreement still needs federal court approval and it is possible that the whole arrangement, which really amounts to a political compromise, will get hung up in legal thickets. Should it stand, though, it is certain to be cited by lawyers elsewhere.
>
> At least three factors appear to have contributed to the Atlanta agreement. First, as the NAACP conceded, the original busing plan ran into resistance from a sizable number of Atlanta blacks. Second, with the quickening of black pride, the belief has grown that black children need not suffer in an all-black school if equal resources for all schools can be assured. And third, everyone faced the plain truth that trying to spread Atlanta's remaining white pupils through the school system would accomplish little but to accelerate the flight of white families from the city.
>
> In Atlanta, it appears that all sides appear to have balanced principle and practicality.

Two days later, in a formal petition, the LDF urged Judges Smith and Henderson to reject the King compromise and, instead, to adopt a revised version of an alternative plan that would make every school in

Atlanta 80 percent black and 20 percent white, essentially the same plan it had urged for the last year and a half. Nabrit, who signed the petition on behalf of the LDF, not only attacked the King plan as "unworkable and inconsistent with sound educational administration," but went on to charge "that the local Atlanta newspapers have carried the accounts of the plan which are biased in favor of the settlement and do not objectively portray the overall impact of the plan or its particular operation. The subjectivity and anti-busing bias of local news accounts throughout recent history of the case is such that the court may not properly rely upon such news accounts as furnishing any legal notice to the class."

The LDF criticism was immediately followed by board member Howard Klein's objection to the compromise. He submitted his own plan. CORE, for the third time, tried to intervene in order to offer its own plan.

In the week before the hearing, the opponents of the compromise plan escalated the attacks on King. Ralph Abernathy, the only major Atlanta black leader who had sided publicly with the LDF, called a meeting of some of Atlanta's black leaders to try to persuade them that the LDF was right. They refused to budge, even after two hours of discussion. King did not attend.

At the same time that the LDF was unable to shake King's extensive support among Atlanta's blacks, it was being blocked by the court on another front. As a plaintiff in the suit, the LDF still had the power to take depositions from other parties to the suit, and it had attempted to use that power to compel testimony from a number of persons, including board member William Van Landingham. On March 21, Judge Smith forbade the LDF from taking such depositions.

Two days later, Margie Pitts Hames, the ACLU's advocate of metropolitan school desegregation, asked the court to allow her to take depositions about "allegations of conflict of interest and impropriety" in the background of the Atlanta school compromise, citing an article in the March 19 issue of Atlanta's alternative newpaper, the *Great Speckled Bird.* The article accused King of selling out the Atlanta business establishment in exchange for loans to his personal business enterprises.

King was incensed. Of course, he said, he had received loans from Atlanta banks over the preceding years. It would have been impossible for him or any other businessman—black or white—to have gone into business without them. Describing the *Great Speckled Bird*'s allegation as "preposterous," he stated categorically that neither he nor any of his companies had received any monies from any Atlanta bank since serious negotiations had begun in February. In past years, he acknowledged, he had received a loan from the Trust Company of Georgia to help finance an office building he was putting up. He had also received from the Citizens' and Southern Bank, of which Van Landingham was a vice-president, an automobile loan and he carried a Citizens' and Southern Bank credit card. He said that the charges were "just an attempt to sabotage the plan . . . by some people who take that position that, if they cannot rule, they must ruin. It's pretty clear to me that these people have gone to the lowest extent they possibly can to smear my integrity and the goodwill I have in the Atlanta community."

The day after the charges were reprinted in the Atlanta daily newspapers, Judges Henderson and Smith denied the LDF motion for a new hearing, which was the only way the LDF could get court consideration for its own plan. Two days later the judges refused to allow Margie Pitts Hames to take the depositions she sought, because, the court said, she had no standing in the proceedings and, moreover, the information she sought was "irrelevant at this point."

After all the fireworks of the preceding two and one-half weeks, the March 29 court hearing seemed pretty tame. The court received petitions bearing the signatures of four thousand parents, overwhelmingly black, supporting the compromise plan. They also received supportive statements from a number of individuals, including Reverend J. E. Lowery, chairman of the board of the Southern Christian Leadership Conference, the organization led by Ralph Abernathy, who was opposing the plan. The LDF's plan was "unreasonable, because it proposes to send scores of black children scurrying all over the city in pursuit of classrooms where there are white children," Lowery said. "Busing just to have a certain number of black students sitting in classes with whites is not meaningful . . . and borders on being racist." Several other black leaders made similar statements.

Judges Smith and Henderson denied a motion by the national NAACP to permit it to intervene in the suit, explaining, "We have constantly denied motions to intervene. We've got more parties and lawyers than we can handle now." The judges also turned down again another LDF attempt to convert what the judges intended to be a hearing on a specific plan into a free-for-all evidentiary hearing in which other plans could be offered and evidence taken on them.

The hearing added little of substance that was not already known, but, for a brief poignant moment, it was highly symbolic. As the proceedings began, the lawyers opposing the compromise plan were lined up at a table in front of and to the right of the judges, while the lawyers for the school board were at another table in front of the judges but to their left. In between the two larger tables was a small table where Ben Spaulding, representing Lonnie King and the Atlanta Branch of the NAACP, sat alone.

Judgment Day: Monday, April 4

> Any plan, whether privately conceived, jointly proposed or court imposed, contains features which are objectionable to certain individuals or certain groups; and there is no way known to the law to satisfy all the patrons of separate schools. This plan, at least, appears to the court to satisfy the overwhelming majority of the plaintiff class. On the whole, the plan is deemed fair, adequate and reasonable.
>
> —Judges Sydney Smith and Albert Henderson, Jr., April 4, 1973

It had taken the court only four days to prepare its ruling, which addressed all the legal points raised during this fourteen-year-old dispute, this "ancient class action," as the court described it. Sustaining the constitutionality of the compromise plan, the judges declared: "In a system with so overwhelming a preponderance of black students, it is not necessary to distribute the remaining minority whites *pro rata* throughout the entire system."

Having sustained the plan as a negotiated settlement acceptable to the parties, the court then explained why the LDF was precluded from objecting to the settlement. The court concluded that once LDF attorney Rindskopf had informed the court that she had "no objection" to the plan, the agreement was legally binding, and described the LDF's attempt to withdraw her authority as "eleventh hour maneuvering."

Response to the court decision was predictable. Declaring that he was "very happy," King hoped "that we can now move to the broader goal of quality education—relevant education for every child. I think Atlanta has a unique situation, one that is not present in many other cities in America. That's why I am presuming that this won't be a precedent, but it will be something which the Atlanta case with its uniqueness had to bring into focus in order to resolve this problem." Calling the decision "a victory for common sense," the *Atlanta Constitution* editorialized that "it is a victory, too, for the white and black leadership of Atlanta, men and women who labored hard in good will to put the plan together."

Rindskopf explained that she didn't "feel that the plan was agreed to by our side, but even if it were, the court has to review it itself to see whether or not it's constitutionally acceptable–and we feel that it is not." Moore attacked the court for its "summary disposition of people who object to the plan and the apparent haste of the court, the court's refusal to even want to engage in dialogue and discussion of pros and cons of the so-called compromise plan." He said that the court's position was determined by the judges' "adherence to local tradition." Organizations and individuals appealing the district court decision to the Fifth Circuit Court included the LDF, with its ally the national NAACP, which argued that the plan didn't go far enough; CORE and Howard Klein, who maintained that the plan went too far; and the ACLU, which contended that an Atlanta-only plan in itself was the wrong approach to a solution.

The Fifth Circuit Court, which initially disapproved the plan, nonetheless ordered it put into effect for the 1973–1974 academic year. At the same time, it directed the district court in Atlanta to hold hearings on the petitions for intervention, which had been summarily refused in the March hearings. About a year later, the district court held a hearing and gave final approval to the plan. Atlanta's school ordeal was over at last.

Four years later, the LDF and the national NAACP have long since withdrawn their arguments against the compromise plan. The metropolitan education suit, brought by Margie Pitts Hames for the ACLU, however, is still in the courts, six years after it was initiated.

Personal Afterword by The Author

As a teacher, a researcher, and as an occasional participant in public policymaking, I wish to record here some of the thoughts that were stimulated by my study of the Atlanta compromise. The themes of this case that most intrigued me are those growing out of the conflict between ideology and practicality. When are national policies and objectives useful in treating local social problems? When is a local problem so unorthodox that it cannot be resolved by national remedies?

What began as a conflict between black parents on one side and the school board and white parents on the other was recast by a group of local negotiators into a joint effort by white parents, black parents, and the school board to devise a solution tailored to fit Atlanta's needs. This was done against the oppostion of national civil rights organizations determined to reach a solution shaped by their perception of national needs.

The LDF and the national NAACP were not entirely wrong. On the contrary, their courageous initiatives and hard-fought struggles for two decades against the evil of racial segregation in the public schools earned them an important voice in the shaping of desegregation plans everywhere in the United States. Besides, what happened in Atlanta *was* important to national efforts to bring about the end of racial segregation everywhere else.

The difficulty the national organizations faced in this case arose not so much from any misplaced zeal or from any arrogance of national office as it did from what seems to me their umimaginative inflexibility. They behaved as single-minded bureaucracies have always behaved when faced with problems that develop in unfamiliar ways. They treat them as essentially the problems that *are* familiar to them.

Had the LDF and the NAACP been less rigid, they might well have taken an entirely different tack with Atlanta. They might have started by recognizing that the configurations of Atlanta's problem—and perhaps not only Atlanta's problem—were different from those problems with which they were familiar. They might have recognized that a city school system that was 80 percent black was not capable of being desegregated by the same methods that had been effective in school systems only 20 percent, 30 percent, or 40 percent black. They should have understood that busing, which had appeared to be in the interest of black parents when their children were in the minority, might not necessarily be so perceived by black parents in systems where their children were in the majority. Indeed, the greater the majority, the less acceptable the kind of busing plan they proposed was likely to be.

Starting from that point, why not try to develop an entirely different national model that might subsequently be used in desegregating the growing number of cities with school systems that more resemble

Atlanta's than they do Charlotte's or Jackson's? They might have considered an alternative desegregation model for cities with both a majority black school population and a majority of black voters. They might have recognized the value of the plan proposed by Atlanta's Lonnie King: (1) a black superintendent; (2) racial parity in administrative and teaching positions; and (3) no all-white schools. This approach may prove more advantageous to blacks in a majority black city than a blind insistence on systemwide racial distribution of students that imposes massive costs on all parties. These costs include inconveniences and lost learning time for both black and white students; the destruction of neighborhood schools (neighborhood schools may appeal to many black and white parents and children alike); the concern shared by both black and white parents about their children going to school in unfamiliar neighborhoods across town; increasing frustrations as the exodus of whites to the suburbs and increased enrollment in private schools each year erode the justification of busing in the first place; and the massive financial cost of busing (a burden on *all* taxpayers), using money that might otherwise be devoted to improving the quality of education for all students.

It is possible that an earlier solution of the sort eventually adopted by Atlanta might well have prevented a substantial part of the white flight to the suburbs from occurring in the first place. Without the threat of massive busing, it is possible, perhaps even probable, that 1978 would have seen an Atlanta school system with larger numbers of both black and white students.

One thing is not subject to conjecture, however. The solutions invented by Atlanta's citizens were responsive to the problems of Atlanta. The solutions proposed by the non-Atlanta participants were not. The outsiders were not in close touch with the reality of that city. How, one wonders, could any reasonable person have believed that, in a system 80 percent black, the racial proportions in *every* city school can reflect the systemwide racial distribution?

The parties to the dispute in Atlanta were all sincere in their respective beliefs, convinced that justice and the Constitution required the outcome each advocated. By their own lights, each was right, and each was attempting to serve what *it* regarded as the public interest. The LDF was right, if "equality" means one thing only—the same racial proportions in each school as exists in a school system as a whole. CORE and the southside white parents were also right, if "equality" means one thing only—that white and black parents have the right to send their children to neighborhood schools or to whatever schools they want. The ACLU was right, if "equality" means that the only way to assign students to each school is on the basis of the racial proportion of the wider metropolitan area as a whole.

Each of these parties was asking that the court give greater weight to one particular ultimate value or criterion over any of the other competing values. That is what policy choice is all about, whether made by legislatures, courts, or individuals. Which value dominates? Choosing one principal criterion to govern a decision inevitably prevents one from selecting another; it is impossible to maximize more than one value at a time.

To have allowed the LDF's value to dominate, the court would have had to discount the parental desire of the southside white parents for schools in close proximity to their homes—the neighborhood schools value. It would also have had to disregard the ACLU's value of distributing students throughout the entire metropolitan area. The ACLU's plan would have left each Atlanta school, both within and without the city, approximately 65 percent white and 35 percent black, while the LDF's outcome would have left the schools within Atlanta 80 percent black and those outside the city 90 percent white. Many Atlanta blacks regarded the ACLU's preferred alternative as unnecessarily burdensome, culturally insulting, and politically weakening; the LDF's alternative, with its similar emphasis on integration rather than educational quality, was seen as equally burdensome and frustrating to black hopes for upward social mobility. With only some exaggeration, the ACLU's aim might be termed the pure integrationist ideal, that of the LDF as the punitive integrationist fallback, and that of CORE as the defeated integrationists' withdrawal.

When viewed against these alternative values, it is not difficult to understand why the judges, as well as most Atlanta blacks and a substantial proportion of Atlanta's whites of good will, chose as they did. While the compromise plan did not conform to every detail of the integrationists' formula, it was much truer to traditional integrationists' doctrine than any of the three major alternatives. The essence of the Atlanta agreement did not lie in its trade-off of widespread student busing in return for a large number of administrative positions for blacks. While the compromise agreement *did* put blacks in many high administrative positions, that was more than anything an incidental consequence rather than a principal intention.

The central value animating the Atlanta NAACP's position was pluralist integrationism that prohibited purposeful segregation by race. It provided black parents with a wider variety of educational choices for their children than would have been available to them under the terms of any of the other alternatives. Black parents—either lower or middle class—could choose either middle-class black neighborhood schools or middle-class predominantly white schools characterized by racial proportions close to those prevailing in the metropolitan area as a whole. They would have had neither option under the LDF or CORE plan, because of the predominance of lower-class blacks throughout the system. By gaining administrative control of the school system, middle-class blacks gained the power of doing something that middle- and upper-class whites, because of their dwindling numbers in the city, had little incentive to do—design new kinds of schools aimed at substantially increasing the quality of educational opportunity for black and white children alike. With such schools, there might even be the possiblity of attracting white children back to the city's schools, especially for families who desire educational quality more than they fear having their children attend predominantly black schools. Such magnet schools, perhaps in the arts or sciences, were clearly in the minds of Lonnie King and others and are now in the planning stage.

Upper- and middle-class whites lost the option of sending their children to totally segregated white schools. But they were reassured by the prospect of white preponderance, as well as overwhelming black and white middle-class dominance, in the schools which their children would attend.

A great deal has been made of the alleged disadvantage imposed by the compromise agreement on lower-class black children. Lower-class black parents were obviously less likely than middle-class black parents to encourage their children to take advantage of the possibility of transfer to the predominantly white northside schools. But the compromise plan *did* give them that alternative, an option that they would not have had at all had the LDF's plan prevailed. They would have been even less inclined to select that option under the ACLU alternative, in view of the much more arduous bus journey. Lower-class black children, it would therefore seem, at least had an open door to the educational and cultural upper mobility that the LDF's alternative would have closed to them.

The real losers were the lower-class white children, who had neither the option of transferring to the predominantly white northside schools (since transfer was only allowed from a school in which a child's race was in the majority to one in which it was in the minority) nor the alternative of continuing in a predominantly lower-class white school. They would have lost out, however, under any of the plans, with the possible exception of the one proposed by CORE.

When one makes racial mix the dominant value in educational decision making, the value of learning must be correspondingly subordinated to the educational disadvantage of both black and white students. Atlanta's middle-class parents were not acting irrationally in opposing the LDF's plan. Instant desegregation without regard to the resulting quality of edcucation, they clearly believed, was less desirable than slower desegregation, which results in better schools for all. That may be cultural snobbery, but it is not racism. There is more than a little common sense in the concerns that motivated Atlanta's black parents. To dismiss those concerns is to blind oneself to the truths about American public education: that our urban public school systems are almost everywhere in shambles; that a good part of the cause stems from the flight of upper- and middle-class whites; that their departure leaves to the middle-class blacks who remain in the public school systems the principal burden of sustaining the cause of learning.

One of the most puzzling questions about the resolution of social disputes revolves around the issue of what is the public interest and how it gets defined. Does the mediator define it? Is one attribute of the succesful mediator that he is perceived as the voice through which the objective public interest speaks? Are there some disputes—Atlanta was not one of them, however—that can be resolved only by someone from the outside, someone who is detached from the local conflict? What happened in Atlanta to permit resolution of its particular dispute by someone not only *in* the local environment, but very much part of the particular dispute? Lonnie King was very much a protagonist mediator. He was both a party to the dispute and a mediating force. Perhaps he was able to play that role in Atlanta, because, unlike most participants in a dispute, he was willing to seize the initiative and because the essential nature of the compromise he urged was perceived to be *against* the interest of the NAACP, the organization he represented.

Are there circumstances in a particular dispute that can determine whether an inside or an outside mediator will work best? The answer to this question depends partly on how the parties to the dispute perceive what is in the public interest. Is there a difference between an aggrieved party who sees the public interest as requiring him to get *exactly* what he wants—in other words, a "maximalist"—and one who wants only something more than he already has—in other words, a "minimalist"? Perhaps there is a third category—someone who is more flexible and realistic. Was the Atlanta suit so difficult to settle because of the "maximalist" position of the LDF? It is true that the suit *wasn't* settled until the "minimalists" and the more flexible negotiators excluded the "maximalists" from the equation.

The unfolding of the negotiations is fascinating. For a month, the local NAACP and the Board of Education members met together and formulated principles of agreement. When the LDF lawyers refused to approve that agreement, the Atlanta black leadership forced the LDF to join the negotiations. Such a widening of the spectrum of demands—the inclusion of the "maximalists"—predictably led to the lengthening of the dispute resolution process, requiring additional intermediate steps before any agreement could, in fact, be consummated. The first was the development of a united plaintiffs' position and the predictable rejection of it by the Board of Education, which then advanced its own negotiating position. Predictably, too, that plan was unacceptable to the plaintiffs. Now that each side had formulated a plan unacceptable to its protagonist, both were ready to begin the serious negotiations.

The principal difference between Plan I, which King had worked out with the school board, and Plan II, the plaintiffs' negotiating position worked out with the participation of LDF attorney Elizabeth Rindskopf, was in the minimal percentage of black students required to be enrolled in a school in order for it to be considered "desegregated"—10 percent in Plan I and 50 percent in Plan II. Looking back on that period, it seems clear that King went along with the LDF demand for more busing, both because he knew it would never be accepted by the school board and because it would have impaired his credibility within the black community for him to have opposed it.

Indeed, one might infer that the price King paid for getting Rindskopf and Moore to join in the negotiations was an agreement to tilt their way, at least for one round, on the crucial sticking point of pupil integration. King knew full well that the board would never buy it, but he also knew that he had nothing to lose by agreeing to it at the proposing stage. For the time being, he got a united plaintiffs' front; if worst came to worst, he could always compromise on that point in the final settlement. If Moore and Rindskopf objected, he could simply let the court decide what to do. Moreover, King had nothing to lose personally by agreeing to go along with the Moore and Rindskopf position on busing. If he had to compromise later, his reputation as an integrationist would be protected because he had made that part of his own proposal. The clincher was that if he backed down on busing later, he could say that that position was opposed in the black community. Finally, King's attack of January 25 on Letson, the newspapers, and the opponents of busing generally was a masterful synthesis of frustration and flank protection. He knew before he ever agreed to the Moore and Rindskopf plan what the board reaction would be, but by attacking the critics of the plan vehemently, he made his later compromise credible.

After all has been said and done, however, the Atlanta school dispute could have been resolved only by persons "in the middle," persons with sufficiently solid reputations for integrity to attract a broad consensus of agreement contrary to long-held ideologies. To a large extent, only such leaders have the power to convince others that a particular dispute solution is in the long-run public interest even when it appears contrary to what the antagonists view as their respective personal short-run interests. Those who serve the public interest in this fashion simultaneously sacrifice for the public good at least part of their personal repute. They are never as popular or trusted after a settlement as they were before the respective costs of the settlement fully register in the minds of the antagonists.

7
Desegregating the Schools in Dayton

Graham S. Finney

On September 3, 1976, the Dayton, Ohio, public schools were peacefully desegregated. Under a federal court order, some twenty thousand black and white children were transported to schools across the city without incident. The national press gave Dayton high marks for the smoothness with which the extensive measures were carried out. Judith Bogart, a community relations consultant who worked on implementing the desegregation plan, said: "When school started, there were fewer problems than usual for the opening of a school year. That was because of the extensive preparation for desegregation."

Desegregation in Dayton did not just happen overnight. This chapter examines the complex events that lead to the sweeping changes in the city's school system and shows how potential community conflicts were overcome through a process of conciliation and open communication. In particular, the role of the personnel of the Community Relations Service (CRS) of the U.S. Department of Justice will be traced.

As 1978 began, the integration of the Dayton schools was continuing successfully—but the battle over desegregation had suddenly erupted again. A series of court decisions led to a judge's order to scrap the desegregation plan, but a higher court issued a stay and kept the plan working until more hearings could be held. Years may go by before the issue is finally resolved—probably by the U.S. Supreme Court.

Note: As indicated in the Introduction, this chapter represents a segment of the long story of the Dayton school desegregation case and is designed to illustrate the role of the Community Relations Service of the Justice Department in a specific situation. It does not fully cover the Dayton school case, since the writing was completed in early 1978.—Ed.

The Background

Since the *Brown* v. *Board of Education* decision in 1954, Dayton faced the eventual desegregation of its schools. That landmark civil rights case has redirected the policies and life-styles of countless school districts across the nation. First used in the Deep South, in cities like Birmingham and New Orleans, application of the *Brown* decision gradually pushed northward, to encounter de facto patterns of racial isolation in the nation's major industrial cities.

Dayton, Ohio, lay directly in that path. Situated in southern Ohio, forty minutes from Cincinnati, Dayton is an industrial city of considerable wealth and local pride. An active business-financial establishment still guides community development. The city has been governed by a nonpartisan commission-manager form of city administration since 1928. Beginning in the days of World War II, Dayton has received considerable numbers of black families from further south. By 1970, its total population of 203,000 was 40 percent black. This minority community lives largely in the city's North End where, for years, blacks have gone to segregated schools.

The Dayton story is not unique but can be compared to the experiences of many other cities. The desegregation of the Dayton schools in the fall of 1976 was influenced by similar events that occurred in Boston, Louisville, Charlotte, and Detroit. The Dayton situation was one that the CRS was well familiar with: The CRS staff had been in all those cities and had learned from each.

The CRS was established by Congress under the Civil Rights Act of 1964 "as an impartial catalyst in settling racial disputes, helping people to resolve their differences through cooperation rather than as adversaries on the streets or in the courts." With strong presidential backing and a real, if fragile, national commitment to make the new laws work, the CRS began its work in the Deep South on both school segregation and public accommodation cases. In those early cases, the CRS honed its techniques and perfected its unique approach to dispute settlement. Social workers and labor mediators were attracted to the new service as were civil rights activists anxious to cement recent legal gains.

As September 3, 1975 approached in Dayton, the resources of the CRS were trained on the city's schools. Conciliator Tommie Jones was the key person on the scene. She was backed up by the CRS midwest regional staff in Chicago under Richard Salem, the director. Salem was a journalist by background and a seven-year veteran of settling conflicts of all kinds. He had taken over the Chicago office in the wake of the assassination of the Reverend Martin Luther King, Jr. His staff of ten professionals was assigned to cover a six-state region. It was a small but experienced team, with considerable background in security, conflict resolution, public relations, and crisis management.

Even without the thorough field assessment his staff members had completed, Salem sensed the scenario about to unfold. He had been on hand in Denver when schools were being integrated and had supervised ticklish court-directed conciliation efforts toward school desegregation in Lansing and Detroit. After those experiences, it did not take much to identify the roots of potential conflict in Dayton.

School desegregation had dominated educational policies and politics in Dayton for a decade. It had been a major issue in the riots that followed Martin Luther King's death when teenage youths burned and looted blocks in the North End. By 1967, the labels "liberal" and "conservative" on the Dayton Board of Education meant, respectively, prodesegregation or proneighborhood schools. By 1975, the conservatives had gained a solid 5:2 majority on the board, even as the city's black population was continuing to grow. A recent migration of poor whites from Appalachia added a touchy dimension to the picture. Numbering thirty thousand in 1975, the Appalachians were ardent supporters of neighborhood schools and backers of the board's conservative position.

By 1975, there were few neutrals left in Dayton on the subject of desegregation. Busing was the code word everyone discussed. Both daily newspapers editorialized on desegregating without further delay. Only the nonpartisan city government was still trying hard to keep its distance from what it considered a school district problem.

What was to follow, therefore, did not result from a single incident, nor from miscalculation by politicians. It was the inevitable culmination of a decade of grappling with an issue that would not go away. Further details of this history are necessary to understand the events that followed and how the CRS would come to play its role.

The Details

Although the Ohio state courts had ruled in 1926 that segregation of pupils and teachers by race was illegal, actual school practice lagged far behind in Dayton. Blacks were excluded from school swimming pools until the forties, and black athletic teams (from schools in black neighborhoods) were barred from interscholastic competition until 1948. In the fifties and sixties, civil rights groups complained bitterly about the location of new school facilities in areas where housing patterns would perpetuate segregation. Their demands for open enrollment, black administrators, and other corrective measures finally forced a board resolution in August 1967, the month following the North End riots: "Every reasonable and constructive measure that can be effected will be taken for the ultimate elimination of racial imbalance in our schools."

In July 1968, an outspoken champion of desegregation was named superintendent of schools by the board's liberal majority. The following May, the superintendent, Wayne Carle, convinced the board to adopt a citywide open enrollment policy. He also dealt with a Department of Health, Education, and Welfare report that charged the Dayton schools with discriminatory hiring practices. The board's response to the report was a commitment to achieve a 70:30 white-to-black staffing ratio in each school in the system. A voluntary transfer policy, supported by the Dayton Education Association, enabled most school staffs to achieve the ratio by 1970. Involuntary transfer by lottery of 107 teachers completed staff integration in 1971.

But these moves, plus the superintendent's own reformist zeal, proved unpopular in the next school elections. In 1969, three members of the Save Our Schools slate were elected to the board on a platform espousing neighborhood schools and opposing cross-district busing. Two years later, in 1971, voting control passed to the conservative bloc.

In the final days of liberal control, the board ordered Carle to draft a plan to desegregate the city school system the following September and to institute metropolitanwide desegregation a year later. They passed a second resolution conceding that past board actions had had segregative results. This admission anticipated the events that followed when the conservative faction took control.

When the new board was organized in January 1971, it promptly shelved the superintendent's newly completed plan that would have bused twenty thousand youngsters. And three months later, the National Association for the Advancement of Colored People (NAACP) brought suit against the Dayton Board of Education. In November 1972, the trial opened in Columbus with federal district court Judge

Carl Rubin presiding. (As the judge was preparing his decision, the new board released Superintendent Carle and hired John B. Maxwell, a Dayton high school principal with thirty-five years in the system.)

In February 1973, Judge Rubin found the Dayton board guilty of violating the equal protection clause of the U.S. Constitution. The decision cited optional attendance zones, racially imbalanced schools, and the current board's rescission of the former board's desegregation resolutions. The judge ordered the board to complete a plan by March 1974 to correct these faults.

Thus began a three-round battle in the federal courts. In each round, the Sixth Circuit Court of Appeals overruled Judge Rubin and ordered the Dayton schools to take more extensive steps to ensure desegregation. In turn, plans for voluntary pupil shifts and reliance on magnet schools and learning centers were ruled out by the circuit court. In its third ruling, in June 1975, the appeals court directed that a systemwide plan be prepared by year's end so that complete desegregation of the system could take place in September 1976.

Judge Rubin appointed an expert to write the plan. He set November 1975 for the plan's completion. Dr. Charles Glatt, a white Ohio State educator and well-known advocate of desegregation, was retained to do the drafting. Glatt was to be assisted by another expert retained by the Dayton schools. The board, concurrently, appealed the latest circuit court's decision to the U.S. Supreme Court.

On September 18, 1975, Dr. Glatt was murdered in his federal court office. A white, middle-aged man was charged with the crime and was later found guilty of Glatt's murder, as well as the random shooting of several blacks in the Dayton area. The senseless killing brought the Dayton school desegregation case to national attention, and it convinced the city's leadership that future acts of violence must be prevented if the city's image was not to be irreparably harmed. But the outlook for achieving peaceful compliance with the federal court's order did not look good.

The CRS Intervenes

With Dr. Glatt at the time of his assassination was Tommie Jones, a woman well known in Dayton school circles as a teacher and outspoken champion of human rights and desegregation. During the Carle era, Jones had offered voluntary intergroup workshops while teaching chemistry and medical technology in the Dayton schools. Only the day before Glatt's murder, she had been named a provisional "conciliator" for the CRS and head of its small Dayton office. Her initial meeting with the court's expert ended in tragedy, shock, and screaming headlines, hardly conducive to a spirit of conciliation.

Jones explained that two years in medical school and later work in clinical pathology steeled her reaction to the murder. But no training could wipe out the murder's impact on her. Given the option to be reassigned to another city, Jones refused. For the next week, she kept her appointments accompanied by her husband as an informal bodyguard. The new federal presence of the CRS in Dayton was thus maintained.

Jones had been personally selected for her delicate assignment by CRS's Regional Director Salem. Her knowledge of the local scene and her enormous energy were viewed as pluses by Salem in light of his previous experience with school desegregation cases. His plan called for pairing Jones with a more conservative white conciliator in Dayton, but budgets and events prevented the latter's appointment from ever being made. From September 1975 on, therefore, this articulate, somewhat driven black woman, with well-known views on desegregation, went about her delicate work alone.

In November, the Save Our Schools platform won two of three seats in the biennial school election. Conservative William Goodwin was renamed to the chairman's role. The victory clinched a 5:2 majority for antibusing advocates. In retrospect, it also assured that the conservatives, since they would be in power, would bear whatever political heat any eventual court decision might bring about.

The heat soon intensified. On December 1, the U.S. Supreme Court refused, without comment, to review an appeal of the Dayton school case. Later in the month, Judge Rubin, after public hearings, ruled that the desired racial balance must be achieved by September 1976, through methods a court-named master and the Board of Education would determine. Dr. John Finger, a Rhode Island professor who had been assigned to replace Dr. Glatt, was named the court's master. Rubin took pains to state that no feasible method of compliance could be developed without "transporting" school children.

After forty-four months, the die was finally cast. A deadline, with the full force of law, was in effect. It was now up to the Dayton leadership to use the next nine months to prepare for all eventualities.

Implementing the Plan

As the court master prepared the details of the actual plan, Judge Rubin moved concurrently to put directional instruments aboard the vehicle he had launched by his ruling. The CRS was to be the stabilizer. On January 13, 1976, the court directed the CRS to: "provide assistance to the City of Dayton and to the parties involved in this litigation in resolving disputes, disagreements and difficulties that may arise in the implementation of the desegregation plan."

Three specific instructions were included in the order. The CRS was to give "organizational and technical assistance in the establishing and functioning of a Citizens' Monitoring Commission" soon to be named by the court. Continuing access to the court itself was also stipulated "as to all matters which bear upon the speedy and harmonious implementation of the desegregation plan." Furthermore, the order made it clear that all parties were "directed to cooperate with the Service and to afford it all reasonable assistance."

The process of conciliation by the CRS was now formally underway. It should be emphasized that CRS's participation was ordered by the court and not requested by the parties involved in the dispute. Conciliation, in CRS terms, takes place when its personnel enter a community dispute—with or without having the prior approval of all parties to the conflict—involving alleged discrimination. In school desegregation cases, frequently, but not always, CRS intervention occurs at court invitation or direction. CRS then moves in to work behind the scenes toward settling potentially explosive situations. A low profile for such work was specified by Congress in creating the service.

The CRS distinguishes conciliation cases from mediation efforts wherein the services of CRS are engaged with the prior support of all parties to help them reach a signed agreement. Many police-community relations disputes—CRS's second largest category of cases—are handled via mediation. In such efforts, CRS operates quite openly and seeks to build strong, supportive public opinion that will enforce the negotiations it has been able to complete. A signed agreement and press release are the marks of a settled mediation case.

The Dayton desegregation case, unlike a mediated dispute, was to be conciliated quietly and from behind the scenes. Jones, as conciliator in charge, had to win over those hostile both to the court order and to her personal intervention. That would not be easy, as she well knew. While black leaders and white liberals were encouraged by her presence, most school officials, for example, remembered her human relations workshops and saw her as no ally during the weeks ahead.

Content to let her past record speak for itself, Jones turned her considerable energy to building a network of communication links throughout Dayton. Whether Judge Rubin knew it or not, and whether Dayton still knows it or not, she appeared whenever it counted, especially when members were being picked for the monitoring commission and when nudges–gentle or otherwise–had to be applied to the innumerable parties to the dispute. While others dealt through bureaucratic structures, Jones learned to use the range and independence of her small office to stay ahead of events and conflict. This may best be seen in her dealing with the monitoring commission and the federal court, during and after desegregation.

The Monitoring Commission

On February 12, 1976, Judge Rubin appointed fifty-five members to a broad-based Dayton Citizens Advisory Board (DCAB) "to monitor the Plan that would be mandated and to assure that it functions in accordance with the order to this Court." His model was the Detroit Action Board, which had performed so well a year before in that troubled city. Through Tommie Jones and Richard Salem, the court had become fully acquainted with the Detroit Action Board and how it might be adapted to Dayton. Representative citizens were named to the monitoring commission for a period not to exceed three years, with the court retaining power to name additional members later. Well-known establishment leaders from business and the professions were suggested to the court through its business connections; grass roots and minority names were largely supplied by Jones and a group of local ministers. The result was a respected cross section of Dayton that would have to function in a very volatile situation.

Public credit for the success of the DCAB is generally given to its chairman, Dr. Robert Kegerreis, president of Wright State University. Kegerreis, a locally respected, nontraditional educator, switched from retailing to education at mid-career. He was nominated for this delicate job by the business community in whose ranks he easily operated while still guarding his independence as a university president. Appropriately, his Ph.D. in business administration had centered on consumer relations.

Throughout the summer and fall of 1976, Dr. Kegerreis acted as the spokesman for those in Dayton who were determined to accept Judge Rubin's decision with minimum discomfort. He explained that he took the job with grave misgivings about the time and energy it would require of him. Among other problems, a new medical school was just about to open at Wright State. Only when Judge Rubin half-seriously threated Dr. Kegerreis's board of directors with contempt if they opposed their president's appointment, did Kegerreis accept the task that consumed his time—and patience—especially during the hectic summer months of 1976.

Jones was often among those trying his patience. Her wide acquaintances and free-wheeling style allowed her to work with many members of the monitoring commission, but not always comfortably with its chairman, whose cautious style bothered her own sense of timing and urgency. The feeling was mutual. Dr. Kegerreis was himself bothered by the gadfly role which Jones enjoyed among members of the large commission. While liking her personally, he feared unpredictable results from her contacts with those members who were passionately opposed to the school board and its policies.

Fortunately, during the intensive days prior to September 1976, these mutual concerns remained well in the background. Soon afterward, however, when Dr. Kegerreis would seek to step down from his position as chairman, the concerns would reappear as the CRS struggled to maintain the stature of the montoring commission during the less dramatic but no less important school adjustment period that followed implementation of the desegregation plan.

The Federal Court

The CRS in the person of Jones also played a key, if less visible, role on behalf of the federal court. She served it as a personal early warning system on all aspects of desegregation, including the performance of the monitoring commission. In doing so, the court's desired appearance of distance from the day-to-day implementation of its order was preserved, even as vital information continued to flow to it through informal channels.

For example, the CRS, working through a subcommittee of the

monitoring commission, made sure that training of school personnel was added to the court order when it appeared in the spring that school administrators were moving too slowly to equip their staff with the skills needed to make desegregation work in the classroom. Later on, again at CRS's suggestion, four young people were added to the monitoring commission by the court before that question became a public issue.

The need for this informational role by the CRS stems from the essential isolation of courts in general when handling an explosive issue like school desegregation. The court's interest and expertise with the subject often lies exclusively in the "muddy territory" surrounding the law of desegregation. The stresses and strains in executing the law are for others to handle. Informed distance is the desired posture of court officers: informed so that improper and excessive rulings are not handed down; distant so that the community rather than the court is made fully accountable for carrying out the latter's rulings. Judge Rubin put it this way in his Dayton decision:

> I believe that it is not the function of the United States District Court to oversee the methods whereby children are instructed. I believe it is not the function of the United States District Court to administer by judicial fiat any social philosophy, however benign. The temptation to do either or both has proved almost irresistible in the field of school desegregation.
>
> Courts deal with rights, not ethical behavior, not social accommodations, but rights, rights guaranteed by the Constitution of the United States. That is and should be the limit of our function.

Preparing for Desegregation

The six months of final preparation for desegregation is best described by examining the posture of selected groups in Dayton and by reviewing the communication links and connections among them. Such a review reveals an underlying network that was able to overcome historic patterns and sharp differences that went beyond mere school desegregation. The CRS played a special role in connecting the pieces of this network. With some, like church and civil rights groups, the task was easy and direct; with others, especially school officials, it was often strained and distant.

Schools

The Dayton schools were, of course, in center stage. Many feared that the schools were incapable of managing the demanding changes imposed by the court. Desegregationists were appalled that the Board of Education continued its legal appeals even in the wake of the Supreme Court's refusal to consider the case. That posture raised suspicion of the board's sincerity and its ability to oversee a peaceful opening of school come September.

Looking back, school officials viewed their preparation quite differently. They argued that peaceful conversion of the system was aided by keeping hopes alive that the ruling might be reversed before September, while working feverishly within the system to assure a smooth transition to desegregated classrooms. The former stance was for the antibusing Board of Education to take; the latter for the board's administrators. This pragmatism became the policy of the new superintendent and was actively fostered as a strategy by Dayton business leaders who feared the blot on Dayton's reputation should desegregation efforts bring more violence.

A young social studies administrator, James Eschbach, was assigned the board's coordinating duties for desegregation. He was encouraged by business advisers to develop a complete timeline for all the critical decisions and logistics necessary in the weeks preceding September 3. These targets were determined and published in March 1976, only three months after the judge's order. The timeline was an invaluable device for marshalling resources and for demythologizing the desegregation process. Its detail removed doubt and established a sense of equity in the arrangements. Eschbach, since reassigned to his regular social studies duties, noted with pride that all but one deadline was met on schedule.

Board administrators also credited voluntary transfers of black and white students with helping to pave the way to a smooth transition. A variety of magnet schools and alternative programs—among them outdoor education and science centers—had been installed as far back as 1972. While critics called them expensive and evasive efforts to put off the day of massive change, school personnel insisted they demonstrated the system's basic responsiveness. Most of those early programs have now given way to the more sweeping changes called for in the desegregation plan.

The heavy cost of desegregation became a large burden on the system, which was already scraping the bottom of its revenue barrel. About $150,000 for garage security and another $150,000 for bus radios were among the special costs absorbed by the Dayton public schools. A Board of Education suit now pending before Judge Rubin contends that the state should pay these costs. With desegregation actions pending in a number of other Ohio cities, his decision will have great significance. Dayton estimated its desegregation costs at $12 million, although many critics argued that the true cost was much lower.

Perhaps the most important fact regarding the Dayton school administration was that antibusing forces were in power at the time of desegregation and were required, by virtue of their office and the pressures placed upon them, to do their duty as public officials. Had the liberal faction controlled, resistance and trouble might well have been more likely.

Business

Dayton's prestigious business leaders sized up the emerging situation in 1975. They avoided becoming polarized regarding desegregation and chose to act as the school system's think tank on the matter. They had contacts that were informal but continuous throughout the period. An atmosphere of mutual trust prevailed. Anxious to preserve Dayton's image as a productive, thrifty city in which to do business, they chose to work closely with school administrators, as they were already used to doing on financial and vocational education matters.

Dayton is home for four divisions of General Motors, one of Chrysler, and one of Firestone. It is the corporate headquarters of National Cash Register and the Mead Corporation. Its banks and retail stores serve a large hinterland. Although the large corporations are now run by corporate managers for the most part, the paternalistic attitudes of the Patterson, Kettering, and Deeds families still dominate business practices regarding community affairs. The Dayton Area Progress Council, the Dayton Chamber of Commerce, the Downtown Dayton Development Corporation, and the Dayton Community Affairs Committee are interlocking arms of this formidable array of power. It was mobilized quietly, but effectively, as September approached.

James McSwiney, chairman of Mead Corporation, the paper manufacturers, played an active role in implementing the desegregation plan. McSwiney was named to the monitoring commission by Judge Rubin and assumed the cochairmanship of the all-important Community Education and Information Subcommittee, charged with mobilizing a positive public response to the court order. McSwiney raised substantial funds ($95,000) from business colleagues and used contacts in his firm to select a person to direct the public relations campaign. Judith Bogart, a seasoned community relations consultant from nearby Cincinnati, was hired. At the time she was retained, Bogart was unknown in Dayton and for this reason was an important complement to Tommie Jones, with whom she worked closely throughout the period. Bogart soon commanded the respect of business and school officials, who were leery of Jones. They praised Bogart's "super well-organized" approach. A network of interacting staff people was greatly strengthened and expanded by Bogart's presence.

While the rest of the nation was caught up in Bicentennial reflections, Dayton spent the summer of 1976 in the more serious business of facing an uncertain fall. A speakers' bureau, media campaigns, a rumor-control center, press releases, brochures, bumper stickers, and posters, were geared toward broadening public acceptance of desegregation. In the community, seminars, workshops, and conferences attracted leadership, parents, and volunteers around the city. Potential trouble spots were identified and strategies composed to prevent their actual occurrence. At precisely the right moment, a citywide coalition of community groups favoring implementation of the court order was organized under the mayor's chairmanship. Even paycheck envelopes were stuffed with a statement from all major employers in the city: Your company expects your best on September 3 and thereafter.

Plainly, the Dayton business community had grave misgivings about the wisdom of the court order, but instead of retiring from the field as its counterparts had done in Boston, it used its own resources to assure a successful outcome. Urging quality education and child safety, the campaign worked well. So did the strategy of working closely with the Board of Education, despite criticism from many sources.

The Media

The Dayton media were vital, but independent, parts of the community relations campaign. Anxious to avoid blame for any incidents triggered by its coverage of preparation for the actual day of desegregation and knowing that the nation's eyes would be focused on Dayton, both the *Journal Herald* and the *Daily News* were fully mobilized by September 3. As one editor said, the newspapers "planned for World War III." Both softened their prior strong endorsements of desegregation so as to be credible to all parties; yet they kept pressure on the school system to prepare for all contingencies.

With the help of CRS staff, editors from Louisville were brought in to share their prior experiences. As a result, both papers prepared detailed protocols to guide their reporters, who were advised when to use the word "riot," what kinds of pictures to take or not take, and how to interview people involved.

The Churches

In a campaign designed to change public opinion, endorsements by groups and organizations played a key role as school opening approached. At one end of the spectrum were the well-organized efforts of Metropolitan Churches United, a nondenominational coalition led by Reverend Robert Kolze.

Metropolitan Churches United had been a consistent advocate of peaceful desegregation since its formation in 1971. It had supported Dr. Glatt's earlier work on desegregation. In March 1976, the group hosted an all-day citywide Conference on Desegregation, which "through coincidence or grace," occurred three days after Judge Rubin's acceptance of the court master's desegregation plan for September 3. The conference sessions were highlighted by speakers from Detroit who recounted their experience of the year before. Tommie Jones and Richard Salem had arranged for the attendance of the speakers from Detroit. As a result of the conference, some 250 key people began serious preparations for the months to follow. Area committees were formed throughout the Dayton area and endorsements from dozens of church congregations were published in late August.

Members of the Metropolitan Churches United were among the most active participants in the monitoring commission, where they were close working allies of Jones.

The Appalachian Community

While support from the religious community was predictable and also vital to peaceful desegregation, an unexpected but equally vital endorsement came from the leading organization in Dayton's Appalachian community in early August. Many now argue that its statement assured the calm that later characterized the opening day of school.

Our Common Heritage (OCH) is an all-volunteer neighborhood organization centered in Dayton's modest East End and chaired by Lela Estes, mother of six and a native of the hills of eastern Kentucky. Estes had long been active in school affairs and, like her organization's membership, was totally committed to neighborhood schools. This position was in keeping with the strong family ties of Appalachian families.

OCH is the kind of organization CRS staff members seek to work closely with in school cases in order to interpret the law and to maintain steady contact. The CRS had successfully worked this way in Detroit with the highly organized Mothers Against Busing coalition. The object of working closely with community organizations is to foster communication and to avoid misunderstanding during major societal changes.

Tommie Jones spent many hours with OCH and other community groups, where she was known only as the agent of a federal agency that was determined to achieve peaceful enforcement of the law. Her assignment coincided with the Appalachians' abhorrence of violence and respect for legal authority, views the group held that were even stronger than its opposition to busing. After one meeting with Jones, OCH issued a "brave endorsement" in support of full compliance with the court order.

The tone of that endorsement caused other community groups and individuals to speak out publicly in support of peaceful desegregation efforts and others to be supportive in more guarded tones. The OCH endorsement set the tenor of the city's mood in the weeks remaining until opening day of school. A bandwagon of support was put in motion that culminated in a telecast by the mayor, James H. McGee, who spoke as head of the Coalition for Peaceful Desegregation, a paper organization created to unify the city.

Dayton City Government

Until the OCH statement, city government had been quiet regarding the desegregation issue. Officials were quite willing to leave it for the schools to handle. In fact, the city and school district of Dayton are not even entirely coterminous. A small portion of the city is outside the school boundary line and the school district spills into several suburban towns. This structural pattern may add logic to a metropolitan desegregation plan at one time envisioned by both the liberal Board of Education and by Dr. Finger, the court-appointed master.

Actually, city government worked behind the scenes during the summer of 1976, again with help from Jones. Desegregation was made the first priority of its community planning, or priority, boards. Under Assistant City Manager Lloyd Lewis, Jr., logistical support was supplied to the schools by the Planning, Public Works, Police, and other departments with roles to play in the coming events. Lewis, a black leader and former head of the City Planning Board, himself became an active member of the monitoring commission and developed a Tactical Plan for Civil Disturbances for use by all city departments in the fall. Jones was constantly in touch with Lewis during the preparation period.

The greatest involvement by city personnel was on the part of the Police Department. The entire complement of five hundred officers was given intensive training under the leadership of Lieutenant Colonel Tyree Broomfield, chief of staff of the department. A nationally recognized expert on security measures and conflict resolution, Broomfield is an anomaly among police officials. Not only is he black, but he is also a former social worker and union official who was first introduced to police work as a human-relations trainer. He was also a veteran of school desegregation work in Boston and Louisville.

Broomfield, along with other professionals, ran dozens of training sessions around the city during the spring and summer of 1976. He is a close confidant of Jones and was thought likely to be the city's next police commissioner, despite some objections to him as an "outsider." Broomfield credited Dayton's success in school desegregation to its "desire to overcome [the] crisis and solve issues" that threatened to disrupt the city's reputation and thus the stakes of all groups involved.

The CRS

Other organizations and individuals helped to prepare for desegregation. The CRS constantly kept in touch with priority boards, established under the Model Cities program and subsequently used to elicit community opinion throughout Dayton. Jones's only assistant was recruited from the staff of one such board. While not a strong element in the emerging picture, labor leadership was also enlisted. National labor leaders were occasionally brought to Dayton to publicly support peaceful desegregation. A tape was made especially for this purpose by George Meany. These arrangements were worked out by CRS officials back in Washington at the request of Jones and Salem.

In all these efforts, the hand of Jones and the CRS was in evidence, sometimes so subtly that its imprint was barely detectible. Hers was, in fact, the only presence that managed to touch base with all the various parties, however she herself was regarded by them. This network capacity proved crucial as events unfolded. One person described Jones's role as a kind of "ombudsman for information." It was indeed the kind of catalytic role of which ranking CRS officials proudly speak.

The catalytic role might also be described as a herding process. The CRS in Dayton worked as a skillful sheep dog would work to get its flock safely into the fold. The fold, in this case, was a desegregated school system and the flock contained many reluctant and contrary-minded persons and groups. Sometimes the process called for biting at the heels of school officials or others, who seemed to be in no hurry to prepare for the plan. Often, it meant running ahead to scout potential troubles. Barking was sometimes necessary, but far less effective than always knowing the destination and working long hours to get everyone safely to it.

Opening Day

By September 3, 1976, preparation for desegregation had been largely accomplished. Opening day was the quietest and most uneventful the Dayton schools had experienced in years. The busing of twenty thousand youngsters—roughly half of the total enrollment—proceeded without reportable incident. Even the usual number of fist fights and lost children dropped dramatically as the plan took effect. Absenteeism, then and subsequently, has been below prior years. Dennis Shere, editor of the *Journal Herald,* had perhaps the biggest problem that day. With nineteen reporters in the field, but with no news worth reporting, Shere had a morale problem on his hands. After weeks of preparation and training, he suddenly knew the meaning of overkill—not that he wasn't secretly pleased. Most everyone in Dayton was proud and relieved that the city had managed to execute so complex and risky an act of change and adjustment.

"The temper of the Dayton community" and a "strong desire to overcome [the] crisis and solve issues" were factors constantly mentioned by blacks and whites alike in reviewing the apparent success with which the desegregation plan was implemented. Despite grave differences and tensions regarding housing policy, police conduct, and other issues impinging on community relations in addition to the school problem, lines of communication remained intact in Dayton during the period of preparation. No interest group felt entirely excluded from the process, as had occurred in other cities facing similar adjustments. And no group wanted to jeopardize Dayton's highly successful development efforts that were producing a steady flow of new jobs and a revitalized downtown.

The basis for a peaceful resolution of the desegregation issue was present throughout the period. Police and federal intelligence reports never uncovered any likelihood of planned violence prior to the opening of school. The insane slaying of Dr. Glatt, itself an isolated incident, perhaps had put an end to such possibilities. Far more crucial, however, was the fact that a solid 5:2, conservative, antibusing majority was in power at the time desegregation occurred. The leaders of potential opposition to the court's order were at the helm and not in the streets as they had been in many other cities.

Finally, a deep respect for legal process was in evidence during the entire period. Whether felt by the head of the monitoring commission, reflected in the endorsement by OCH, or implicit in the black community's recurring use of the courts to solve its grievances, it is plain that confidence in a functioning legal system minimized possible conflict and brought about initial conciliation of the case. That same confidence would also protract any final settlement, as subsequent events illustrate.

Events Following Desegregation

The Dayton school story did not end on September 3, nor did the role of the CRS in that city. Subsequent events have kept the file open and proved that deep sores do not just disappear.

In December 1976, the U.S. Supreme Court remanded an Austin, Texas, school desegregation case on the grounds that the circuit court's remedy was more extensive than required to meet that city's needs. The import of the ruling was not lost on the Dayton Board of

Education, whose attorney was instructed to petition the Supreme Court to review the full necessity of the changes Dayton had recently implemented. When the brief was filed, the Supreme Court agreed to hear the petition.

By doing so, the prospect for some sort of de-desegregation of the Dayton public schools loomed to some as a distinct possibility. In the days that followed, the CRS was obliged to play a brand new role. Any reversal by the high court was certain to spark unpredictable events. Steady leadership was badly needed.

Even before the high court's decision in the Austin case, the monitoring commission was struggling to define its role during the period of adaptation to the Dayton plan. There were sporadic reports of incidents involving discipline problems and suspensions in individual schools. Yet, to many members of the commission, the crisis seemed over; they wanted be relieved of a time-consuming role. While at first piles of monitoring reports from individual schools went unanalyzed for lack of staff, soon such reports became infrequent for lack of monitors. Attendance at commission meetings dropped. Morale was low.

Richard Salem and Tommie Jones became more concerned when it was learned that Dr. Kegerreis had requested the court to release him as chairman, citing pressures at Wright State University. Kegerreis even wrote a letter to his fellow members, thanking them for their services and implying that their job was done. Whatever their views of the chairman's style, both Salem and Jones were convinced that his resignation would destroy the monitoring commission since no one of like stature was available to replace him.

Shortly into 1977, the CRS officials got in touch with key members of the monitoring commission that had succeeded so well in September. They especially urged business leaders to bolster the commission in anticipation of possible troubles ahead. They cited the risk of allowing the commission's leadership to devolve to liberal groups alone. A court statement, reaffirming the need for the commission, appeared as these talks quietly took place, no doubt the result of CRS prompting.

The winter of 1977 could not have been a poorer time to reenlist business support for desegregation. The worst winter in memory had crippled Dayton and forced the closing of factories and schools. Despite the Supreme Court's intervention, desegregation faded into the background amid this natural catastrophe.

Nevertheless, the urging of Salem and Jones paid off. In early spring,

Chairman Kegerreis tabled his resignation and reconvened the commission, this time to concentrate its attention on in-school adaptation to the plan. The CRS was asked to help the group prepare a first-year report and to aid a reconstituted school monitoring committee under Reverend Kent Organ's chairmanship. To that end, the commission met with school officials in mid-May to request current data about internal problems such as discipline and violence.

The very same day of the meeting, the *Daily News* broke a story that rekindled lingering anger and anxiety. In the story, leaders of the local American Friends Service Committee (AFSC) charged that suspensions of black students were running twice the rate for whites in the Dayton schools. Discriminatory administration by school officials was strongly implied.

The AFSC stood outside the network represented on the monitoring commission so its charges took all parties by surprise. School Superintendent Maxwell replied to the charge by stating, in effect, that statistics can be made to say most anything. On behalf of CRS, Salem was also asked to comment on the charges. It was a time for the herd dog to bite some heels. Salem did so with deliberate force, so as to reactivate the supporters of peaceful desegregation in Dayton. He said quite flatly that higher rates of suspensions were inevitable in the aftermath of desegregation and cited data from Louisville in making his point. The comment made clear the necessity of constant monitoring by community leadership during a long and natural process of adjustment.

The Supreme Court Acts

The Supreme Court heard the Board of Education's request in late April and received, at the same time, an opinion from the Attorney General that the implemented plan remain unchanged. In June, the Supreme Court sent the Dayton case back to Judge Rubin for more hearings, ruling that the desegregation plan could not stand on the basis of the violations found by Rubin's court during previous hearings. The high court noted, however, that the plan should remain in effect for the coming school year—September 1977 to June 1978—subject to further orders from Judge Rubin.

Rubin felt that the Supreme Court wanted him to determine the answers to two key questions: (1) Was the scope of the systemwide desegregation plan equal to the severity of the problem, or did it exceed it? (2) Was the school board actually guilty of having brought about segregated schools? After a number of hearings, Rubin, in December 1977, surprised many segments of the community by throwing out the entire desegregation plan and advising the school system that it could go back to the old system in February. The NAACP asked for a stay while it appealed the decision, but Rubin rejected the move. Then the Sixth Circuit Court of Appeals received the NAACP's request on appeal and granted the stay in January, pending its study of Judge Rubin's order cancelling the plan. As a result of the appeals court action, the desegregation plan remains in effect as of 1978–somewhat precariously.

As soon as Judge Rubin threw out the plan, Dr. Kegerreis disbanded the monitoring commission.

The sixth circuit court was expected to rule on the case in the spring or summer of 1978. The side that loses may then bring the case back to the Supreme Court.

By that time, Tommie Jones may be in Cleveland, where a major and potentially explosive desegregation battle is developing. Jones was honored with a distinguished service award from the attorney general for her work in Dayton. Salem transferred her to Cleveland, but he noted that the CRS will keep an eye on developments in Dayton and stands ready to provide technical assistance if needed.

There is a general feeling on the part of some in Dayton that the higher courts will not allow the entire desegregation plan to be scrapped. But some people are concerned about the future. Community relations consultant Bogart noted:

> The long-term effects of the desegregation plan could have been very positive–parents were getting involved in the schools again on both sides of town. They were concerned about the quality of education, and I thought that was one of the most positive elements of this. But without some kind of organizational structure to keep them involved–with no one working on this now–that worries me.

Salem believes that the likelihood of serious conflict is minimized today as compared to two years ago. Dayton, he said, is a city working at its problems.